Burnham Norton Friary

Perspectives on the Carmelites in Norfolk, England

Supported by:

Norfolk Archaeological and Historical Research Group
Norfolk and Norwich Archaeological Society
Norfolk Archaeological Trust
Norfolk Record Office

The Gatehouse at Burnham Norton friary, 1898, photograph by E M Beloe, junior. Collection: ref: 30129075430398

Image courtesy of Norfolk County Council Library and Information Service -- Enjoy thousands of Norfolk's unique history at www.picture.norfolk.gov.uk

Burnham Norton Friary

Perspectives on the
Carmelites in Norfolk, England

edited by Brendan Chester-Kadwell

Oldakre
Press

Oldakre Press

63 School Road, Drayton, Norwich, NR8 6EG Norfolk
oldakrepress@gmail.com

First published 2019

ISBN: 978-1-9162869-0-0

Copyright © the contributors.

The moral rights of the authors have been asserted.

Brendan Chester-Kadwell has asserted his moral right under the Copyright, Designs and Patents Act 1988 to be identified as the editor of this work.

Without limiting the rights under copyright reserved above, no part of this publication may be reproduced, stored or introduced into a retrieval system, or transmitted in any form or by any means (electronic, mechanical, photocopying, recording or otherwise) without the prior written permission of both the copyright owner and the above publisher of the book.

A description of this book is available from the British Library
and from the Library of Congress

Typeset in Gentium Basic and Gill Sans MT by
Oldakre Press, Norwich, UK

Printed in the UK by ImprintDigital.com, Upton Pyne, Exeter, Devon.

Contents

List of figures and tables — vii
Foreword by Caroline Davison — xi
Preface by Brendan Chester-Kadwell — xiii
Notes on the Contributors — xvii

Part I Burnham Norton Friary: landscape, settlement and site analysis

1 Imagined coastlines – coastal change at the port of Burnham
   Jonathan Hooton — 2
2 The Burnhams from the fifth to the fourteenth centuries
   Andrew Rogerson — 21
3 The medieval friary site at Burnham Norton and its landscape context
   Brendan Chester-Kadwell — 45
4 Results of recent archaeological surveys of the Burnham Norton site
   Giles Emery — 69
5 The existing remains including Friary Cottage and Our Lady's Well
   Stephen Heywood — 85

Part II The Norfolk Carmelites and their cultural context

6 From hermits of Mount Carmel to Whitefriars in England *c.* 1200–50
   Helen Clarke — 102
7 The urban context: investigation of Norwich Whitefriars
   Rachel Clarke — 127
8 Benefactors great and small: late medieval wills relating to Burnham Norton Friary -- *John Alban* — 155
9 The Carmelite journey 1247–1538: with a focus on Burnham Norton
   Brendan Chester-Kadwell — 175

Combined bibliography — 198

Part III Annex: The Medieval Carmelite priory at Burnham Norton: a chronology -- *Richard Copsey* — 213

List of Main Topics — 252

Index of Significant People relevant to the friary and the Carmelite Order — 254

Figures and tables

Figures

1.1 Pre-glacial east–west trough underlying the North Norfolk coast	2
1.2 The Burnhams, extract from Faden's map of Norfolk 1797	8
1.3 A comparison of the coastlines of Faden (1797) and the O S (1954)	9
1.4 North Norfolk ports trading with Newcastle (1508–11)	13
1.5 Detail from the Plan of the Marshes, Norton and Deepdale 1825	18
2.1 The Central area of the Burnhams	22
2.2 Distribution of Early Saxon finds	26
2.3 Copper alloy button brooch, mid-fifth–mid-sixth century, area A	26
2.4 Copper alloy equal-armed brooch with stamped decoration, mid to late fifth century, area A	27
2.5 Gilt copper alloy mount, earlier seventh century, area B	27
2.6 Copper alloy 'axe-shaped' mount with garnet inlay, earlier seventh century, area B	27
2.7 Distribution of Middle Saxon finds	30
2.8 Copper alloy Ansate brooch, eighth century, Area A	31
2.9 Copper alloy Ansate brooch, eighth century, area A	31
2.10 Copper alloy Ansate brooch, eighth century, area B	31
2.11 Copper alloy hooked dress fitting inlaid with niello, ninth century, area A	31
2.12 Copper alloy sword scabbard chape, later ninth century, area A	32
2.13 Lead weight with fragments of eighth-century gilt copper alloy decorated object set into each end, late ninth century, area A	32
2.14 Lead weight with fragment of eighth-century gilt copper alloy decorated object set into one end, ninth century, area A	32
2.15 Copper alloy strap end with inlaid niello and silver wire, ninth century, area A	33
2.16 Copper alloy Anglo-Scandinavian disc brooch, tenth century, north of Docking Road	33

3.1 View of the site from the west front of the fourteenth-century church to the eastern precinct wall	44
3.2 View of the standing remains from the north	44
3.3 Modern Burnham parishes	46
3.4 Conjectural medieval landscape of the estuary of the River Burn	48
3.5 View of the coastal area at Inclosure	49
3.6a The public road system pre-Inclosure (1821)	50
3.6b The public road system after enclosure	52
3.7 Land management post-enclosure, 1825	54
3.8 Conjectural medieval landscape of the possible location of Bradmer	57
3.9 Conjectural medieval landscape of the friary site after 1253	59
3.10 Friary site precinct landscape with gauged measurements	61
3.11 Friary site in the fourteenth century	63
3.12 Site of the conventual buildings showing gradients	64
3.13 Plan of the fourteenth-century church with measurements	65
3.14 Plan of the thirteenth-century church with measurements	66
4.1 Brian Cushion's 1995 Survey	71
4.2 Brian Cushion's 1995 Survey with additional features identified by magnetometry	74
4.3 The east wall during repair work	76
4.4 The eastern gateway	76
4.5 Test-pitting at Burnham Market Primary School	81
4.6 Metal detecting at Burnham Market Primary School	82
5.1 Brian Cushion's 1995 Survey	85
5.2 The gatehouse from the north-west	87
5.3 The gatehouse interior looking west	88
5.4 A boss in the west bay	88
5.5 View of the Gatehouse from the east through the church doorway	89
5.6 The priory ruins from a 1794 engraving	90
5.7 The priory ruins from a 1794 engraving (reversed)	90
5.8 Detail from a repair specification for the Gatehouse	91
5.9 The church façade	92

5.10 The boundary wall on the north side of precinct photographed in 1992	93
5.11 The north façade of Friary Cottage before the works of 2011/12	95
5.12 Friary Cottage, interpretive plan	95
5.13 Friary Cottage, the north-east quoins	96
5.14 Friary Cottage, blocked puthole, the south section of the east gable-end	96
5.15 Friary Cottage, the south elevation before alterations	96
5.16 Plan of Hulne Friary, Alnwick	98
5.17 Aerial view of Hulne Friary, Alnwick looking south-east, remains of the church in the foreground	98
6.1a The Christian states of the Levant c. 1241	102
6.1b Location of the Hermitage of St Mary of Carmel	102
6.1c Hermitage of St Mary of Carmel, looking west to the coast and Haifa peninsular	102
6.2 Distribution of friaries in England c.1250, showing Carmelite hermitages	105
6.3 The hermitage of St Mary of Carmel with early and late phases of construction outlined in green and red respectively	107
6.4 Remains of the church of St Mary of Carmel, from the north west	107
6.5 The hermits gathered around the Well of Elijah on Mount Carmel	108
6.6 Plan of Hulne Friary, with the standing walls in solid black	110
6.7 Hulne Friary, the thirteenth-century window in the nave	112
6.8 Hulne Friary, the thirteenth-century window in the choir	112
6.9 The fourteenth-century bridge over the River Medway at Aylesford	113
6.10 Aylesford Priory, projected plan of the thirteenth-century church	114
6.11 Aylesford Priory, the modern church and shrine of St Simon Stock	115
6.12 Aylesford Priory, the outer court or 'curia', showing part of the stone built guest house and much restored western range	116
6.13 Aylesford Priory, the outer gatehouse dating from the fifteenth century	116
6.14 Lossenham Friary, map of the area in 1801	118
6.15 Lossenham Friary, fragment of the base of a small column of Caen stone	118
6.16 Lossenham Friary, with the River Rother as precinct boundary	120
6.17 Lossenham Friary, bridge over the River Rother, Rye to London road	120
6.18 Burnham Norton Friary gatehouse and west front of the church	122

Appendix: Inventory of Lossenham: objects used in church	125
7.1 Location of friaries in Norwich and Carmelite houses in Norfolk	126
7.2 The Carmelite friary and its precinct, based on documentary research and excavated evidence	132
7.3 Detail plan of Norwich Whitefriars showing excavated and conjectured building remains with interpretations	133
7.4 The 'Anchorite's arch' with new office building behind, from south	136
7.5 Overhead 'working shot' of the great cloister under excavation, from south-east	137
7.6 Taps and tap key	139
7.7 Norwich Whitefriars overlaid onto First edition O S map, 1885	140
7.8 The extant undercroft in 1978 showing fifteenth-century vaulting	142
7.9 The Arminghall Arch	144
7.10 Detail of cloister buttresses	145
7.11 Painted window glass: a lion	146
7.12a Page holder	147
7.12b Strap ends and book fittings with a saltire design	148
7.13 A gilded needlecase	149
7.14 Example of one of the monastic graves	151
7.15 View north from the Cathedral spire showing the urban infill of the former friary site	153
8.1 Coat of arms of de Hemenhale, *c.* 1300, in Threxton church	157
8.2 Coat of arms of de Calthorpe, *c.* 1418, in Ashwellthorpe church	157
8.3 The testament and last will of Elsabeth Norton, 1499	168
8.4 Act of probate to the testament and last will of Elsabeth Norton, 1499	168
9.1 The seven sacraments font, St Mary's Church, Great Witchingham, Norfolk	187

Tables

1.1	Ships from the Burnhams in the sixteenth century	16

Foreword

Norfolk Archaeological Trust (NAT) has been looking after Burnham Norton Friary since 2010 as part of our work to protect Norfolk's significant archaeological or historic sites at risk. We take monuments into our care, repair them, provide interpretation, and open them for everyone to enjoy; and we actively engage with local communities so that they can be involved in the future conservation of the sites that they treasure. This is the background context which produced the NAT's 'Imagined Land' project and, in turn, the papers that have been drawn together by Oldakre Press in this absorbing book.

In the first few years of managing the Friary NAT focused on repair and maintenance – we cleared scrub from the church earthworks; re-discovered the precinct walls, which were lost in a tangle of brambles, then recorded, repointed and consolidated them; instigated minor repairs to the stonework and roof of the gatehouse; and established a hay meadow with paths. Once this was done we felt it was time to celebrate the site with the local community.

This was the inspiration for NAT's National Lottery-funded two-year-long 'Imagined Land' project, the second year of which (2018) focused on the Burnham Norton Friary site. We needed to understand the history and development of the site better, and we wanted to get to know the local communities and invite them to explore the site with us. The project aimed to combine research with creative arts, using what we learned about the landscape, the buildings and the people who lived and worked there, to weave stories and develop characters for the grand finales: a Village Pageant and an evening of Carmelite Music, both devised and created with local people.

An important early step in development of the project was an approach to the Norfolk Archaeological and Historical Research Group (NAHRG) for support in delivering the research phase of the project. At Burnham, Brendan Chester-Kadwell, his NAHRG colleagues, and members of the local community organised two very successful day schools which brought together for the first time the expert speakers whose work has been collected together for this book. Both days were over-subscribed, the village hall at Burnham Village Hall packed to capacity, evidencing the strong local interest in this enigmatic site. A highlight for me was the afternoon field trip down a muddy track by the marshes, to explore the potential site of the first foundation at Bradmer, its exact location keenly debated by several contributors.

As well as these workshops, the project funded a geophysical survey of the area managed by NAT, and the recording of some fascinating oral histories of local people who remember Burnham Norton in the twentieth century. During the programme of archaeological test-pits in the school grounds a stunning Anglo-Saxon decorated belt fitting was uncovered by a pupil – a reminder that there is much to understand about the history of the site and its context prior to the establishment of the Friary. These activities sparked the imagination of the local community, including pupils at the school who can see the Gatehouse from their assembly hall. Some of them had never explored the site before the project, despite its position on the other side of the road!

The publisher must be congratulated whole-heartedly for drawing the resources together to produce this book, developed from the Imagined Land workshops. The fact that several of the main county organisations with an interest in archaeology are supporting its publication emphasises the growing awareness of the Friary's significance, and the importance of making this scholarship more widely available. I know that Burnham people who were involved in the project will be the first in the queue to acquire their copies! From NAT's point of view, this drawing together of material from a broad range of disciplines has provided us with new perspectives which require further investigation – the development phases of the main buildings, the significance of the site's location in relation to the Burnham group of settlements, the river, the pilgrimage route to Little Walsingham, and the kind of lives the friars lived there – which will inform the way we manage and interpret the site in the future. The ideas in this book provide us with an inspiring foundation from which to formulate specific research questions about the site, which we will pursue in partnership with the local community in the coming years.

Caroline Davison

Co-Director, Norfolk Archaeological Trust

May 2019

www.norfarchtrust.org.uk

Preface

'Put

Your hand on stone. Listen

To the past's long pulse.'[1]

The Carmelite Friary at Burnham Norton, a lost past's ruin in a deserted field, challenges our imagination and invites us to seek its hidden history. In this volume a number of investigators take up this challenge from different perspectives with the intention of shedding new light on this very unusual site. The aim of the book is to present what is known of the friary site, its landscape and historical context, as well as the available survey material recorded to date. Hopefully the book will become the starting point for discussion and further research and be a benchmark for future work.

The Carmelites who first came to England in 1241 were seeking a new home from the continued turbulence of the Holy Land following the fall of the Kingdom of Jerusalem to Saladin in 1187.[2] These hermits from Mount Carmel were given permission by king Henry III to settle in England and the first four houses were established soon after. Burnham Norton Friary was first founded between 1242 and 1247, the fourth house in the list of Carmelite foundations (Egan 1992: 2). These first four foundations of Carmelite houses in England were all on rural sites. However, Burnham Norton friary was re-founded in 1253, between the date of the establishment of other East Anglian houses at Cambridge (1247) and Norwich (1256), at a time when Carmelite foundations were being built on sites associated with urban centres. Burnham Norton Friary seems at odds with this trend, but hopefully this reappraisal will help to explain why this is not necessarily the case. There is reason to believe that in some respects the medieval Burnhams (taken as a group of close knit parishes) had some of the attributes of more pronounced urban centres elsewhere (Chapter 2). However, its rural location has helped to preserve the integrity of the site to a degree that is rarely found in the intense urban setting of other friaries.

The friary buildings above ground have not survived well, although the (restored) fourteenth-century gatehouse is particularly fine and the west front of the church is still standing, but in an incomplete form. Other above ground remains can be seen within a cottage (now known as Friary Cottage) to the north of the footprint of the church, and a large part of the original precinct wall also survives in the landscape. Unlike most friary sites, no further re-building or development has taken place and so the potential for undisturbed below ground archaeology is high. One of the aims of the book is to facilitate the case for a fuller on-site investigation of this important scheduled monument, building on the geophysical survey by David Bescoby, undertaken as part of the Imagined Land project in 2017.

Following its dissolution in 1538, the site of the friary and its standing buildings went into private ownership and its associated lands absorbed into local manorial holdings. At some point most of the friary buildings were demolished and the church was reduced and converted into barns, which stood on the site until the nineteenth century. These barns appear on the tithe map of 1838, but not on the 6 inch Ordnance Survey first edition later in the century. The earl of Orford (the then owner) restored the gatehouse in 1840 or soon after (Bryant 1914: 22). The area within the precinct wall had been divided between two tenants in the nineteenth century when it was still part of the Orford estate. In the twentieth century the Holkham estate purchased both elements of the site and the part containing Friary Cottage was sold off as a private residence. From the time of the Dissolution, the site has been used for agricultural purposes, except for a short period during the First World War when, apparently, it was employed to accommodate German prisoners of war engaged on local agricultural work in 1917 (Sabine 1994: 9).

The book offers a multi-disciplinary approach. Each contribution explores a specific aspect that sheds light on a subject related to the friary, but they are not linked as a continuous narrative and on some issues there are differences of interpretation. The structure of the book partly reflects the papers presented at the two study days mentioned in the Foreward, but there is also some additional material. The volume is in three sections that collect together related topics, as follows:

Part 1 – This section looks at the landscape and medieval settlement context of the friary site, together with analyses of previous surveys, archaeological assessments and a description of the standing remains.

Part 2 – The second section explores the broader cultural context of the Carmelite Order, its engagement with English society in Norfolk and beyond, and the relationship between the friars and the local Burnham community.

Part 3 – The Annex, by the Reverend Dr Richard Copsey O. Carm, contains a Chronology of Burnham Norton Friary and a list of friars associated with Burnham Norton in the Middle Ages. This contribution was prepared prior to the writing of this book, but has not previously been published. However, it is an extremely useful addition and one that is reproduced here with gratitude to the author.

After the Annex there is a list of main topics, and an index of people relevant to the story of the Carmelite Order and the foundation of the friary at Burnham Norton as described in this volume.

A number of experts have contributed to the book: the specialisms include archaeology, landscape history, geography, architectural history, and medieval history. There is still, however, room for further scholarship. It is hoped that in time more information and analysis can be added.

Burnham Norton Friary: Perspectives on the Carmelites in Norfolk is aimed at a wide audience. It is written for all those interested in the history and archaeology of Norfolk, regardless of their level of knowledge of county sites. However, it also has a wider appeal for the growing scholarly interest in friaries in general, and for the links that can be made between the different regions of the British Isles to which the friars themselves reached out during the Middle Ages. The inter-disciplinary nature of the book should also broaden its interest. The production of the volume has engendered an infectious enthusiasm amongst those who have taken part and it is hoped that something of that will also infect the reader!

General Acknowledgements

This book represents the efforts of a large number of people who have contributed to the project from its inception as two study days, through to the production of the present volume.

The study days were part of the Imagined Land project in the Burnhams and thanks must go to the project manager, Simon Floyd, and the then director of the Norfolk Archaeological Trust, Caroline Davison, for their encouragement and support. Many members of the local community also gave practical assistance on both days. In particular, thanks go to Richard Worsley (chairman of the local project steering group); Gill Francis for organising refreshments; Dr Sally Francis and 'Lyn Stilgoe for their contributions to the field work element of the days; Tim Fisher, the project's co-ordinator at Burnham Market Primary School, for the use of school premises; and Mark and Flic Lowe for access to Friary Cottage and its grounds. Thanks go to Tony Bradstreet, Secretary and Events Officer for the Norfolk Archaeological and Historical Research Group, for his contribution to marketing the study days.

The editor would also like to offer his thanks to those who generously gave their time to speak at the study days, all of whom also agreed to write chapters for this book. Their names appear in the contents pages and under the list of contributors, so need not be repeated. However, thanks go to Dr John Alban for his additional contribution, and to Dr Richard Copsey for supplying the material for the Annex.

It is most encouraging that so many of Norfolk's county organisations are supporting this publication. Thanks go to Caroline Davison, now Co-director of the Norfolk Archaeological Trust, for the support of her organisation and for agreeing to write the Foreword. The Norfolk Archaeological and Historical Research Group and the Norfolk and Norwich Archaeological Society have given grants to assist in the publication costs. This has meant that the cost to the public has been kept to a reasonable one and has also allowed for a good amount of coloured illustration. Gary Tuson, the County Archivist of Norfolk, has generously supported the project from its inception. The Norfolk Record Office has supplied copies of key archival material for inclusion in the book with permission to quote from and to reproduce original documents.

The copyright of the individual contributions belongs to their authors and they are printed here with their permission. Where the copyright for individual figures belongs to other than the authors, the copyright holders are acknowledged either with the pertinent illustration, or otherwise within the text of the relevant contribution. However, special thanks go to the following:

Dr Cristina Gnont, Director, and Dr Maria Mangiavacchi of the Pinacoteca Nazionale Di Siena, for permission to reproduce an image of the art work by Pietro Lorenzetti showing the hermits of Mount Carmel around the fountain of Elijah ('Eremiti carmelitani presso la Fonte di Elia, Particolare della Pala del Carmine').

Jenny Glazebrook, managing editor of East Anglian Archaeology, for giving permission on behalf of the copyright holders (Norfolk Historic Environment Record, Norfolk County Council) for the following: Fig. 89 from Brian Cushion & Alan Davison, 2003, *Earthworks of Norfolk,* East Anglian Archaeology 104 (Chapters 4 and 5, this volume).

A number of authors have made reference to material from Leicester Archaeological Monograph 23: *In the Company of Preachers – The Archaeology of Medieval Friaries in England and Wales,* and thanks go to Deirdre O'Sullivan for permission to use Figure 3.32 on page 167 (illustrator, Susan Ripper).

Emeritus Professor R D Pringle of Cardiff University for giving permission to use Peter E. Leach's drawing in his book, *The Churches of the Crusader Kingdom of Jerusalem: A Corpus,* vol. 2 (CUP 1998), fig. 67 in Chapter 6 of this volume (redrawn by Pat Kadwell for the author's purposes).

Dr Neil Chroston of the School of Environmental Sciences, University of East Anglia for giving permission to reuse figure 6 from 'Geometry of Quaternary sediments along the north Norfolk coast, UK: a shallow siesmic study' by P N Chroston, R Jones and B Makin, (1999) volume 136 of the *Geological Magazine,* in Chapter 1 figure 1.1.

Whilst every effort has been made to establish the copyright holders of the material reproduced in this publication, if there are any unforseen copyright issues please contact the publisher.

Pat Kadwell for the following maps and plans: Chapter 1, figs. 1.1, 1.3-5; Chapter 2, 2.1, 2.2 and 2.7; Chapter 3, figs. 3.3, 3.4, 3.6a and b, 3.8-14; Chapter 6, figs. 6.1a and b, 6.3 and 6.10 redrawn.[3]

The editor would like to thank Susan Curran of Curran Publishing Services Ltd for her contribution to the production of this volume. Thanks go to John Alban and Pat Kadwell for their help with the bibliography, and also to Mrs Penny Harris for agreeing to proof read the text.

A number of people have offered their professional advice and observations on the content of many of the contributions. Thanks therefore, go to the Reverend Dr Sean Connolly, Dr Richard Copsey, Elizabeth Rutledge, and Professor Tom Williamson. Of course, responsibility for the cogency of the book remains with the editor.

Brendan Chester-Kadwell

Norwich, 2019

Notes

1 Lines taken from from 'Stanton Drew' by Ursula Askham Fanthorpe (1929-2009). (Fanthorpe, U. A. 2010 *New and Collected Poems*, © Enitharmon Press, page 38). Thanks go to Enitharmon Press for permission to quote.

2 Although the Holy Roman Emperor, Frederick II (1194-1250), had regained Jerusalem for Christendom in 1229, it was never fully secured and there followed a decade of anarchy. Richard, earl of Cornwall (the brother of King Henry III of England) arrived at Acre in October 1240 to find the Christian states in chaos. He stayed until May 1241, during which time he provided welcome leadership and 'he [had] behaved with great wisdom and tact and had made himself generally accepted as temporary viceroy of the kingdom' (Runciman 1955: 219). It was with some of Richard's knights that the first Carmelites arrived in England.

3 Maps and redrawn plans make use of OS OpenData, VectorMap District data, Terrain 50, OS 1st edition 6 inch 1906, NHER data. The terrain and lidar maps were accessed from Dr David Bescoby's surveys. Programs used include: QGIS, ArcGIS Explorer, CorelDraw, Adobe Photoshop, Adobe InDesign, Google Maps. All other map and plan sources are acknowledged in the text.

List of Contributors

Jonathon Hooton, MA

Jonathan Hooton studied Historical Geography under Professor H C Darby at Selwyn College, Cambridge, where he gained an MA in Geography in 1977. He has taught geography and environmental science for much of his career and led many field trips to the north Norfolk Coast. In 1996 with the help of the Blakeney Area Historical Society he published *The Glaven Ports, a Maritime History of Blakeney, Cley and Wiveton* and has continued to research shipping along the north Norfolk Coast.

He has also been active in the Norwich Society, being Chairman of the Society from 2015-17, and is also a fully qualified City of Norwich Tour Guide where he leads tours and gives talks. Among Jonathan's other interests are folk music, Morris dancing, cricket and landscape history. He is married with two children and lives in Norwich.

Andrew Rogerson, BA, PhD, MCIfA, FSA

After gaining a degree in History and Archaeology at Liverpool in 1970 Andrew spent three years' of digging in the UK before settling in Norfolk as a founding member of the Norfolk Archaeological Unit. He remained there, through a series of the usual institutional name changes, until retirement in 2017. Though his first fieldwork project was the excavation of part of the Roman small town at Scole, his interests lie in the Anglo-Saxon and medieval periods. Amongst his significant, and published excavations were *Morning Thorpe Early Saxon cemetery*, and *Middle Harling and Fullers Hill, Great Yarmouth*.

His final two decades of employment were largely taken up with the recording of finds made by metal detectorists and amateur archaeologists for the Historic Environment Record and the Portable Antiquities' Scheme. This is a sector of archaeological activity in which Norfolk leads the field.

Brendan Chester-Kadwell, MSocSc, MA, PhD, PGCert. Building Conservation

Brendan Chester-Kadwell is a landscape historian specialising in the historical development of rural settlement, particularly those associated with coastal wetlands. He has published on settlement in the Eastern High Weald, an area that includes the Rother Upper Levels and is currently researching the development of wood pastures in the High Weald in the context of early settlement. His PhD thesis (University of East Anglia 2010) was on 'A Sense of Place in Rural Settlement'.

Brendan also has a background in medieval theology and church history and has undertaken post-graduate research at Birmingham University in ecclesiology (a subject on which he has also previously lectured). He is currently researching the impact of liturgical change on medieval church design and compiling a compendium of angel roofs in Somerset. He is also, of course, the editor and a contributor to this volume.

Giles Emery, BA, MCifA

Giles' archaeological career began after graduating in Archaeology from the University of Southampton in 1998, when he worked for a range of archaeological units across the south-east. He settled in Norfolk in 2002 as a Project Officer for the Norfolk Archaeological Unit. In 2009 he founded Norvic Archaeology to pursue an independent career, which has also allowed greater involvement in community outreach work. When not working on commercial projects, he is often found working alongside volunteers for the Caistor Roman Project.

He was the principal archaeologist for the Norfolk Archaeological Trust's community based Imagined Land Project at Burnham Norton and Tasburgh, and Site Director of the University of East Anglia's Operation WALBEA, working with volunteers and military personnel to investigate the WWII American airbase at Thorpe Abbotts. He is also a Leader of the Norwich branch of the Young Archaeologists' Club.

Stephen Heywood, L ès L, MA, FSA

Stephen Heywood took his first degree at the Faculté des Lettres, Aix / Marseille in History of Art and Medieval Archaeology. At the University of East Anglia his MA dissertation was on Romanesque Architecture in East Anglia. In 1982 he won the British Archaeological Association prize Essay on the Ruined Church at North Elmham. He is an elected fellow of the Society of Antiquaries and has published widely, largely on East Anglian medieval architecture.

For several years he was a listing inspector in Norfolk for the Department of the Environment (now Historic England). He then worked as historic buildings' officer for Norfolk County Council from which he has now retired. He sits on the Norwich Diocesan Advisory committee and the Norwich Cathedral Fabric Advisory Committee.

Helen Clarke BA, PhD, FSA

Helen Clarke spent much of her career as a Senior Lecturer in Medieval Archaeology for the Institute of Archaeology at University College London. She specialised in the archaeology of English medieval towns, about which she has written many articles and books. Currently, she is investigating the architectural and historical development of the medieval Carmelite friary (Whitefriars) of Sandwich, Kent. The research includes an investigation of the origins of the Carmelites in their middle-eastern homeland, and their early years in England when they founded four religious houses, Burnham Norton being one of them.

Helen's contribution to the present volume anticipates work to be published in Resurrecting Whitefriars: Sandwich's lost friary, which is in preparation.

Rachel Clarke, BA

Since graduating from Sheffield University with a BA (Hons) in Archaeology and Prehistory Rachel has gained nearly 30 years' experience in professional archaeology, predominantly as a fieldwork Project Officer working in the east of England. After joining Oxford Archaeology (then Cambridgeshire County Council Archaeological Field Unit) in 2004, Rachel directed a range of projects, developing a particular interest in medieval and post-medieval archaeology.

Rachel has published in local, regional and national journals/series and in 2014 left 'the field' to take on the role of Post-excavation Editor, editing grey literature reports and providing support and training for less-experienced colleagues in addition to continuing to author and edit publication articles and monographs.

John Alban, BA, PhD, DAA, RMARA, FSA, FRHistS, FHA

John Alban is Honorary Senior Lecturer in the School of History at the University of East Anglia and was formerly County Archivist of Norfolk, 1997-2013. He has served as a Director and Trustee of the East of England Museums, Libraries and Archives Council and as Chairman of the East of England Regional Archive Council, and is currently a Trustee of the Norfolk Archives and Heritage Development Foundation.

Previously City Archivist of Swansea, he also taught Continuing Education courses in local history, medieval Latin and palaeography for over two decades at the Universities of Swansea and Cardiff.

His PhD thesis (University of Liverpool, 1976) was on 'National Defence in England, 1337-89' and he has published extensively on aspects of local history, heraldry, archives and the Hundred Years' War. He holds fellowships of the Society of Antiquaries, the Royal Historical Society and the Historical Association.

Richard Copsey, O. Carm., MA (Oxon.), PGCE, STL, PhD.

Fr Richard Copsey is a Carmelite friar who entered the Order after teaching physics for some years. Following his ordination as a priest, he was awarded a PhD in psychology and then had various roles in the English Province as a teacher and lecturer.

In 1992, after three years as prior provincial, and following a lifetime interest in history, he was invited to join the Carmelite Institute in Rome as editor of their journal Carmelus. He returned in 1999 to become Catholic chaplain in Aberdeen University and now serves in the parish in Faversham.

He has published a series of books and articles on early Carmelite history and contributed 47 entries on individual Carmelites to the (Oxford Dictionary of National Biography (ODNB). Currently, he is preparing a Biographical Register of Carmelites in England and Wales 1240-1540 for publication.

Part I

Burnham Norton Friary: landscape, settlement and site analysis

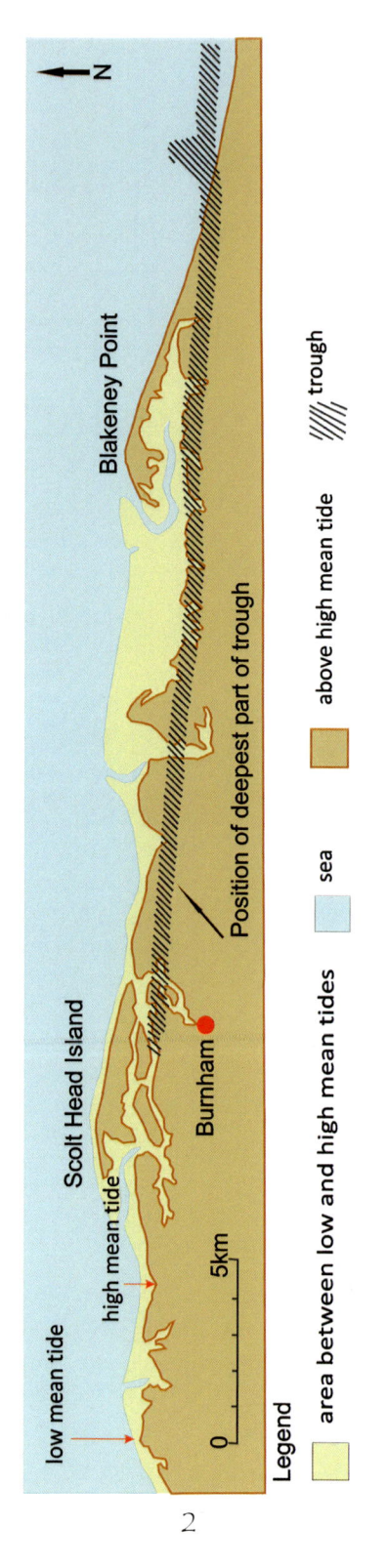

Figure 1.1 Approximate position of the pre-glacial east–west trough underlying the North Norfolk coast Map based on Chroston et al., 1999, 'Geometry of Quaternary Sediments along the Norfolk Coast, UK: a shallow seismic study', *Geological Magazine*, vol 136, no 4, p 473 fig. 6; reproduced with permission.

1

Imagined coastlines – coastal change at the port of Burnham

Jonathan Hooton

Introduction

This chapter attempts to analyse how different the Burnham Norton coastline might have been when the Carmelites first arrived in North Norfolk, and to describe the changes that have occurred since then. It also examines the issues that need to be considered when 'imagining' past coastlines.

The geomorphological processes that shape and change our world operate relentlessly, but very slowly.[1] Since the Carmelites arrived at their first site in Burnham in 1247, only a little over 750 years ago, is it reasonable to assume that the coast they saw was more or less what is there today?

There are four major factors that are responsible for altering the coast over time – erosion, deposition, sea level change and human activity – and the North Norfolk coastline is particularly responsive to all four. The geology of the coastline is neither very cohesive nor resistant to the forces of erosion, which include waves, wind and rain. Rapid rates of erosion also produce a lot of sediment, which means some areas can grow quickly as well. Norfolk is also very low-lying and therefore extremely responsive to sea level change.[2] Humans have also been active in attempting to alter this particular coast since at least Roman times.

The evolution of the North Norfolk coast during the recent geological past

It is perhaps useful to start with a general overview of the North Norfolk coastline over a larger timescale. The current coastline of the British Isles took shape roughly 6,000 years ago after the rise in sea level following the most recent Ice Age. The East Coast of the British Isles runs largely north-south, with the general direction of longshore drift moving material southerly under the influence of tidal currents and the dominant (the most powerful wave with the longest fetch) north-easterly wave. The major exception to this is the North Norfolk coast, which juts out on an east-west alignment. Recent boreholes have revealed a broad trough in the underlying chalk running west east underneath the present coastline which may account for this alignment, although at its western end, north of Burnham Norton, it is broad and shallow and not as well defined as elsewhere (Chroston et al. 1999: 472).

It has been suggested that this trough had a fluvio-glacial origin, having been cut by melt water from the melting ice sheet, but Chroston, Jones and Makin think it is likely to have a preglacial origin, and postulate that the linear North Norfolk coast was caused by east-west faulting in the underlying chalk basement which was exploited by an ancient river system and later by meltwater (Chroston et al. 1999: 473) (Figure 1.1).

Whatever the cause of the north Norfolk coastline, it does form a barrier to the generally southern movement of sediment down the present-day East Coast, and in the words of Professor Steers:

> acts as a great groyne so that material from Lincolnshire and further north, to say nothing of that raised from the shallow floor of the sea, becomes banked up against the coast (1948: 346).

The coastline at Burnham then is one of deposition, and the only erosion taking place is largely confined to resorting and moving the sediment that is already there.

The section of coast north of the Burnhams is part of what geographers describe as a barrier coastline, dominated by Scolt Head, which Steers believes is the best example of a barrier island on the British coast (1981: 4). The coastline is characterised by a high tidal range and low wave energy, as well as having a very gentle offshore gradient (Andrews et al. 1999: 221).[3] This leads to large areas of sand being exposed at low tide. Sand is then blown inland and may accumulate around shells, pebbles or obstacles. A bank of sand may emerge that is above the high tide mark. If this is not destroyed by storms, vegetation may colonise it, stabilising the feature and trapping further sand. This can result in a permanent bank which usually adopts a crescent shape along this coastline. This process is happening at the present time in Holkham Bay. The sheltered low-energy environment behind the barrier island then encourages the development of a saltmarsh which further increases sedimentation. The process of longshore drift can then resculpt this feature.

The prominent direction of drift on this section of coast is westerly for the coarser material, like shingle. However, current thinking is that the net movement of the finer sand is actually from west to east, aided by tidal currents and wind. Sand will bleed across channels from west to east and fix on to the western end of a feature such as Scolt Head. This then provides a platform for the coarser material, which is brought in the opposite direction from the east, by wave action, which is often eroding the eastern end. In this way, Scolt Head and other smaller barriers move to the west (Pethick 2000).

These barriers are also moving inland at an average of about 1 m a year. This movement is not constant and usually only occurs during a tidal surge. A surge tide with strong northerly winds will drive the waves over the top of the shingle ridge and/or dunes, eroding the seaward side and driving sediment inland over the marshes (May 2003: 10). A surge tide might not occur for 30 years or so, but then the barrier ridges might retreat up to 30 m. Evidence for this process can be seen in salt marsh sediment appearing on the seaward-facing beach. These processes are currently shaping the coast, and have been operating for at least the past 6,000 years.

The probable coastline that the Carmelites experienced

So what was the coastline like in the early 1200s when the Carmelites arrived? It was probably not strikingly different from the present day, except that there was little or no embankment. Certainly Cracknell says of the area to the west that 'By the time of the Norman Conquest most of the Wash coastline had been successfully embanked and it looked very much as it does today' (2005: 49). The biggest notable difference would probably have been the wider, deeper estuaries of rivers, like the Burn, which drained northward towards the sea. These rivers might originally have been tributaries of a pre-glacial river that occupied the west-east-running trough in the underlying chalk along the course of the present coastline (referred to earlier; see Figure 1.1). Chroston, Jones and Makin state that 'there may well be channels cutting into the trough that are associated with the northward draining rivers of the Burn, Glaven and Stiffkey' (1999: 472). Certainly these estuaries were wide and ran much further inland than at present, and the Burn may well have been navigable at high tide to Burnham Overy town (and hence the Carmelites' second site) for small ships.

At about the same time, the River Glaven was tidal inland as far as the watermill at Glandford (Hooton 1996: 19) and there were references even as late as the first half of the nineteenth century that the waterwheel at Glandford mill had been seen turning backwards, allowing sea water to penetrate into the fresh water of the Glaven upstream of the mill during exceptionally high tides (*HLRO* 1846). There would also have been a larger tidal prism (amount of sea water enclosed behind the barrier islands covering the salt marshes as well as the estuary) than at present. During high spring tides this would lead to a large volume of water draining back through the channels during the ebb tide, and the increased scour would prevent the estuary from silting up. This would have been even more effective during a surge tide.

Scolt Head would have been well established, although farther out to sea and more to the east than at present, as the positioning of the laterals indicates a continual westerly movement. However, it would have provided a sheltered area for shipping in the channels behind it. Most of the settlement would have been inland, surrounding the banks of the estuary of the Burn. Therefore the coastal marshland would have led to a bleak, isolated environment potentially attractive to the Carmelites when they first settled at Bradmer in around 1247.

However, the climate was changing. The medieval warm period led to sea level rise and increased storminess. There is no consensus on the exact start or finish of the period, but Cracknell divides it into two periods which he terms 'A false dawn 1000–1200' and 'Fearful tempests 1200–1400' (2005: 50-1). Certainly there would have been a time lag between the improving climatic conditions and the start of the effects of climate warming. It is likely that the rise in sea level, however much it was, had little visible effect on the Burnham coastline. This is because it is likely that salt marsh growth was able to keep pace with sea level rise. This was certainly the finding based on a recent study of the growth of Hut Marsh, behind Scolt Head, where the average rate of vertical accretion was nearly 4 mm per year, whereas sea-level rise was only 1.5–2.0 mm per year (French and Spencer, quoted in May 2003: 14).

Therefore it appears that the Carmelites came to Burnham when the benefits of the medieval warm period outweighed the costs. However, certainly most experts seem to agree with Cracknell, that the thirteenth and fourteenth centuries were a period of damaging storms. The worst effects of this would have been an increase in the severity and frequency of coastal flooding caused by tidal surges.

There are several factors that cause the destructiveness of surge tides in the North Sea. Tides vary in height in a predictable way; tides move down the east coast of Britain from north to south, pulling the water with them; water collects in the southern North Sea because it is funnel-shaped; the only way for the water to escape is through the narrow straits of the Channel, causing a bottleneck. When these factors coincide with a deep depression moving over the North Sea bringing strong northerly winds, water starts to accumulate in the southern end of the North Sea and sea levels can increase between 5 and 6 m above normal, thus threatening low-lying coasts and estuaries.

The Carmelites' move from Bradmer to Burnham Norton

Could it be that some serious storms and flooding between 1247 and 1253 helped convince the Friars to move the site of their friary? This must obviously remain conjecture, especially since the precise location of Bradmer, the first site, is not known. This happened to the Carmelites in Suffolk during the next century, when they relocated from Minsmere to Leiston in 1363 'as a result of the sea flooding they had endured at their previous site on the coast' (Cracknell 2005: 66). The Norfolk coast did suffer damage from a great storm on 1 October 1250, when the sea broke through the dunes between Happisburgh and Winterton according to Cracknell (2005: 64). Matthew Paris described it thus: 'What was more destructive, the disturbed sea transgressed its usual bounds, the tide flowing twice without any ebb', and later that at Winchelsea, 'more than three hundred houses in that village, with some churches, were thrown down by the impetuous rise of the sea'. It is not stated whether Burnham was affected, but Paris goes on to say that 'Holland in England, and Holland on the continent also, as well as Flanders and other level countries adjoining the sea sustained irreparable damage.' Holland in England refers to Lincolnshire, so the flooding seemed fairly extensive. He also mentions that the rivers were 'forced back and swelled to such a degree' that inland valleys suffered flooding as well (1852: 391-3). In summing up the year that the friars moved, Paris also says, 'In this year, too, the sea and rivers several times overflowed their usual bounds, doing irreparable damage to the adjacent country.' Whether this was a contributory factor to the moving of the friary site or not, the friars must have been relieved that by 1287 they were farther inland. This was because during that year, according to Lamb, there were five great storms (two in January, two in February and one in December) which caused much loss of life throughout Norfolk (cited in Cracknell 2005: 64).

There are no early maps of this stretch of the coast to substantiate these claims. The first accurate map of the coast did not appear until the end of the eighteenth century. William Faden's map of Norfolk was surveyed between 1790 and 1794 and published in 1797 (Figure 1.2). This map is very helpful in visualising the past coast, since the marshes and estuary are coloured in blue. Here it is easy to see the barrier coast, with the low spring tide mark, a long way offshore, exposing large amounts of sand available for accumulating onshore around the offshore barriers. Although these offshore bars are not in the exact positions they were in the thirteenth century, the protection they afforded for the coastline and harbours, and the large sheltered areas of salt marsh that develops in their lee, gave a very similar appearance that would have been familiar to the first friars that arrived in North Norfolk. By Faden's time, the River Burn would have been shut off by a bank across

Figure 1.2 The Burnhams, extract from Faden's Map of Norfolk 1797. Source: Macnair (2005).

its mouth from Burnham Norton to the road leading to Overy Staithe (the sluice in the bank being clearly labelled); however, the blue shading gives an idea of the size of the medieval estuary. This would have flooded every high tide, with the ebb producing a scour that kept the river channel deeper than today. Also it would have flooded a larger area all the way inland as far as Burnham Thorpe under storm surge conditions. All of the inhabitants of the Burn valley would have felt more closely connected to the coast than the present day, when the sea can appear a long way distant behind reclaimed marshland and the extensive nature reserves that are there today.

Figure 1.3 presents a plan version of a comparison between the coastlines at the end of the eighteenth century, using William Faden's map of 1797, and a post-Second World War (1954) Ordnance Survey map.[4] It shows that apart from the substantial area of marshland reclaimed by Thomas Telford in 1825 the only other changes are fairly minor and relate to the offshore bars, in particular Scolt Head. This island has grown to the west and gained larger laterals as well as moving inland.

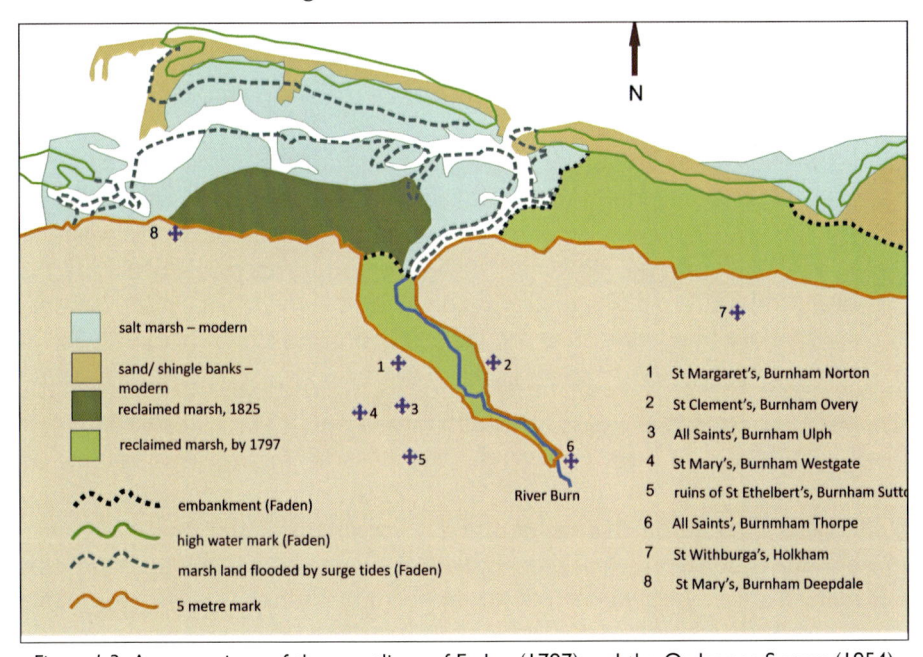

Figure 1.3 A comparison of the coastlines of Faden (1797) and the Ordnance Survey (1954).

The medieval port of Burnham

These deeper channels were exploited of course by shipping. Burnham was a port. Although earlier maps do not exist, documents referring to the maritime trade, and later to the embanking of the marshes, help paint a picture of what the coastline was like and how important it was to the inhabitants.

That the Burnhams were considered an important settlement in North Norfolk can be inferred from their inclusion in the Gough map. This map is thought to date from around 1360–70, although later overwriting is thought to date from the fifteenth century. Burnham appears near the coast in the form of a single building and the name 'burndon', the etymology being *burna* (a stream) plus *'ham'* (a farm). It is placed near the coast almost equidistant between Walsingham and Lynn. There is little indication that it was a port or had a friary, but the same applied to the single building that denoted Blakeney, which was a thriving port with a Carmelite friary (Linguistic Geographies n.d.).

The Elizabethan shipping survey of 1565 illustrates maritime activity of the period (NRO 523). The entry for 'Burnh'm Depdell and Burnh'm Ovry'y at Burnh'm Norton' states that 'The sayde townes are situate nigh a haven adjoyne to two Cryckes ther called Burnh'm Rodested.' This would seem to indicate that the 'Rodested' referred to the area at the east end of Norton creek, which was sheltered from the open sea by the eastern end of Scolt Head island and the dunes around Gun Hill. From this area of refuge, channels or 'Cryckes' ran to Burnham Overy Staithe and Burnham Norton, and in earlier times up the Burn valley to the friary. Although Burnham Deepdale can be accessed by a rather tortuous Norton creek – which might have been more navigable in past centuries, it appears as a much wider and straighter channel called East Creek on Faden's map – it would seem more logical for any ships from Burnham Deepdale to have used the Brancaster channel at the western end of Scolt Head island. However, as will be seen from later documents, it was rather difficult to distinguish which vessels belong to which settlement, and it was more likely that they used all of them from time to time.

The place name element 'burn', as already mentioned, comes from a stream. At no time in the past was this a large river, it was an estuary which filled with water on high spring tides quite a way inland. This volume of water flowing out to sea on the ebb tide kept the channels deep and usable. Medieval craft were much smaller and flat-bottomed, so that they were able to sit in the mud flats at low tide. These craft were also at the mercy of the weather, so a sheltered 'Rodested' was important when they were liable to be driven onshore in northerly gales. Scolt Head Island therefore was as much a benefit as the estuary was to medieval craft.

The etymology of Scolt Head island is obscure. Steers devotes a chapter to it in his book (1934 [1960]). Names on maps do not go further back than the late eighteenth century, and the name cannot be traced further back unless it comes from Skottermuth, the old name for Brancaster Harbour. If that is the case then it is possible that it comes from Scout, meaning a projecting ridge, as in Kinderscout in the Peak District. It may also come from the old English *sceald*, meaning shallow, or from *scald* – scald head is also the common name for hounds-tongue which is common on Scolt Head. There are also several other unlikely suggested origins.[5]

The name 'Skottermuth' is found in the Patent Rolls for March 1301. Edward I (1239–1307) was in the process of assembling a fleet to gather at Berwick-on-Tweed by midsummer to fight the Scots by writing to the bailiffs of the ports to provide ships. Skottermuth and Brunnemuth were expected to provide one ship. This must refer to the channels at either end of Scolt Head island, leading to the landing places of Brancaster and Burnham Deepdale in the west and Burnham Norton and Overy in the east. All of these areas were considered as one administrative unit, as were Thornham and Holm, and 'Hecham and Flichene', which were also tasked to provide a ship. To put this into context in Norfolk, six ships were expected from Yarmouth, three from Lynn and two from Blakeney (*CPR* Edward I, 1895: 583).

Burnham ports during and after the Carmelite friary

Burnham was still an important harbour during the period of the Carmelites' expansion. The medieval warm period had probably started around 1000 AD but because there is always a time lag involved, it was not until the thirteenth century that the effects of a changing climate were felt. Although it is likely that the barrier islands and their marshes kept pace with any rise in sea level, that change would have kept water levels higher in the channels, and the increase in the storminess of the thirteenth and fourteenth centuries led to flood events which kept the channels well scoured as the storm water ebbed back to the sea. As Cracknell put it, 'Along the north coast of Norfolk the rise in sea level must have been a boon to the small ports that lay behind the protecting spits of Blakeney and Scolt Head' (2005: 65).

Certainly there is evidence that Burnham was trading overseas at this point. In August 1294 a commission was appointed to look into the complaints of Reynbricghtus and Folcardus de Greninge, two German merchants, who stated that 'certain persons' stole goods out of their ship when it was in the 'port of Brunham' in Norfolk (*CPR* Edward I, 1895: 114). How much the friars were involved with the port is difficult to assess, but they were certainly benefiting from the buoyant trade and activity since only four years later, in June 1298, that they were given a rood of meadow by Walter de Calthorp 'for the enlargement of their place' (*CPR* Edward I, 1895: 354).

During the latter part of Edward II's reign (1307–27) there was a lot of conflict and much lawlessness. Again, a German ship heading for Hull was attacked and goods stolen, off the coast near Blakeney, in 1322. It appears likely it was attacked by two ships, judging by the names and home ports of those accused. This assumption is given more credence by the fact that they were to be tried by a jury from Suffolk and another jury from Norfolk. At least ten of the accused came from Burnham and three from 'Depedale', and others from Wells, Thornham, Titchwell and Hunstanton. They included a Thomas Mirihel of Brunham and a Thomas Mirihel of Brunnemuth. This was probably a mistake by the scribe, and there was only one Thomas Mirihel who lived in one of the Burnhams but operated out of the port known as Brunnemuth (*CPR* Edward II, 1904: 159).

Earlier that year, Edward II had been preparing for another Scottish campaign against Robert the Bruce. In March the bailiffs of Burnham were requested, along with many other ports, to send armed men and victuals, in as many ships as they could, to the Humber (*CCR* Edward II, 1895: 524). A month later, those same bailiffs were requested to go to Lynn to listen to orders from the bishop of Norwich and Walter do Norwyco (the treasurer) and to discuss what subsidies they could offer (*CCR* Edward II, 1895: 536). By June of that year the king wanted five more ships, but at least this time he was willing to reimburse the expenses. Burnham was expected to provide one of these five (*CCR* Edward II, 1895: 463). A month later, Burnham was included in a request to many ports to 'cause to be sent to the King in the north, new and old corn and other victuals from time to time with all possible speed' (*CCR* Edward II, 1895: 670). Whether he received any from Burnham is not recorded.

Further requests for ships, two years later, hint at the usual trade carried out by the larger ships. In May 1324 ports (including Burnham) were requested to retain and make ready for naval service all ships capable of carrying 40 tuns of wine and upward. This indicated that Burnham was considered a port capable of trading with larger ships as well as fishing vessels. They were to be retained to be ready to set out in the king's service within three days of being summoned. This enforced inactivity must have caused much resentment, since in July that year the mayors and bailiffs of a variety of East Anglian ports, including 'Brunham', were asked to retain only enough ships 'as shall suffice' and to allow the rest 'to go to Poitou or Gascony, as the masters of the ships shall elect, for the exercise of merchandise'. Although there is no direct evidence, it does imply that Burnham was a port that dealt in overseas trade with the French Atlantic ports and was capable of berthing ships of 40 or more tons in size (*CCR* Edward II, 1898: 183–84 and 201).[6]

In the nearby Glaven valley ports it is possible that the Carmelites prospered from the maritime trade. The so-called Blakeney Chapel, sited on Thornham's Eye (or island) was conveniently placed at the mouth of the River Glaven, leading to the ports of Cley and Wiveton. Here dues could be collected and prayers offered up for a safe journey. Although the name

Blakeney Chapel is old (in 1596 a document refers to it as 'an old house called the Chapell': Lee 2006: 3), there is no definite evidence linking this with the Blakeney Carmelite friary, or indeed with any form of religious ownership. However, excavations show that the foundations of the main structure dated to the fourteenth/fifteenth century and that the building had had 'substantial time and money spent upon it'. There was also evidence of a track leading south-westwards, in the direction of the Carmelite friary. The conclusions were that the results had 'not presented any conclusive proof that the site contained a chapel or an ecclesiastical building of any type, however, nor could it be refuted' (Lee 2006: 8, 18–19). The positioning of the friary site at Burnham was not in such a strategic position to control trade, so it is likely that the major benefit of the Burnham ports to the friary was in the supply of goods from afar.

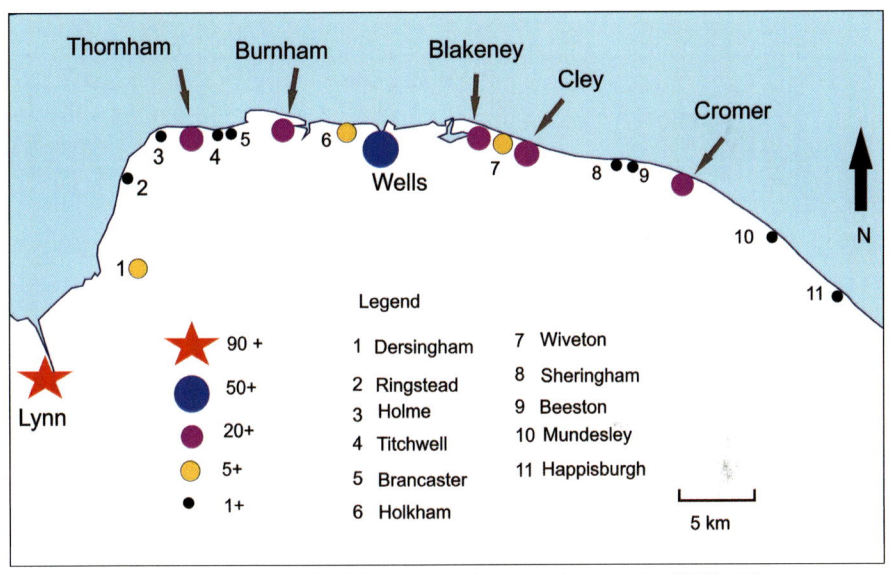

Figure 1.4 North Norfolk ports trading with Newcastle (1508–11).

The Burnham ports and the fifteenth-century coal trade

By the fifteenth century, the scanty evidence so far indicates that the rising sea levels of the medieval warm period kept a variety of channels behind the shelter of Scolt Head island deep enough to support a regular trade in coastal and continental European goods; and that these settlements maintained a fleet of ships of the size that could be used by the sovereign for warfare. It is only towards the end of the friary's existence and in the years immediately after the dissolution of the monasteries that there is a little more evidence that can shed some light on the trade and coastline of the Burnhams. The first piece of evidence comes from the Newcastle upon Tyne Chamberlain's

Accounts for the collection of tolls from ships covering the period 1508–11 (Fraser 1987). These accounts record ships coming into Newcastle for coal. Newcastle was supplying coal to ports from Edinburgh to Portsmouth, as well as abroad, including many of the East Anglian ports.

Figure 1.4 illustrates the comparative size of ship movements along the North Norfolk coast between 1508 and 1511.[7] It uses coloured, proportional symbols to represent the number of voyages to Newcastle mentioned in the Chamberlain's Accounts, for a period of three years and three months, from the ports along the Norfolk coast.

Not surprisingly, Norfolk was dominated by Lynn (104 ships) and Yarmouth (305 ships), with their large river systems, supplying inland settlements (Wright 2000). However, because the overland movement of coal was so difficult and expensive, many of the North Norfolk creeks, including Burnham, sent ships for coal. During the period May 1508 to August 1511 45 ships left the estuary of the Burn to bring back coal; if we consider the period 1 July 1508 to 30 June 1511 (exactly three years) there was an average of about 15 trips a year (Wright 2000).

Although the ships are described in the accounts as being 'of Burnham' or 'of Holkham', it becomes obvious that the same ship, with the same name, same master and the same cargo capacity, often served both ports. Therefore it is necessary to consider the level of trade for the whole estuary, which here included Brancaster, Burnham and Holkham. It is difficult to assess the exact number of ships, since many of the ships had the same name. It is fairly safe to assume that the *Cristoffer* of Burnham and the *Cristoffer* of Brancaster, which both made two trips to Newcastle in 1510, was the same ship since the master for all four trips was Nicholas Bodom and each time she returned with 13 chaldrons of coal. However, this might not be the *Cristoffer* of Holkham which made eight trips from 1509–11 with John or Thomas Mansser as the master, and returned with either 15 or 16 chaldrons of coals.

The shipping trade was obviously a family affair. A third Mansser, William, was master of the *Nycolles* of Burnham. There may well have been a *Nycolles* of Brancaster, with Nicholas Bodom as master, since this vessel seemed to ship three more chaldrons of coals. Or was it the same vessel with Nicholas willing to take a greater risk by overloading his ship? As well as the Manssers and Nicholas and William Bodom (sometimes Botham), there was William Petten (or Pepyn) who was master of the *Trinitie* of Burnham, and there are two references to a William Pell (or Pen) who was master of the *Cristoffer* during the last three months of the Chamberlain's accounts. Although it is impossible to be certain, there were probably six different vessels using this estuary during this period.

It is easier to be more definitive about the cargoes. Some vessels did arrive empty, but usually they took small amounts of grain – mainly barley, but sometimes wheat, rye or malt, and on two occasions 'mascillyn' (meslin, a mixture of wheat and rye). The return cargo was always coal. The only exception during this period was when William Mansser, in the *Nycolles* of Burnham, returned with 7½ weys of salt in September 1510 (Fraser 1987: 173).

These ships carried between 6 and 16 chaldrons of coal, which might give an indication of the depth of water in the channels during this period. By comparing tonnage with chaldrons carried later in the sixteenth century and then adjusting the figures by the fact that the weight of a chaldron rose steadily from 18 cwt *c.* 1420 to 53 cwt *c.* 1700, John Wright makes a convincing case that the chaldrons of coal carried in a ship of this period were 80 per cent of its tonnage (2000).

Therefore the largest cargo coming to Burnham (16 chaldrons) indicates a ship of around 20 tons. These vessels would have been flat-bottomed and able to settle in the channel at low tide. It is interesting to note that nearby Thornham was able to accommodate ships carrying 38 chaldrons, which would mean a vessel approaching 50 tons.

Shipping surveys of the second half of the sixteenth century

The next documents to give an indication of the size of vessels and importance of Burnham as a port are the shipping surveys in the second half of the sixteenth century. Although these occur after the dissolution of the Burnham friary they are worth considering as the coastline, port and channels would not have changed that significantly in the time period. The Special Elizabethan Commission of 1565 placed Burnham Deepdale, Overy and Norton together and described the port thus: 'The sayde townes are Situate nigh a haven and adjoyne to two Crykes ther called Burn'm Rodested' and later 'Ther are shippes that pteyne to ye said town or be occupied in cayeng corne northwrde w'thin ye Realme of recarye Coales to ye number of 2' (NRO 523).

The ships listed were in two categories: ships for Iceland (the larger ones) and Crayers and boats of burden. Both of Burnham's ships were in the latter category. This would indicate that the estuary here was smaller and shallower than at neighbouring Wells (which had seven Iceland ships, the largest being 80 tons) and the Glaven, where Blakeney, Cley and Wiveton had ten Iceland ships between them (the largest, the *Mary Grace* of Cley, being 100 tons). Neville Williams pointed out that by the second half of the sixteenth century neither Wells nor Burnham had any resident customs officials: masters were supposed to make the 20-mile journey to Lynn to custom their goods. However, he did say that 'Wells possessed a considerable fleet of traders and one writer thought Burnham the best harbour between Harwich and Newcastle' (1988: 5).

This means that it is impossible to discover from the Lynn port books, introduced after 1565, which entries related to ships from these ports. A lack of customs officials also might be of advantage to those wishing to ship goods illegally, and later Williams comments, 'there are indications of corn being smuggled north (to Scotland) from Lynn and Burnham'.

There are two other Tudor surveys, in 1572 and 1580, that mention ships from Burnham, and all three are summarised in Table 1.1. This appears to indicate a slow decline in both size and tonnage of ships as the century progressed. However, tonnage measurement was not an exact science and the surveys were not always easily comparable; for instance the 1580 survey ignored ships smaller than 16 tons. Neville Williams also made a thorough search of the Kings Lynn port books for 1586/87 for vessels not mentioned in the 1580 survey, and concluded that in the period 1582–87 the shipping at that port had increased by a further 1,324 tons (or 26 new ships). He went on to state that 'Burnham had similarly increased its shipping by 482 tons (or a further thirteen ships) in those five years. The development of the coal trade lay at the root of this expansion' (1988: 222–3). He does not expand on how the Burnham ships were identified, but where detailed records survive, a comparison of these records with the port books frequently show that they understate the trade, as in the neighbouring Glaven ports (Hooton 1996: 81).

Table 1.1   Ships from the Burnhams in the sixteenth century.

Year	Name of ship	Tonnage	Owners
1565	Goddes Grace	30	Thomas Baxter
	Kateryn of Burnh'm	42	Robert Hargate & Richard Cap
1572	Anne	40	Edward Gerost?
	Swallow	40	Christopher Moore
	George	10	John Saffore
	Mayre	10	Robert Read
	Trynite	10	James Smythe
1580	Marie Sysley of Burneham	20	John Shorte and Robert Smythe
	Saker of Burneham	20	John Smyth and Ed Smythe

Sources: NRO 523; CSPD vol 22 1566-79; Smith and Baker (1982/3: 143–50).[8]

The effects of embankment on the coastline

Although the trade of the north Norfolk ports still seemed buoyant in the 1580s, changes were afoot that would see them lose their prominent position. Ships were getting larger and less able to cope with the Norfolk creeks, especially as the focus of trade began to change from the North Sea to the Atlantic. Also, engineers were beginning to think about reclaiming the marshland. Although this started to take place around 100 years after the Carmelites were dissolved, these changes had a profound effect on the Burnham coastline and economy; it would be fruitful to end this chapter by considering the impact that embanking had on the imagined coastline.

It is likely that some embanking occurred during the medieval period (Albone et al. 2007: 107). Also, at some time a bank with a sluice went across the River Burn; the staithe at Burnham Overy, nearer the sea, took over the maritime functions from the older site of Burnham Overy town. Although this necessitated the transhipment of goods over the embankment into smaller boats in order to be moved inland, it made riverside sites like the friary safer from flooding. However, it is not known when this took place, and it might well have occurred after the Dissolution.

The first dateable embanking that took place was in 1630, when Sir Philip Parker embanked a saltmarsh in Burnham Overy, called the Piles and containing 104 acres. It was described as 'bounded by the sea bank on the N., the harbour on the E., a line drawn from Burnham Overy to the "key" on the S. and Crinkleshaw Creek on the W' in Walter Rye's 'Maritime history of Norfolk' (NRO MC 106/11). Whether this refers to the 'Piles bank' on Faden's map is unclear. This is in the parish of Burnham Norton, not Overy. It may be possible that this was the northern bank, but only if the 'key' mentioned in the southern boundary was that of Burnham Norton and 'Crinkleshaw Creek' (as yet, unidentified) referred to the channel leading to Burnham Norton. The eastern boundary would then make sense as the harbour channel. Wherever this particular enclosure was, within the next ten years more enclosure took place along the north Norfolk marshes from Holme to Salthouse, and much of it involved the Dutch drainage engineer Jan van Haesdoncke.

At Burnham van Haesdoncke had joined with William Neve to enclose and drain some of the salt marshes, and in 1641 forty 'poor fisherman, inhabitants of the towns of Burnham Norton, Burnham Deepdale and Burnham Overy' petitioned the House of Lords complaining about the damage done to their livelihoods by the embanking (Historical Manuscripts Commission 4th Report, 1874, reprinted in Smith 2012). The petitioners estimated that the area enclosed was about 1,000 acres. The 40 poor fishermen were involved in dredging for oysters, most of which were bought and then resold in

London by a local entrepreneur, Thomas Hooper. Their complaint was that 'severall odle channelles and havens are so straytened and stopped' that their ships (described as small cobble boats) could now no longer approach the settlements and they were forced to carry the oysters on their backs for up to 3 furlongs to the detriment of their trade. It is interesting to note that they mention that 'whereas formerly shipps of great burthen could have come upp unto our gates to loade and unloade there burthen' this was no longer possible. This implies that the Burnham ports no longer engaged in coastal trade with larger vessels. Throughout the petition the only vessels mentioned are 'our small Cobble Boates which are dayly imployed att Sea in dragginge of Oysters', and the petitioners complained of 'having noe other meanes of livelihood but dragging of Oysters and fishing att Sea'. They also were fully aware of the effect that the embanking had on the channels that were still open when they stated that 'the said Channells doe continewally everie day more and more syltt upp'. This was because the embanking prevented the marshes flooding at high spring tides and tidal surges, when large volumes of water would ebb off the marshes, naturally scouring the channels and keeping them deep (Smith 2012).

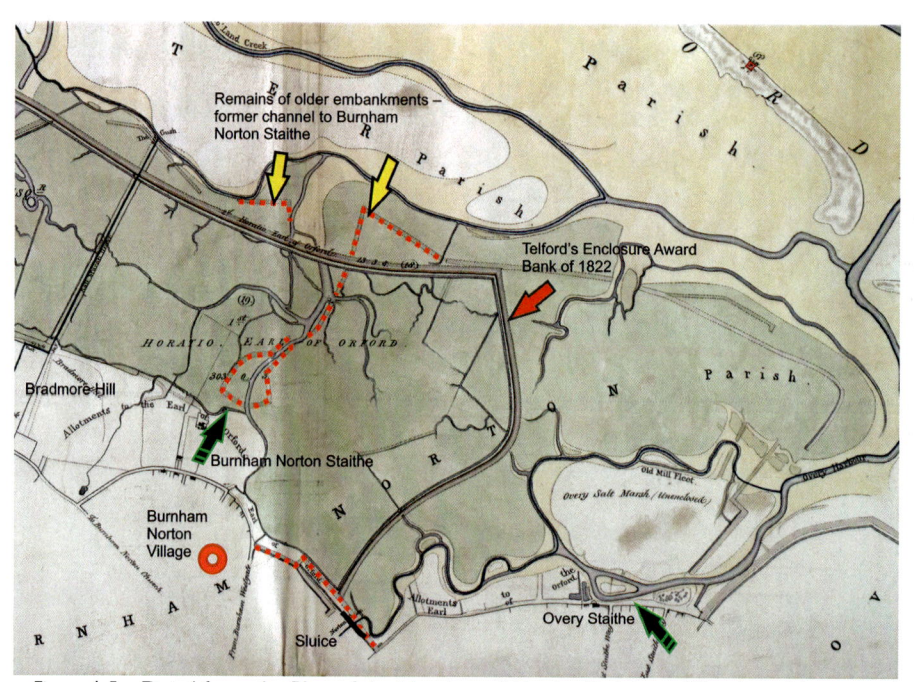

Figure 1.5   Detail from the Plan of the Marshes within the Parishes of Burnham Norton and Burnham Deepdale 1825 by J Dugmore.
The annotations point out the remains of older embankments.

It would be interesting to know if this embanking cut across the channel that led to Burnham Norton key, an area of marshes later referred to as Norton Broad. These embankments run north to south either side of a channel that led to the Old Quay just north of Marsh Farm. The Norfolk Heritage Explorer refers to these banks as post medieval flood defences. These banks, plus other remains of old banks, can be clearly seen on the map of 1825, which shows the bank built by Telford as a result of the Enclosure award and which is still there today (NRO C/2FSca 2/2F060/3: see Figure 1.5).

Conclusion

The Carmelite friars settled on this coast towards the end of the medieval warm period, with rising sea levels and violent storm surges which kept the tidal inlets scoured and usable by 'ships of Burthen'. They would have recognised a busy port with vessels of 20 to 45 tons employed in the coastal trade and occasionally trading overseas. The masters of these vessels probably used the creeks leading to Holkham, Overy, Norton, Deepdale and Brancaster from time to time. By the time of the Dissolution, the Warm period was over and the cooler conditions of the Little Ice Age were approaching. This, combined with a move to larger ships and a change of focus in trade from the North Sea towards the Atlantic, led to a decline in the coastal trade and a switch to fishing from smaller boats. Sea walls and embanking culminating in Telford's fine bank produced a coastline which must have looked very similar to that of today.

At present, sea levels are rising, land sinking, and longshore drift is continually making minor adjustments to the shape and positioning of the offshore features. Today it seems that the onshore movement of material and the continual growth of salt marshes (as witnessed by the recent dune barriers, and back shore salt marshes growing in Holkham Bay) is capable of keeping pace with sea level rise. Whether this will remain so in the future is open to debate. With the deliberate breaching of embankments and restoration of salt marshes starting to take place on the East Anglian coast, it might not be long before the coastline becomes more like one that the first Carmelites might have felt more familiar with.

Notes

1 The landscape in seismically stable areas, not subject to earthquakes and volcanic eruptions, can be seen as relatively unchanging or fluidly dynamic, depending on the timescale that is being considered. A steady erosion rate of 1 mm a year appears barely perceptible during a lifetime; it would result in the retreat of a coastline of a mere 10 cm if you lived to be 100. However over a million years that same rate of retreat would lead to a loss of a kilometre, and a million years is a very short time in the life of the planet (4½ billion years). Of course erosion rates often vary from year to year, and some coastlines erode much faster than that. In Norfolk, Happisburgh is a good example, having lost 17 m of cliff in one storm!

2 This could be due to eustatic change (changes in the volume of water) or isostatic change (a relative change due to sinking or emerging of land) or in Norfolk's case, a combination of both.

3 The current tidal range is 6.6 m for mean spring tides at Hunstanton, and the coast between Scolt Head and Blakeney has an average wave height of 0.2–0.3 m.

4 The information was taken from Faden's map of Norfolk (1797, surveyed 1790–94) and one of the last inch to the mile Ordnance Survey Maps (1950, fully revised 1954) because they both used the same scale allowing for easy comparison. The position of the eight church sites, present on both maps, was aligned to allow a comparison of the surveyed coastlines.

5 Scald Head is also an old name for ringworm of the scalp, and it is suggested that the patchy cover of vegetation might suggest ringworm. Another meaning is land likely to be scorched by the sun on the highest part of a field. Scaldy is also used to describe land affected by drought, and was used in this fashion by William Marshall in connection with Norfolk in his *Rural Economy* in 1787.

6 Size of vessels was measured by the amount of cargo they could carry, and the unit adopted in England was the Bordeaux wine cask or tun. Although this was a measure of capacity, in time it came to have a standard equivalent in weight similar to the modern 'ton' measurement. After a lengthy examination of fifteenth-century documents Dorothy Burwash concludes that 'it is clearly permissible to treat figures given in fifteenth-century records as expressing something very close to modern cargo tonnage', although it must be remembered that there was no accurate way of measuring the tun and the masters probably depended on experience to estimate cargo-carrying capacity (1969: 88–95).

7 Taken from Fraser (1987). The symbols indicate the relative importance of the trade as suggested by the number of ships from each port.

8 NRO 523 is a facsimile and translation of a survey of the "several havens, creeks and landing places in the county of Norfolk" which is located at The National Archives, Calendar of State Papers Domestic (*CSPD*) under Elizabeth I Volume 37, 1547-80. The originals were also repurposed by Robert Lemon (London, 1856). The second reference is a 1572 Shipping Survey entitled "Merchant Shipps in England AD 1572" found in the Calendar of State Papers Domestic, Elizabeth I, Addenda Volume 22, 1566-79. It has also been repurposed by Mary Ann Everett Green (London 1871). The third reference is from the published papers of Nathanaiel Bacon of Stiffkey. It is a certificate of maritime resources in Norfolk and is entitled "An abstracte of the certificate sent to the Lord Admyrall in Novembre 1580."

2

The Burnhams from the fifth to the fourteenth centuries

Andrew Rogerson

Introduction

Brunham or *Bruneham*, the 'river village or estate', was probably so named at an early stage of Anglo-Saxon period, in the fifth or sixth century (Williamson 2005). The tautologically named River Burn must thus have been of major importance from the beginning. For the medievalist the Burnhams stand out from the crowd of Norfolk places, and in the sixth or seventh century would have 'formed a single territorial unit, covering an area of nearly 40 square kilometres' (Williamson 1993: 92–3). David Dymond considered the possibility that this land block, 'abnormally large for an East Anglian township', was even more ancient, and 'was the remains of a sizeable Romano-British estate' (1985: 62).

At the present day four civil parishes, Market, Norton, Overy and Thorpe share the name, while Deepdale lies in the civil parish of Brancaster. The names Sutton and Ulph might have largely fallen by the wayside in official administrative nomenclature but have survived in the name of an ecclesiastical parish. Amongst East Anglian places only the South Elmhams in north-east Suffolk share such a multiple name usage and such a proliferation of rural parish churches (Clarke 1921: 132). In the thirteenth century there were nine churches in the Burnhams, forming a veritable, almost urban concentration, in what Dymond (1985: 82) called an 'extreme case'.[1] Entries in the Domesday survey of 1086 are numerous and complex, and the manorial history convoluted and baffling. It is telling that Allison began the last paragraph of his seminal work on medieval village desertion in Norfolk with the sentence 'The Burnhams, in north Norfolk, pose several problems' (1955: 162).

Although there was no major town here in the Middle Ages, there were two monastic foundations, a house of Carmelite friars and an Augustinian priory. It is, however, the Burnhams' pre-Norman Conquest or Anglo-Saxon significance that in recent years has provoked such intense interest, thanks entirely to the contribution of archaeology, in the way of surface finds, field surveys, excavations and landscape analysis. The terms 'Early Saxon', 'Middle Saxon' and 'Late Saxon' are employed in this chapter solely as simple chronological indicators or periods, and do not imply any judgements on racial or cultural distinctions: Early Saxon early fifth-mid/late seventh century; Middle Saxon mid/late seventh-mid/late ninth century; Late Saxon mid/late ninth-eleventh century.

When Norfolk's archaeological database (the Sites and Monuments Record, SMR, now known as the Historic Environment Record, HER[2]) was first compiled at the newly founded County Archaeological Unit between 1973 and 1975, it contained only one reliable record concerning Burnham before the Norman Conquest: the discovery in 1962 at the primary school in Friars Lane of fragments of an Early Saxon copper alloy Great Square-headed brooch 'thrown up by [a] cultivator into [the] school fences'. In the same year a single sherd of possibly Middle Saxon pottery was found close by.[3] David Yaxley with his typical eloquence considered the history of the Burnhams 'difficult to disentangle', but had very little archaeological data to fill in the pre-Norman background (1977: 58–9).

During the 1980s this state of ignorance or absence of information began to become transformed thanks to the efforts of a schoolmaster and amateur archaeologist, John Smallwood. With his band of A-level pupils from King

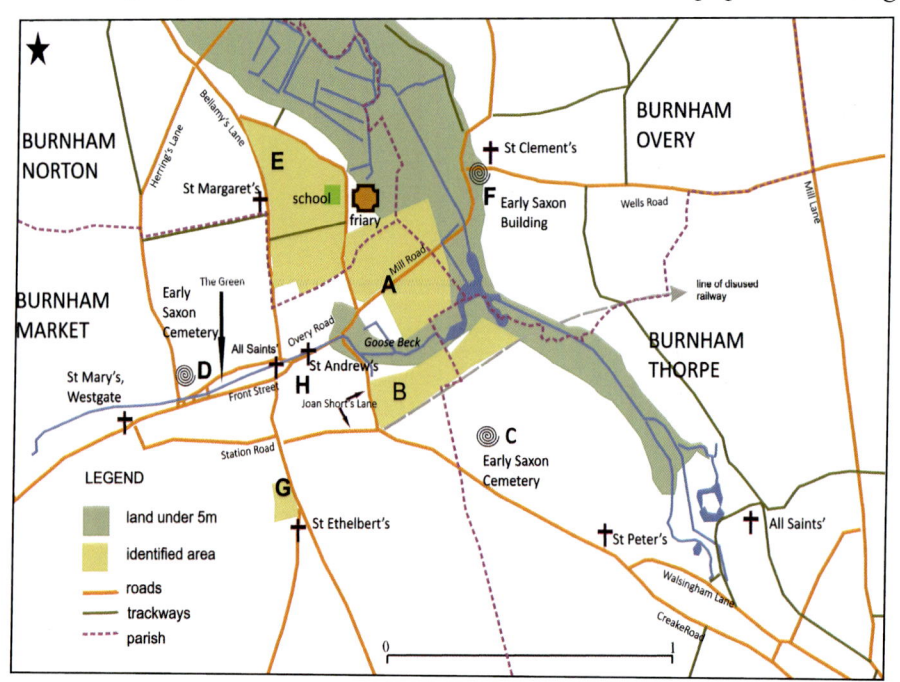

Figure 2.1 The central area of the Burnhams.

Edward VI School, King's Lynn, he began a campaign of fieldwalking in three fields on the north and south sides of the Goose Beck, a stream which rises to the west of St Mary's Westgate to run through Burnham Market and join the River Burn south of the Corn Mill. (Locations mentioned within the Burnham landscape are marked areas A, B, C, D, E, F, G and H on Figure 2.1.)

The two northern fields (area A) lie on both sides of Overy Mill Road, and the southern field is bounded by Joan Short's Lane on the west and the course of the dismantled West Norfolk railway to the south. Finds from the Mesolithic onwards were recovered from these fields, while the pre-Roman Iron Age was the earliest period recorded in the field south of the Goose Beck (area B). Most of the finds in the northern field of area A were recorded towards its eastern end, where there was surface evidence of a Romano-British settlement including signs of a masonry building. More importantly for our present purposes were the substantial amounts of Early, Middle and Late Saxon pottery found in all three fields.

From 1990 onwards these remarkable discoveries were supplemented by the work of two metal detectorists, David Fox and Philip West. All three fields were searched, and many significant finds of metal objects spanning the Early, Middle and Late Saxon periods were recovered and recorded. Some of these were recorded in the SMR in time for the first authoritative survey of Middle Saxon Norfolk to include Burnham as one of a very select number of 'productive' sites in the county (Andrews 1992).[4] Material recovered with the use of metal detectors continues to be reported to the HER. Since the early 1990s a number of formal excavations carried out in advance of redevelopment have also made major contributions to our knowledge of the archaeology of the Burnhams, and these are summarised below. In 2002 an auger survey conducted by Mike Godwin in the valley of the Goose Beck between areas A and B showed that conditions were in place for a small harbour and landing place by the fourth century. The survey is unpublished, but can be consulted in the HER and is summarised by Davies (2011: 234).

In 2007–9 during the preparation of a PhD thesis on early medieval West Norfolk, Gareth Davies carried out a geophysical (magnetometer) survey in the southern field of area A and in area B, along with detailed fieldwalking in area B. The analysis of the results, combined with a detailed review of all records of fifth to eleventh-century finds from these fields and from all Burnham parishes, has proved to be of great significance (Davies 2010, 2011).

The Early Saxon period

Roman settlement in the Burnhams was widespread and probably as dense as in many Norfolk parishes, but no site of special importance has yet been identified. The Roman shore fort of Branodunum and its associated civilian settlement in neighbouring Brancaster was of great importance in the later phases of Roman occupation, but unlike its sister establishments at Caister-by-Yarmouth and Burgh Castle it seems, on present evidence, to have played a very minor role in the post-Roman period.[5] This reduction in status was probably caused by the rise of the Burnhams, the result of the emergence of a more sheltered, convenient and safer harbour in the Goose Beck.

The prolific ceramic and metal fifth to seventh-century finds from areas A and B include objects imported from the Continent, the presence of which may perhaps indicate that trade and exchange took place on site. The whole collection is difficult to interpret in the absence of excavation. The many female dress accessories, especially brooches, suggest inhumation cemeteries, since such metalwork normally occurs in small quantities on excavated habitation sites.[6] The quantity of pottery, however, much of it undecorated and domestic rather than funerary in character, is more indicative of settlement. The latter interpretation is supported by a ceramic loom weight from area A and by geophysical anomalies recorded in B which might possibly be identified as Early Saxon timber 'sunken-feature' buildings, or SFBs.[7] Conversely three ring-ditches, ploughed-out remains of probably Bronze Age barrows, also in area B and recorded by aerial photography and geophysical survey, favour burial: Early Saxon reuse of prehistoric burial mounds for this purpose was quite normal. Perhaps the safest assumption is that the area of these fields was used for a variety of activities, domestic, commercial and funerary. Two other nearby sites were certainly inhumation cemeteries during this period.

Upslope from here, about 600 m to the south-east of the Goose Beck and in Burnham Thorpe parish, an Early Saxon cemetery (location C), first recorded under most unpleasant and unfortunate circumstances, is known only from surface evidence. In early 1997 14 large backfilled disturbances in an arable field were reported by the farmer, and a site visit produced several broken objects including spearheads discarded in a hedge and a brooch fragment. Within a few weeks a group of spearheads, shield bosses and a sword, said to have been found in Norfolk, were purchased from a London dealer, and a Great Square-headed brooch with a similar provenance was sold at auction in Cologne. Through the good offices of the two purchasers these items were submitted to Norwich Castle Museum for the purposes of recording. It is very likely that they had been stolen from this site by clandestine nocturnal metal detecting. More recently recorded finds of the Early Saxon period include further brooch fragments and a sword scabbard chape of Continental manufacture. The cemetery appears to have passed out of use before the end of the sixth century.

Most surprising has been the discovery – by formal archaeological excavation carried out between 2012 and 2015 ahead of building works – of an inhumation cemetery about 600 m west of fields A–C, and just to the north of North Street and north-east of the Foundry (location D). Burial began in the middle of the fifth century and continued for about 200 years. With a minimum of 438 individuals recorded, males, females, juveniles, infants and neonates, the Foundry Field cemetery forms the largest group of Early Saxon inhumations to have been examined archaeologically in Norfolk. Its importance is also considerably bolstered by the relatively good preservation of the skeletal material in a region where the opposite is the norm. An unusually large number of 'deviant' or abnormal burials were present, including decapitations, and in one grave the skull was held between the occupant's hands. Within the site lay a probably prehistoric ring-ditch, and a substantial prehistoric ditch, aligned east-to-west and remaining visible as an earthwork in the Saxon period, served as the cemetery's northern boundary. The national significance of this site has been recognised in the designation of the unexcavated outer parts as a Scheduled Monument. A full report is being prepared for publication, and the only detailed information at present publicly available can be found online at www.historicengland.org.uk/listing/the-list/list-entry/1458971.

If the large amounts of Early Saxon metal objects from areas A and B do indeed represent two cemeteries, then the total of four in such a small area is remarkable, though not without parallel. Similar concentrations of burial areas in 'funerary landscapes' are known, for example, at Oxborough, Norfolk (Chester-Kadwell 2009: 147–8, pl. II) and Eriswell, Suffolk (Chester-Kadwell 2009: 18, pl. III; Hines and Caruth, forthcoming). A group of three fields in Norton to the north-west of area A (location E) has produced small numbers of Early Saxon metal finds, though a negligible amount of pottery. It has been suggested that these are evidence of settlement (Chester-Kadwell 2009: 158, pl. VIII; Davies 2011: 226).

In 2015 undoubted evidence of fifth to seventh-century occupation was recorded during small-scale excavation in advance of swimming pool construction at Church Hill Farm, Burnham Overy, in the form of a substantial SFB (location F). This remains the only record of Early Saxon activity in this parish on the east side of the Burn, and publication is awaited.

In contrast to the above-mentioned sites, single Early Saxon finds have been recorded in a number of places within the outer areas of the Burnham parishes (Figure 2.2). It is likely that most are casual losses, but they do serve to underline that activity was not restricted to the central zone. None has been recorded in the former parish of Deepdale.

The sum of all this evidence, the greater part of which comes from surface

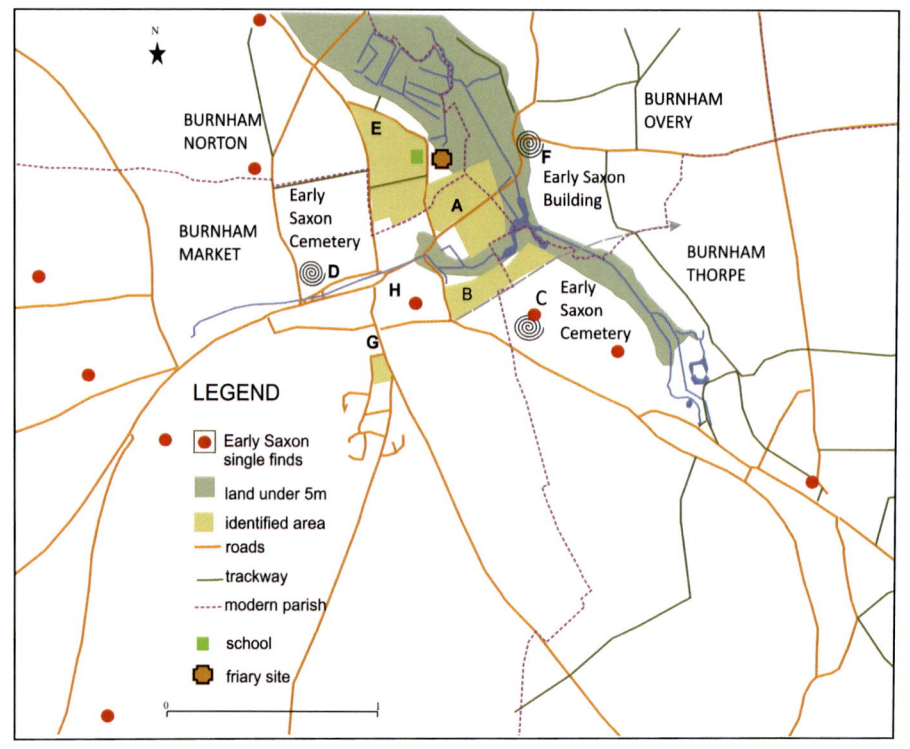

Figure 2.2 The distribution of Early Saxon finds.

artefact collection and non-intrusive surveys, strongly indicates that in the sixth century Burnham had become a populous place of more than local importance, centred upon areas A and B, where activity other than funerary took place: domestic, industrial and perhaps mercantile. This importance was to continue, though its nature was to change, into the following centuries.

A few Early Saxon finds are shown in the following Figures 2.3 to 2.6.

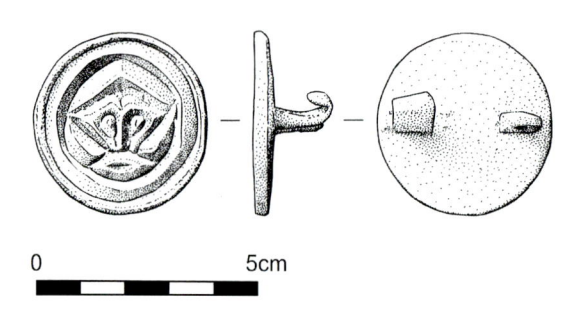

Figure 2.3 Copper alloy button brooch, mid-fifth–mid-sixth century area A © Norfolk County Council (NCC).

The illustrations in Figures 2.3 to 2.6 and 2.8 to 2.14 were drawn by Steven Ashley

Figure 2.5 (above) Gilt copper alloy mount, earlier seventh century, area B. © NCC

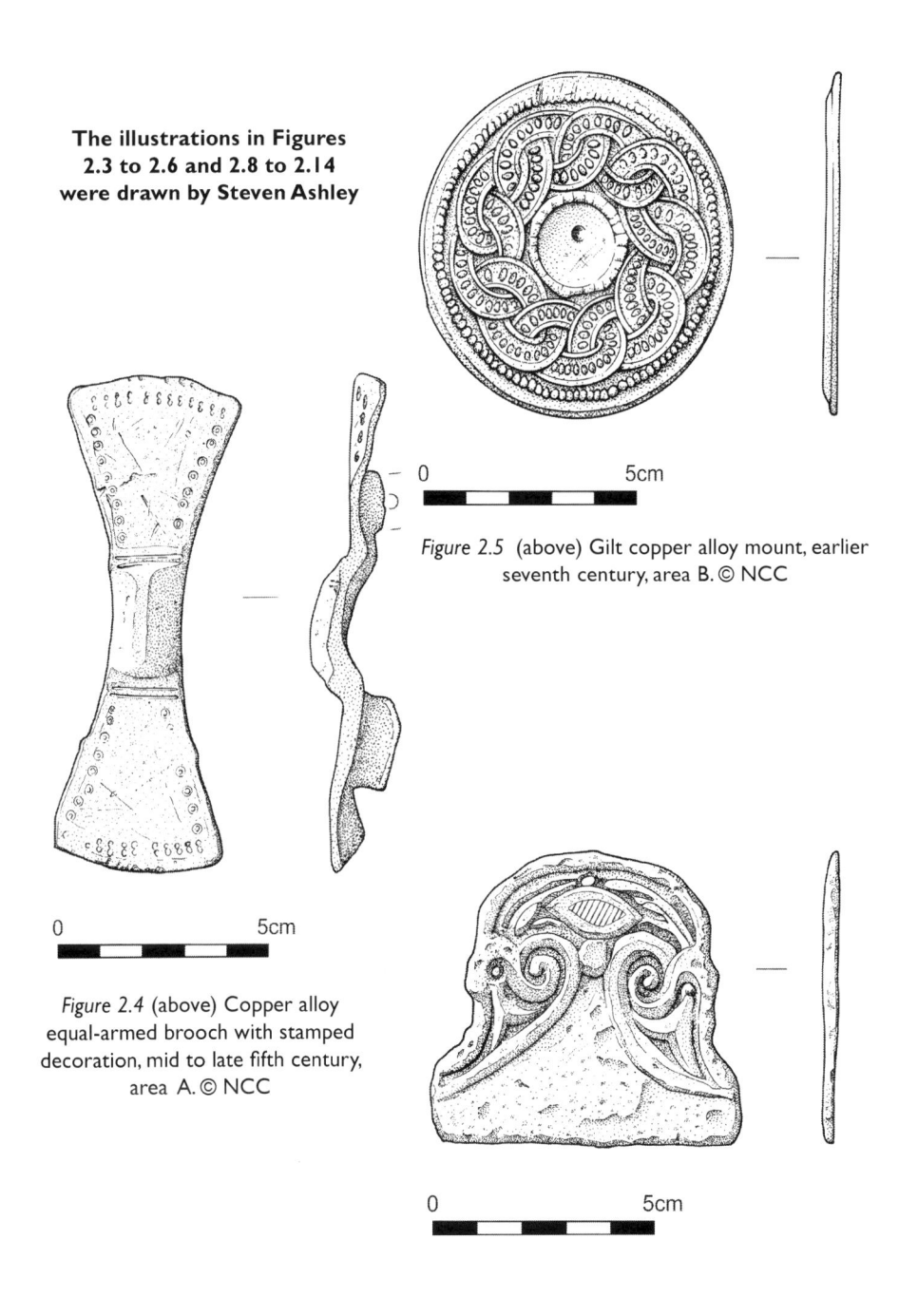

Figure 2.4 (above) Copper alloy equal-armed brooch with stamped decoration, mid to late fifth century, area A. © NCC

Figure 2.6 (above) Copper alloy 'axe-shaped' mount with garnet inlay, earlier seventh century, area B. © NCC

The Middle Saxon period

The Middle Saxon period, broadly coterminous with what historians of early medieval Europe have called the 'long eighth century', was a time of great change in England too, in the governmental sphere, religious organisation, cultural matters, economic affairs, land tenure, and perhaps above all in agriculture (McKerracher 2018: 2–6). East Anglia in this period, as in the previous period, is very poorly served by extant documentary sources (Hoggett 2010: 22–3), and as a result information derived from material evidence remains essential.

The practice of burial with grave goods ceased shortly before or at the end of the seventh century (Bayliss et al. 2013), so that thereafter cemeteries, the most readily located and identifiable site-type of the previous period, are no longer the main indicator of human presence. New places of interment were established, and these are normally unrecognisable without formal archaeological excavation, and in some cases may lie on ground now occupied by parish churches and their graveyards (Moreland 2000: 85–7). The total number of burials firmly dated to this period comes nowhere near reflecting the true size of the population, and as Helena Hamerow has remarked, 'Where and how the majority of the population of eighth- and ninth-century England was buried therefore remains a mystery' (2012: 123).

Settlement sites take over as the main source of data, with the assistance from *c.* 720, in East Anglia at least, of an industrially produced and durable pottery type, Ipswich ware (Blinkhorn 2012). Metal artefacts, especially dress accessories, also became more widespread in settlement contexts than they had been in the Early Saxon period. Variations between sites in the quantity and quality of these objects and of coins, measurable even without excavation and from surface collection only, has encouraged much discussion on the hierarchy of settlements and their functions within the economy of the 'long eighth century'. The debate continues (Wright 2015: 173–85).

'Burnham is the best W Norfolk candidate for the site of a landing place and beach trading site during the middle Anglo-Saxon period' (Davies 2010: 111). The landing place in question is again within the major concentration of finds in areas A and B (summarised in Rogerson 2003: 114–15). Interpretation of this site, and other unexcavated sites of broadly similar characteristics around the North Sea littoral, as places whose primary function was trade, has not met with universal acceptance. Deckers, for example, casts doubt on one – De Panne in Belgium, near the French border – which he saw primarily as a burial place from as early as the fifth century:

the cemetery presumably served as a meeting place for the population of the hinterland, attracting occasional exchange, particularly during the late seventh to early ninth centuries (2010).

The centrality of the Burnham site is emphasised by the pattern of the original parish boundaries. Those of Norton, Sutton/Ulph and Overy meet in the northern field of area A, with that of Overy traversing the river to do so. Westgate extends to the west edge of area A, Thorpe takes in the eastern part of area B and borders the south-east edge of area A. This sharing-out of the site probably reflects the partition of the estate of Brunham which began in the late seventh or eighth century, with the establishment of boundaries which were later to define parishes. The directional place-names, Norton and Sutton, clearly refer to a central place, represented by areas A and B (Blair 2018: 193–6). Overy, 'over the river' (Old English ēa, river), is 'over' from the same place. Tim Pestell (2003: 128; 2019: 13) has suggested, with the support of Overy being a royal manor at Domesday, that Burnham might 'conceivably' be identified with the royal vill of Bruna where, according to an early twelfth-century source, Edmund was consecrated King of the East Angles in 856.

In area B seventh-century metal finds were numerous. There is a marked fall-off in the eighth century, while pottery continued to be prolific. Early eighth to mid-ninth-century pottery was also strongly represented in both fields of area A, but here many metal objects were also recorded, including a run of 17 coins from c. 670–760. Such a total – large compared with most contemporary assemblages – must be indicative of trade, and reflects the commercial importance of the site. It is surely significant that area B has not yet yielded a coin of this date range: it had become a normal or 'unspectacular' site (Davies 2011: 236). From the nine decades between c. 760 and the middle of the ninth century, a period of sparse coin loss in many places, only one coin has been recorded within the three fields, a denier of the Carolingian Emperor Louis the Pious, dated c. 822–40 and found in the southern field of area A. This coin might, of course, have arrived there at a later date.

Elsewhere within the Burnhams, evidence of Middle Saxon activity is currently more muted. Archaeological excavation in Sutton, the 'south-tūn', has shown that settlement developed there from the eighth century. This was quite discrete from the central site but formed part of a cluster around it, along with Norton, Westgate and Overy.[8] In 1997–8 an area of 0.84 hectares (area G) was examined on the west side of Creake Road, about 150m north of St Ethelbert's church.[9] Middle Saxon evidence, restricted to the southern part of the area and nearer to the church, comprised two substantial ovens of uncertain use and 62 pottery sherds, many of which were recovered from the upper fillings of Roman boundary ditches (Davies 2011: 229–31, fig. 124). The excavation remains unpublished, though its context in the historic landscape has been explored by Percival and Williamson (2005). Further evidence of Middle Saxon occupation was recorded a short distance to the south, to the west of Beacon Hill Road, in 2006–7.

Between 1999 and 2002 during small-scale unpublished excavations in the former parish of Burnham Ulph on the south side of Overy Road at its junction with Ulph Place, sufficient amounts of Middle Saxon pottery were found to suggest eighth to mid-ninth-century settlement in the immediate vicinity to the south of the Goose Beck (area H). Single pieces of metalwork follow the general pattern of the Early Saxon period. Their occurrence in various parts of the Burnhams again indicates a human presence away from the centre (Figure 2.7 below).

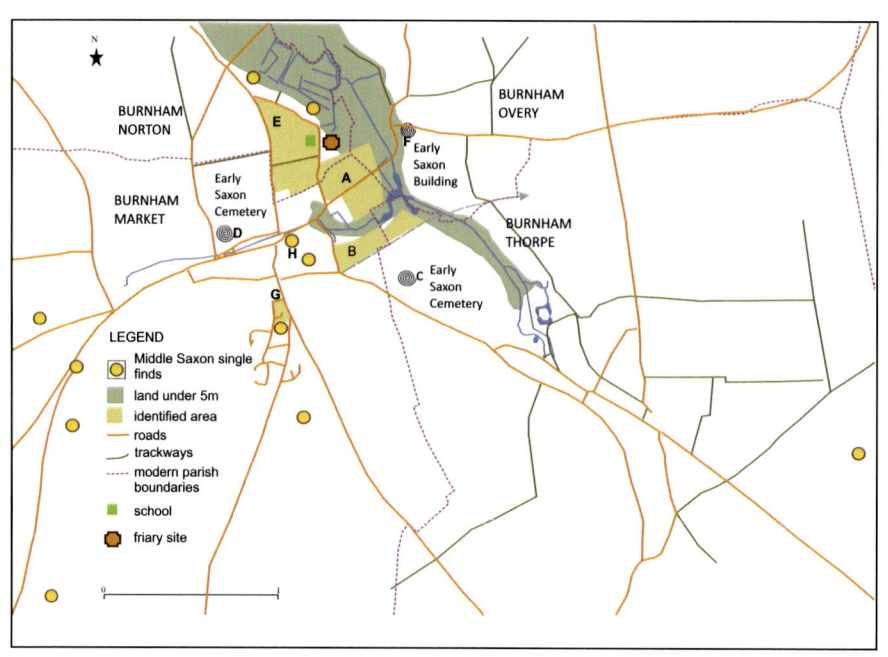

Figure 2.7 The distribution of Middle Saxon finds.

It should be noted that no Middle Saxon object or archaeological deposit has yet been recorded in either Burnham Overy east of the river or the former parish of Burnham Deepdale. However, given the random processes which govern most archaeological discoveries, this absence of evidence may not be permanent.

Some Middle Saxon finds are shown in the following Figures 2.8 to 2.15.

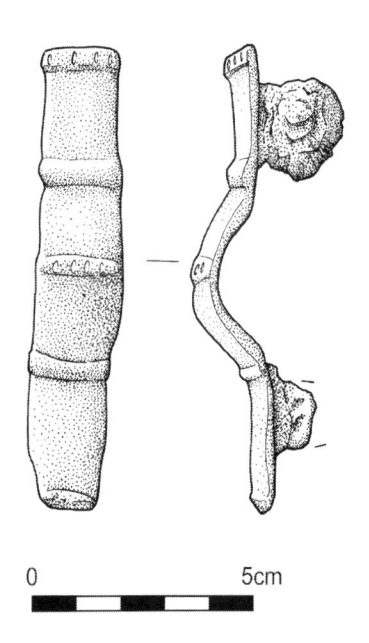

Figure 2.8 (above) Copper alloy Ansate brooch, eighth century, Area A.
© NCC

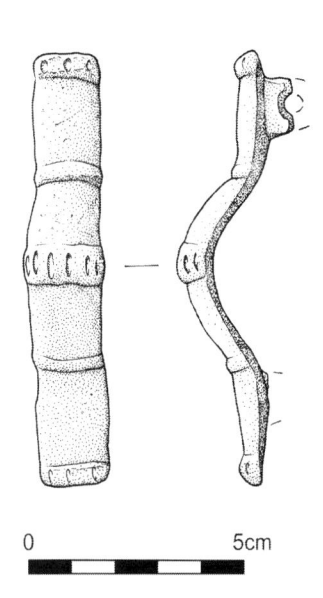

Figure 2.9 (above) Copper alloy Ansate brooch, eighth century, Area A..
© NCC

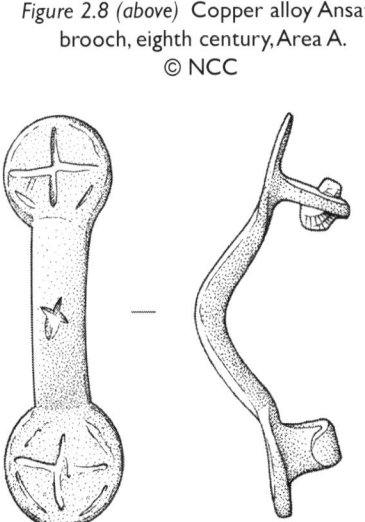

Figure 2.10 (above) Copper alloy Ansate brooch, eighth century, Area B.
© NCC

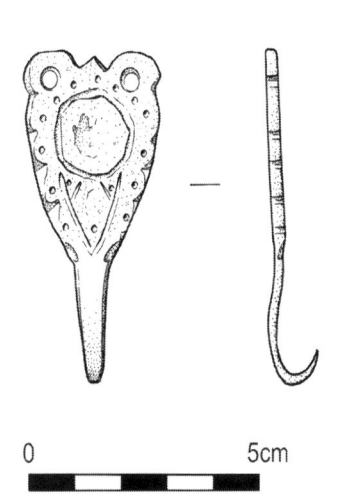

Figure 2.11 (above) Copper alloy hooked dress fitting inlaid with niello, ninth century, Area A.
© NCC

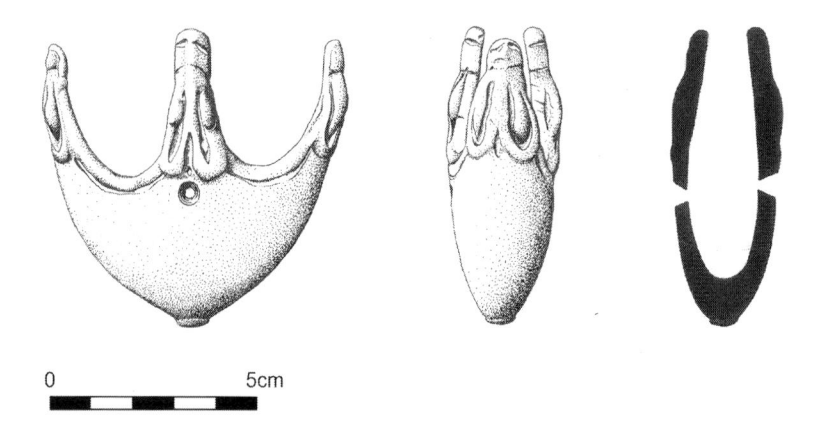

Figure 2.12 (above) Copper alloy sword scabbard chape, later ninth century, Area A. © NCC

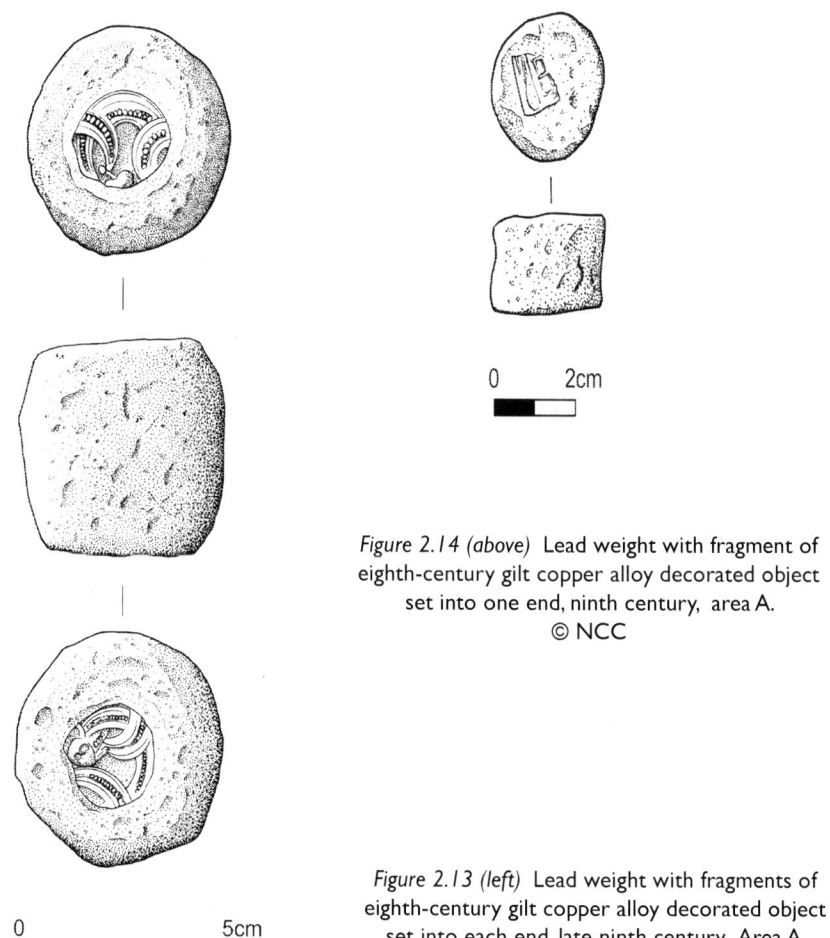

Figure 2.14 (above) Lead weight with fragment of eighth-century gilt copper alloy decorated object set into one end, ninth century, area A.
© NCC

Figure 2.13 (left) Lead weight with fragments of eighth-century gilt copper alloy decorated object set into each end, late ninth century, Area A.
© NCC

Figure 2.15 Copper alloy strap end with inlaid niello and silver wire, ninth century, Area A.
© NCC image from Portable Antiquities Scheme/ Trustees of the British Museum.
Licenced under a Creative Commons Share-Alike agreement (CC BY 3.0).

Figure 2.16 Copper alloy Anglo-Scandinavian disc brooch, tenth century,
north of Docking Road.
© NCC image from Portable Antiquities Scheme/ Trustees of the British Museum.
Licenced under a Creative Commons Share-Alike agreement (CC BY 3.0).

The Late Saxon period

The Late Saxon period might be said to have begun with the arrival of the Vikings in East Anglia in 865, although a date of 850 was established in the 1950s as the point at which Middle Saxon Ipswich ware pottery gave way to Thetford-type ware. There is, however, no firm date for this ceramic changeover, which in any event would not have taken place instantly. On the murder of the East Anglian king Edmund in 869, there followed two Anglo-Saxon puppet rulers, Ethelred and Oswald, known only from their coinage. With the creation of the Danelaw in 880 the former kingdom remained under Viking rule until the reconquest by Edward the Elder of Wessex in 917. Arguments, using the evidence of archaeology and place-names and more recently of genetics, have continued for many years about the scale of the Scandinavian immigration, either the mass settlement of soldiers and their followers or the imposition of a warrior elite on a large indigenous population. At present the former interpretation is in the ascendancy. Very recent detailed work on assemblages of metal objects associated with the Viking Great Army in Lincolnshire and Northumbria strongly suggests that it was very large, as large as the Anglo-Saxon Chronicle claimed (Hadley and Richards 2018, Richards and Haldenby 2018). Without doubt the division of the Great Army that settled in East Anglia was also substantial.

The central site in areas A and B continued to act as the focus of activity during the main part of this period. Finds from area B showed a very strong bias towards the tenth century, with a marked Viking presence. Apart from a dirham, an Arabic silver coin dated 912–13, the majority of objects were dress accessories, and included both purely Scandinavian and hybrid Anglo-Scandinavian examples. In area A fewer metal finds of the Late Saxon period were recorded, but they did include some with probable Viking associations, such as a copper alloy ingot and three lead weights inlaid with fragments of Anglo-Saxon decorated copper alloy. Pottery, on the other hand, was plentiful. The latest coin was a penny of Edward the Elder (899–924). It is probable that the population of the central site began to decline in the eleventh century, and it might have dwindled away by the Norman Conquest.

Some linear anomalies, boundary ditches, recorded by geophysical survey in the southern field of area A and in B may belong to the Middle or Late Saxon periods, though without excavation their dates cannot be confirmed (Davies 2010: fig. 10; Davies 2011: figs. 128, 131–6). An east–west feature in area A aligns quite well with the western end of Overy Road, North Street/Front Street and the Market Place, and rather discontinuous north–south ditches might suggest property divisions on either side. Anomalies in area B comprise part of a rectangular enclosure and droveway towards the west as well as a curvilinear feature at the east end.

Away from the central site, signs of Late Saxon activity, from both surface finds and archaeological excavation, are more plentiful, as a result of greater visibility caused by an increase of pottery in circulation and of a growing population. Though there was somewhat meagre surviving evidence of Late Saxon buildings in the large-scale excavation west of Creake Road in Sutton, intense activity was indicated by ditched enclosures and large quantities of ceramics (area G). Further signs of contemporary activity were recorded to the south of the west side of Beacon Hill Road. The site examined at Ulph Place/Overy Road (area H) also produced good evidence for occupation in this period, as has the more recent work at Foundry Place (area D).

Through a paucity of both positive and negative evidence we are not in a position to map the pattern of Late Saxon settlement in the Burnhams. Many more excavations would be needed in and between present-day built-up areas, as well as widespread systematic field surveys, in particular fieldwalking, the collection and plotting of pottery sherds and other artefacts from the surface of arable fields. In the meantime, it is reasonable to assume that most settlement was nucleated rather than dispersed, and lay in quite close proximity to the churches.

In East Anglia the late tenth and eleventh centuries saw the foundation of most of the parish churches that are known from medieval documentary sources. This would have been the case in the Burnhams, though only one (unnamed) church in Thorpe was recorded in the Domesday survey. We can be much surer about the disposal of the dead during this period. Though there are no archaeologically recorded examples, there is no doubt that the deceased inhabitants of the Burnhams, as elsewhere, were now normally buried in churchyards or in graveyards to which churches were later attached. It remains possible, however, that there were more than nine churches, and therefore places of burial, around the time of the Norman Conquest. Some might have been short-lived and not survived the parochial reorganisations under Archbishops Lanfranc and Anselm. Such undocumented churches and churchyards are sometimes revealed during archaeological excavation, for example in Norwich within the area to be occupied by the royal castle (Ayers 1985; Shepherd Popescu 2009: 96–101).

Church foundation might have encouraged further subdivision and the creation of new boundaries within Brunham, with Ulph and Westgate carved out of Sutton, Deepdale splitting off from Norton, and Thorpe being detached from Overy.[10] Partition of a different kind also took place. East Anglia was subdivided into fiscal and administrative units known as hundreds in the tenth century, and in 1086 Brunham lay in two of them, with Thorpe and Overy in Gallow and the remainder in Brothercross (Barringer 2005).

St Clement's in Overy differs from its six fellow extant parish churches in possessing a cruciform ground plan. Dating to the late eleventh or early twelfth century, this arrangement might indicate that this church's origins were also different. At an earlier date, perhaps in the Middle Saxon period, it might have been a minster or monastery catering for a large parish (parochia) at a time before the proliferation of small parishes served by local churches founded by local landowners which began in the tenth century (Morris 1989: 93-167). The extent of this parochia might have had a close relationship with the early estate of Brunham. However, the cruciform plan could simply reflect William the Conqueror's direct ownership of the manor or its transference to William d'Albini, a major tenant-in-chief, by William II (Blomefield 1807, Vol. 7: 19). It is noteworthy, in view of St Clement's proximity to the central site on the Goose Beck, that dedications to this saint occur frequently in Scandinavia and in England in coastal and riverine locations and places associated with commerce (Morris 1989: 175-6; Linnell 1962: 15, 42).

Domesday Book of 1086, which also includes details of the situation 20 years earlier, contains the earliest written records of the Burnhams (Brown, 1984). There are nine entries, and in 1086 there were six land holders: the king, Ramsey Abbey and four tenants-in-chief (William de Warenne, Roger Bigot, Hugh de Montfort and Robert de Verly). Thorpe is named in two entries, and Deepdale (Depedala without the prefix Burnham) in one. In the remaining six the only place-name employed is Burnham. The recorded population in all entries amounted to 199 in 1066 and 186 in 1086. These figures record heads of households only, and a generally accepted multiplier of 4.5 gives impressive population totals of around 896 and 837.[11] These figures are high in comparison with others in this area of Norfolk. The Burnhams along with North Creake, where there were 55 householders, stand out noticeably from sparse surroundings on one published map of Domesday population densities. Williamson and Skipper reasoned that the lush valley of the Burn was able to maintain many more people than the dry flanking upland with its sandy soil cover and underlying chalk (2005).

The king's holding was the largest, with 64 householders in 1066 and 56 in 1086. Interestingly one was a named female free tenant called Oia. The two smallest holdings, both with only four householders, were held by Roger Bigot and his tenant Thurstan son of Guy. One was in Deepdale. Arable land comprised 16 carucates and 130 acres.[12] How much this amounted to in hectares is uncertain, but areas under the plough would have been considerable and dwarfed the mere 2½ acres of meadow. The number of plough teams declined between the two above dates, demesne teams from seven to six, men's (that is unfree tenants) teams from nine and a half to four, and those of the sokemen (a category of freemen) from four to three. In addition, there was one team in both of two outlying dependencies or berewicks of the royal manor. There was no great extent of woodland, with sufficient, shared by three holdings, to fatten 20 pigs, but woodland was sparse in north-west Norfolk generally. Seventy-five pigs were listed, but there many more sheep, 1,125 in 1066 and 1,026 in 1086. Heads of cattle amounted to only four, and there were 18 cobs (horses) and a solitary ass. There were four and a half mills, probably all water-powered, shared between four holdings, and two salt pans.[13]

By 1066 the Burnhams were certainly a major centre of population, but they had not achieved borough status as had Norwich, Thetford and Great Yarmouth, with their free citizens known as burgesses. Although urban status had not yet been achieved there might well have been a market here, as in most parts of the county (Dymond 1985: 88). The failure of the Domesday survey to record one is not evidence of absence: a market at Downham Market was documented in 1050 but does not appear in 1086 (Dymond 1985: 156; Williamson 1993: 135). A market was recorded at Holt, half a market at Dunham and a quarter of a market at adjacent Litcham (Darby 1971: 146).

The twelfth to fourteenth centuries

In or very shortly after the close of the eleventh century a transformation in the disposition of settlement occurred over what might have been a quite brief period of time. The central place (areas A and B) ceased to be permanently occupied, and the presence of only sparse spreads of metalwork and pot sherds shows that the area was turned over to arable. Excavations at Ulph Place on the south side of the Goose Beck (area H) revealed layers of silt deposited during the medieval period in what had been a wide valley. The Goose Beck harbour had ceased to be usable, and shipping was forced to find alternative landfall further towards the open sea. The area of North Street, Front Street and the Green, which had probably until this time been an area of common pasture edged by a few dwellings and marked by a church at either end, became 'an enormous green/market place' (Williamson 2006: 113) at the centre of a thriving community. The edges were rapidly built up, and at some stage in the twelfth or thirteenth century encroachment through the permanent fixing of market stalls led to the filling-in of the eastern half and the creation of North and Front streets (Yaxley 1977: 68; Penn 2005).

Apart from the churches, the friary, Peterstone priory and the wayside cross in Overy, there are no medieval architectural remains visible in situ in the Burnhams. Vernacular buildings, except perhaps for some of manorial status, would have been constructed of timber, and fragments surviving within later rebuilt structures have yet to be identified. Other physical evidence, so far derived from excavations, aerial and ground surveys and surface collections, forms a very small proportion of what is known of the Burnhams in the Middle Ages, although medieval features and finds have been recorded in every archaeological excavation.

It is fair to assume that from the late eleventh to the end of the thirteenth century – a time of population increase throughout England – Westgate and Ulph coalesced into Burnham Market, with Sutton as an expanding suburb along the Creake road. Settlement in Norton might have shifted away from St Margaret's Church both south towards the Market Place and north to be nearer to the mouth of the Burn. The population in Overy Town, the area around St Clement's Church, might also have dwindled at this time as a result of movement north to the Staithe, while Thorpe expanded along the Burn Valley and Deepdale probably experienced some growth. One very small archaeological excavation in 2000 close to the water's edge at East Harbour Way in Overy Staithe revealed traces of thirteenth to fourteenth-century activity. Until a great deal more formal excavation and systematic field survey is carried out firm detail on the disposition and density of settlement will remain sparse, while much could also be learned from documentary sources. A single example of this state of affairs will suffice: the location of only one manor house is recorded on the HER, the moated site adjacent to the churchyard of All Saints, Thorpe. One other was known to Blomefield (1807 Vol. 7: 33): Polstede Hall, which 'Stood in a close', perhaps off Herrings Lane.

The forces behind the emergence of Burnham Market as a town during the course of the twelfth century and beyond, population increases and agricultural development, would have been similar to those in other places, and both manorial lords and members of a thriving commercial class must have played their parts. Little can be known of the role of merchants at this date, and the complexity of the manorial situation, already evident at Domesday, prevents much being said of the latter. Blomefield (1807 Vol. 7: 7–40) – the major secondary source for medieval Norfolk – is intractable and incomplete, and has been judged 'sketchy notations' by the editors of a major work on the neighbouring parish of Holkham (Hassall and Beauroy 1993: 26). Sub-infeudation, the fission of manors, and the granting of lands to monastic houses, made the already complicated structure at the time of Domesday far more complex during the twelfth and thirteenth centuries. The manorial state of play in the late thirteenth century is best known in Thorpe, whose Hundred Roll return of 1279–80 has partly survived: there were four tenants-in-chief and nine sub-manors (Hassall and Beauroy 1993: 61).

The earliest reference to a market at Burnham is of May 1209, when one quarter of the market occurs in a long list of holdings specified in a legal document or 'Final Concord' settling a dispute between Walter de Gimingham and Juliana his wife, and Hugh de Polstead and his wife Avis (Dodwell 1958: 100–3, no. 210). Walter and Hugh were lords of Polstead Hall manor in Westgate, which Blomefield considered was descended from the Domesday holding of Hugh de Montfort (1807 Vol. 7: 32–3). In 1223 Robert de Narford was granted the right to hold an annual fair in Burnham Thorpe (Letters 2002: 240). In 1256/7 Hugh de Polstead and Juliana de Gimingham, a widow, took 'stallage', that is, were paid rent for stalls, in the market of Burnham. In 1271 the lord of the Warenne manor in Thorpe, Sir William de Calthorpe and his wife Cecilia, received a royal grant of an annual three-day fair and a weekly Saturday market in Burnham, and in 1272 Richard, son of Thomas Sniterton was granted the right to hold a Wednesday market and three-day fair there (Blomefield 1807, Vol. 7: 12 and 35; Letters 2002: 240).

Charters granting rights to hold markets and fairs, which in reality were already in operation, were often issued by the crown (Dymond 2005). The Calthorpes' right to hold a market was confirmed in 1274/5, and in 1286/7 they, along with Ralph de Hemenhale (Hempnall), his wife Emma and John de Gimingham were found to hold a Saturday market, take stallage and tolls from every cart passing over the causeway at Burnham (Blomefield 1807, Vol. 7: 35).[14] In 1347 the crown granted another Ralph de Hemenhale the right to hold a fair in Burnham annually on 23 July and the following four days (Letters 2002: 240). The above grants are strong indications that the Burnhams enjoyed a buoyant economy in the thirteenth and the first half of the fourteenth centuries.

The comparative wealth of the nine parish churches can be judged from two major thirteenth-century ecclesiastical fiscal records, the Norwich Taxation of 1254 and Pope Nicholas's Taxation of 1291–2 (Hudson 1910: 123–4). In 1254 the income in tithes of the nine ranked, in descending order, St Clement Overy, St Margaret Norton, All Saints Thorpe, St Mary Westgate, All Saints Ulph, St Ethelbert Sutton, St Mary Deepdale, St Peter Thorpe, and St Andrew. The income gap between the first and the ninth was yawning: in 1254 St Clement was reckoned at 50 marks (£33 6s. 8d.) and St Andrew at 20s. (£1). The order was unchanged in 1291–2 but the final two had dropped from the list. They were already poor, but survived in some form until falling populations had rendered them unwanted: St Peter was to be annexed to All Saints Thorpe in 1364, and St Andrew to St Clement in 1421 (Blomefield 1807, Vol. 7: 14–15 and 29).

The Augustinian priory of Peterstone in Overy next to the border with Thorpe began life as a hospital some time before 1200 under Augustinian rule. The founder is not known, though Blomefield (1807, Vol. 7: 24) surmised that it was one of the de Cheneys of Rudham, who were later patrons. It soon achieved the status of a priory, and the names of three priors are known from the first half of the thirteenth century. This house, dedicated to St Peter, was never large or rich, and appropriated only two parish churches (Beeston St Andrew and West Lexham). It suffered badly in the fourteenth century, and was annexed by Walsingham Priory in 1449 (Cox 1906: 391). According to a fifteenth-century source, an obscure 'local order peculiar to Norfolk', the Order of Peterstone, independent of the Augustinian general chapter, comprised this house, Great Massingham, Weybridge in Acle and Beeston Regis (Knowles and Hadcock 1953: 150; Heywood 1989: 227–8). Pestell (2004: 198) noted Peterstone as one of several East Anglian monastic houses set up in the twelfth century close to important Middle Saxon sites. The lack of imposing ruins of this minor monastery was succinctly summarised by Le Strange: 'The slight remains are mixed up with the farm buildings of Peterstone Farm. There is very little to see' (1973: 103).

The wealth and population of the Burnhams compared with each other and with other townships can be assessed in records of the lay subsidies (national taxations on moveable wealth) which were levied in 1327, 1332 and 1334.[15] In the returns for first two years the names of individuals and their assessed wealth are listed, while in 1334 a single figure is given for each township as a whole. Though detailed interpretation is fraught with difficulty because of undervaluation, inconsistency and evasion, cursory but cautious examinations of the returns are instructive (Hadwin 1983). Transcriptions of those for 1327 and 1332 have been published (Hawes 2000–1: 26–8, 180–1, 506, 514). For the almost complete returns for 1327 the six townships can be listed, in descending order of population: Westgate and Ulph 65 taxpayers, Overy 45, Sutton 32, Thorpe 30, Norton 29, Sutton 32 and Deepdale 12.[16] Averages of assessments per taxpayer varied greatly between places, again in descending order and expressed in shillings and pence: Deepdale 3s. 2d., Norton 2s. 10d., Westgate and Ulph 2s. 6d., Overy 2s. 4d., Sutton 1s. 3d., and Thorpe 1s. 1d.[17] The list in descending order of total sums due is rather different: Westgate and Ulph, Overy, Norton, Sutton, Deepdale and Thorpe, the sums ranging from £8 2s. 5d. down to £1 14s. 7d.

The 1334 lay subsidy – a national tax charged on each township – has been more extensively studied than the previous two, because the records survive far more completely and perhaps because, in the absence of long lists of individual taxpayers, they are more easily digestible (Hudson 1895: 273, and 280; Glasscock 1975: 198–9). As before, comparison with surrounding townships in the case of the Burnhams is made slightly more difficult because they lay within two hundreds. Westgate (including Ulph though this was not specified) paid the highest sum, £12 10s., followed by Overy, Norton, Sutton, Thorpe and lastly Deepdale, which paid £2 5s. In contrast to the lay subsidy, a tax on individuals, the poll tax was introduced in 1377 and levied again in

1379 and 1381. The Norfolk receipts for 1379 survive most fully. All people over the age of 16 were named (Fenwick 2001: 96-1-3). The basic rate per head was 4d., but the very much larger sums paid by a very small number of manorial lords renders comparison of township totals unnecessary.[18] Population totals are perhaps more informative: Westgate ('cum villis': that is, including Ulph) 57, Thorpe 55, Norton 47, Overy 37, Sutton 21, Deepdale 19.

The levels of taxation set in 1334 were to remain in place until 1449, when reductions were made to take account of the ravages of the Black Death and subsequent pestilences in the intervening time. The total reduction for Brothercross hundred was 20.8 per cent of the 1334 figure. The two largest townships, Westgate and Overy, had clearly suffered the most, and received reductions of 28 per cent and 37 per cent . Deepdale and Norton had fared better, with more average reductions of 18.5 per cent and 21.7 per cent . The overall reduction for Gallow hundred was 17.8 per cent . Sutton was below the norm at 16.7 per cent while Thorpe had come upon hard times with an allowance of 28.6 per cent. It is clear that any correlation with the 1379 poll tax population figures is impossible.

Trade and commerce have been mentioned above in discussions of the central Early to Late Saxon site and of medieval Burnham Market, but because of the sparse documentary sources and a lack of archaeological evidence, disappointingly little is known about the degree to which the Burnhams and other minor Norfolk ports were involved in coastal or international trade or in maritime fishing during the Middle Ages (Rutledge 2005). A suggestion of links with the Baltic is given by a find from an archaeological excavation in the north German port of Greifswald, an amber signet of one Ada de Bernham which was lost in *c.* 1260 (Ayers 2016: 3). There was certainly a port at Burnham in 1294 (*CPR Edward I, 1292–1301*: 114). Bornam was one of those ports whose fishers were forbidden to fish around Iceland in 1415 for a period of one year. Others included major east-coast ports along with Blakney, Craumer and Dersingham (*CCR Henry V*, Vol. I: 297). However, for details of the Burnhams' role in maritime trade during the fourteenth century see Chapter 1.

Postscript

The Burnhams constituted a place of considerable significance in the first few post-Roman centuries and then settled back during the Middle Ages into the life of a minor market town and small sea port with an interest in fishing, some of it carried out in deep waters. Our knowledge of the period before the Norman Conquest is almost exclusively based on archaeological data, some of which has been garnered though systematic excavation, and from the Domesday Survey. Especially after the twelfth century, written sources play a major role. There is every hope that much will be learned from new fieldwork in the coming years, and although there is little chance of hitherto unknown documentary material coming to light, thoughtful analysis of what survives may yield fresh insights into the processes by which Bruneham, the 'river village or estate' became the remarkable place it is today.

Notes

1 A tenth church, St Edmund, has been claimed (Batcock 1991: 53, 151), and appears in the Norfolk archaeological database (the HER), with a possible site suggested by the discovery in 1957 of two human burials on the site of what is now known as St Edmund's Hall, Market Place. These were undated and are most likely to have been southern outliers from the Early Saxon cemetery at Foundry Place. The confusion arises from St Mary's Church Westgate, which was divided into two portions, with an incumbent each: one, St Mary, under the patronage of Coxford Priory, and the other, St Edmund, under lay control (Blomefield 1807, Vol. 7: 37–9). John de Ridlington, parson of the church of St Edmund Westgate, was party to a final concord of 1329, and land in Burnham St Edmund was cited in another of 1333 (Hassall and Beauroy 1993: 587, nos. 33 and 36). Property in Burnham St Edmund was mentioned in a deed of as late as 1525 (Blomefield 1807, Vol. 7: 20). In the Middle Ages there must have been two defined areas for the payment of tithes, but only one church. The two portions, however, might well point to two separate churches in the Late Saxon period.

2 Unpublished archaeological data noted in this paper is taken from the HER, of which there is a simplified online version, www.heritage.norfolk.gov.uk/. Reports of a small selection of the finds recorded in recent years are also held on the online database of the national Portable Antiquities Scheme: www.finds.org.

3 Suggestions of the survival of Late Saxon masonry fabric in two churches, St Mary Westgate and St Margaret Norton, are also included in the HER database. These buildings were probably constructed in stone for the first time in the second half of the eleventh or early twelfth century, 'building in stone was virtually unknown or not practised in East Anglia before the Normans' (Heywood 2013: 262).

4 The epithet 'productive', then recently coined by numismatists to describe sites on which large numbers of coins were recovered, was still used in 2005 when ten places in Norfolk, including Burnham, were so labelled (Rogerson 2005). It has since fallen out of favour because 'a huge range of site-types [is] hidden beneath this label' (Davies 2010: 91): in other words it is a misleading simplification and 'unhelpful' (Wright 2015: 152–3).

5 Anglo-Saxon finds from the Roman fort and its surrounding settlement are very scarce: a late fifth-century brooch and two Middle Saxon objects, part of a ceramic vessel imported from the Rhineland or northern France, and a brooch. A few pieces of tenth and eleventh-century metalwork have also been recorded. A little farther west a group of timber fishwiers in the intertidal zone on Holme Beach demonstrate the vigour with which maritime resources were exploited during the sixth to ninth centuries (Robertson and Ames 2010).

6 Early Saxon male burials were furnished predominantly with ferrous grave goods, notably spearheads and shield bosses. Metal detecting does not normally recover ancient iron objects, so that male inhumations are under-represented in assemblages recovered by such means.

7   Best seen as reconstructions at West Stow Anglo-Saxon Village and Country Park near Bury St Edmunds.

8   Names for places clustered around an administrative centre, with the combination of a directional qualifier such as north or south with a generic -tūn became widespread from the second half of the eighth century in Kent, Mercia and Wessex (Blair 2018: 1967), and probably also did so in East Anglia.

9   Ethelbert, king of the East Angles, was murdered in 794. Pestell (2004: 96) considered that this church might have been dedicated as a chapel subsidiary to the main church of a royal manor. Ethelbert's cult might have spread very quickly, but some church dedications may not have come about until well into the tenth century or possibly even later (Butler 1986: 46).

10 The place-name element thorp, of Scandinavian origin, has normally been considered to denote a small, secondary or dependent settlement (Ekwall 1960: 468–9). More recently, it has been argued that its use in the late ninth and tenth centuries might have been more specific, and have been associated with places specialising in arable agriculture and involved with the introduction of open-field farming (Cullen et al. 2011).

11 One unfree tenant and half a carucate held by William Warenne were in Holkham but pertained to Burnham and were valued there (Darby 1971: 119).

12 If the traditional but far from standard estimate of a carucate as 120 acres were to be used this would come to 2,050 acres or 830 hectares. This is a very small proportion of the present area of the Burnhams. Much of the difference can probably be explained by large expanses of upland and lowland pasture and waste.

13 These were the only Domesday salt-pans on the north coast, all others being in the east or west of the county (Darby 1971: 136, fig. 32).

14 A bridge was built in 1421–2 to help travellers on the highway between St Andrew's parish and St Clement's (Blomefield 1807, Vol. 7: 28).

15 It is not appropriate here to enter into detailed comparisons with other places in the area, but one small observation may be of some interest. In Brothercross hundred, which included Deepdale, Norton, Thorpe and Westgate/Ulph, 721 individuals were listed under 23 townships. Taxpayers in the four Burnhams numbered 136 (18.9 per cent of the total) and their combined assessments amount to 23.6 per cent of the total of the hundred.

16 In 1327 within Brothercross and Gallow hundreds only East Raynham, Tattersett, Fakenham, North Creake and South Creake excelled Westgate/Ulph in numbers of taxpayers, with 66, 68, 68, 84 and 106 respectively.

17 These figures might suggest that the two poorest communities, Sutton and Thorpe, were so because they lay outside the market and farthest from the sea, so they were more dependent on agriculture. However, this was not the case, and the differences can be explained by the inclusion of wealthy individuals, including those of seigneurial status, in some townships and not in others. Only one person was assessed at above 1s. 6d. in Sutton (John Capell at 5s.), and the highest individual amount in Thorpe was 2s. 6d. At the other end, the first two names in the Deepdale list were assessed at 13s. 2d. and 9s. 5d., and the first two in Norton at 9s. and 12s.

18 For example, in Burnham Westgate Edmund de Ryngham (?Raynham) knight was assessed at 20s. and John Buttrous armiger at 3s. 6d., while the total for all 57 taxpayers was 43s. The largest amount paid by any inhabitant of Norton and Deepdale was 1s.

Figure 3.1 View of the site from the west front of the fourteenth-century church to the eastern precinct wall

Figure 3.2 View of the standing remains from the north.

3

The medieval friary site at Burnham Norton and its landscape context

Brendan Chester-Kadwell

Introduction

Burnham Norton Friary is situated within a rural landscape. The narrow local lane, Friars Lane, that passes to the west of the friary site runs northwards towards the coast road and the current village location of Burnham Norton. To the east the River Burn, which flows through a wide shallow valley, is now a rather inconsequential stream. The land rises steadily to the west and the medieval church of St Margaret, while to the east the parish church of St Clement, Burnham Overy Town, is a dominant element in the landscape across the valley of the Burn from the friary. The nearly complete entry gate and the remains of the church cluster up against Friars Lane within a large field which is still partly enclosed by the fourteenth-century precinct wall. The site would seem even more isolated if it were not for the primary school for the Burnhams which has been built opposite, to the west of Friars Lane. Situated more than a mile away from the present-day coastline, it is difficult to imagine the friary as an occupied site on the edge of a busy estuary, as it was when it was founded.

This chapter explores three aspects of the landscape context of Burnham Norton Friary. First, it analyses the medieval landscape and identifies historical developments that have produced the landscape of today. These changes, it is argued, challenge our perceptions of the friary's original setting. Second, it offers a detailed assessment of the topography of the friary site itself and the implications for how the site developed, and attempts to explain, for example, why the principal buildings are located as they are within the friary precinct. Third, the upstanding remains are discussed in the context of the relationship of the church and the surviving gatehouse. Very little is known about the detail of the layout of the friary buildings on this site, and even the identification of the surviving buildings has been a matter of controversy. It is argued that the analysis of the topography of the site will help to make this identification less uncertain.

The present-day topography of the Burnhams

Historically, this area had its origins in a Middle Saxon estate that later became subdivided (Williamson, 1993: 92–3). This subdivision became crystallised later in the Middle Ages with the establishment of the ecclesiastical parishes of St Mary, Burnham Deepdale; St Clement, Burnham Overy; All Saints, Burnham Thorpe; St Ethelbert, Burnham Sutton; St Margaret, Burnham Norton; All Saints, Burnham Ulph; and St Mary, Burnham Westgate.[1]

Today Burnham Norton is one of a number of civil parishes that make up an identifiable area of North Norfolk around the lower reaches of the River Burn. These modern civil parishes include Burnham Market, Burnham Overy and Burnham Thorpe as well as Burnham Norton, and they cover all of the territory of the Burnhams with the exception of Burnham Deepdale, which

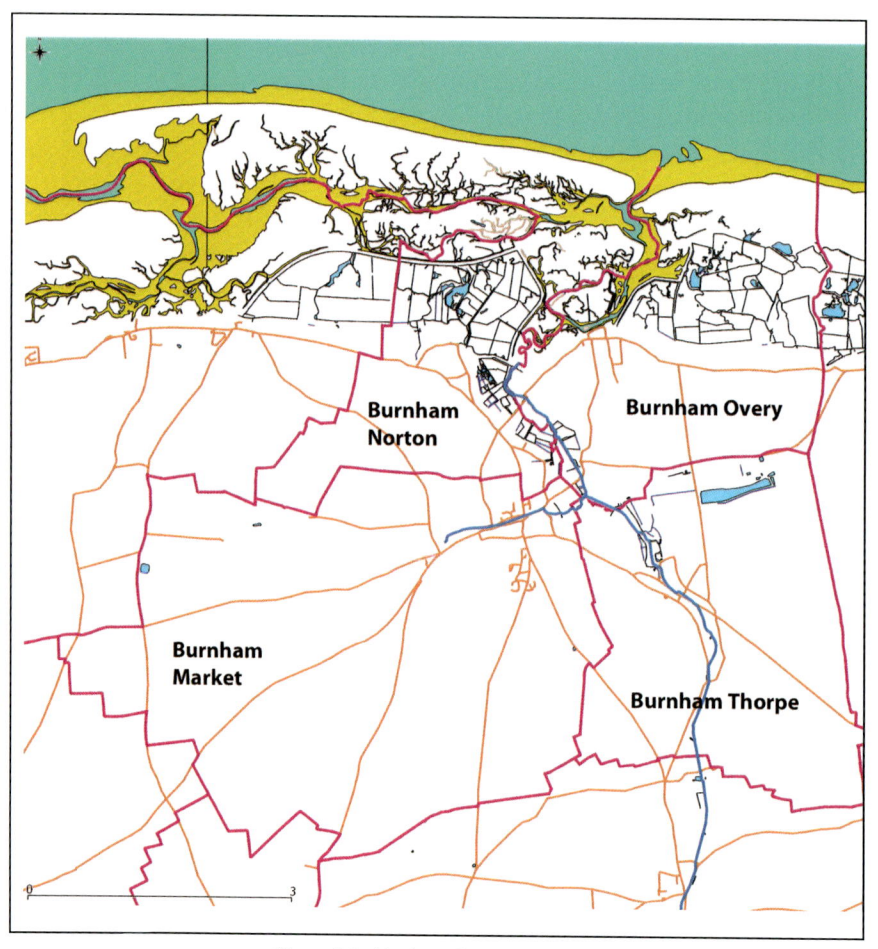

Figure 3.3 Modern Burnham parishes.

is now in the civil parish of Brancaster. The largest contemporary settlement is Burnham Market – an amalgamation of the three medieval parishes of Burnham Westgate, Burnham Ulph and Burnham Sutton. Burnham Norton lies to the north of Burnham Market; Burnham Overy is located across the valley of the Burn to the east. Burnham Thorpe is to the south where the river valley broadens out into what was in earlier times a tidal estuary. Despite these subdivisions, the Burnhams as a group of closely related settlements retain community cohesion and identity. What links these settlements topographically is their relationship to the River Burn and the (salt) marshes that lie to the landward side of Scolt Head.[2] This was as true in medieval times as it is today.

The present form of Burnham Norton village seems to be largely post-medieval, although resettlement from the area around St Margaret's began in the later Middle Ages (see Chapter 2). The local population, who were at least partly dependent on fishing, the cultivation of oysters and other salt marsh produce, found it more advantageous to live nearer to the salt marsh and waters open to the tidal stream. The installation of the sea sluice in the seventeenth century and the reclamation of the Burn estuary to the east and south of the village probably confirmed its location. The relocation of Burnham Norton village is an important clue to how the settlement pattern of this landscape has changed since medieval times.

The medieval landscape context for Burnham Norton Friary

Key features of the medieval topography are explored here under the headings: The riparian and coastal landscape, Disposition of medieval routeways, Settlement patterns, and Agriculture and land management. Post-medieval changes are also reviewed following each analysis of the main themes. These include changes to the coastal morphology and the estuary of the Burn, major alterations to the local road system, and the introduction of agricultural enclosure. All these aspects have radically altered the landscape that would have been familiar to the friars at Burnham Norton and the communities that they served. (See Figure 3.4 for a conjectured medieval landscape of the River Burn.)

The riparian and coastal landscape

In the Middle Ages along the Norfolk coast, as elsewhere in the south-easterly quarter of lowland England, the approximate dividing line between areas that may be considered as permanently dry land and those areas prone to permanent or occasional inundation was the 5 m contour.[3] Areas lower

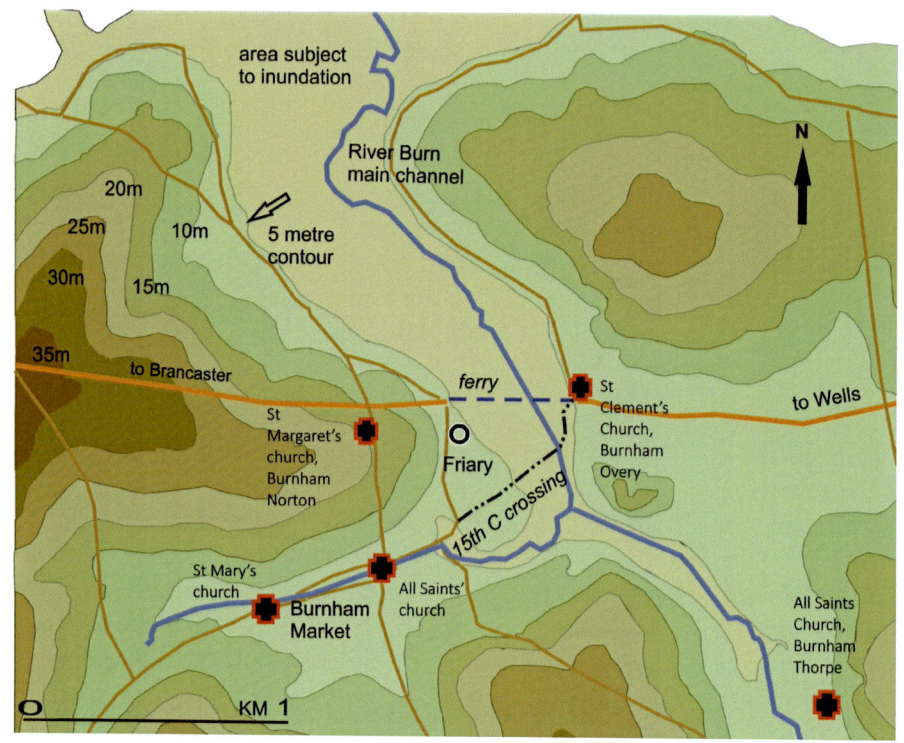

Figure 3.4 Conjectural medieval landscape of the estuary of the River Burn.

than this would have been affected by marine tidal flows, which at extreme high tides or tidal surges could have led to serious flooding. Extensive areas of marshland below the 5 m contour along the coast at Burnham were a distinctive feature of the medieval landscape. Although there is evidence of some attempts to modify the marsh landscape in the later Middle Ages – either to protect specific marshlands or perhaps to embank the channels – these works appear to have been minor (Albone et al. 2007: 107).[4] The extensive areas of medieval waste created by the salt marshes and along the margins of the Burn valley formed a significant resource to the settlements on the dryer land.

The valley of the Burn north of Burnham Thorpe was a significant tidal estuary which at its widest point near the coast was approximately 600 m wide. High tides in the estuary would have led to the build-up of fresh water draining off higher land in the catchment area of the Burn, which would have been aggravated during periods of heavy rain. However, the estuary also provided navigation for ships, and Overy Town was a successful port during the period that the friary flourished (Rutledge 2005: 78–9; see also Chapter 1). The maritime connection meant that the friary was more accessible than it might otherwise have been, not only for visitors or passing pilgrims, but also for goods that could often be moved more conveniently by water.

Post-medieval coastal and waterway modifications

The landscape has been radically changed by human intervention from what it was during the later Middle Ages when the friary flourished. The mechanisms for coastal change are explained in some detail in Chapter 1. However, it is often the engineering solutions for land improvement that have proved crucial in landscape terms. There were attempts to drain the marshes between Norton and Scolt Head Island during the seventeenth century, which in the end were abandoned after local opposition (Smith 2014: 42). However, a sea wall and sluice across the mouth of the Burn estuary may have been installed before 1700, once Overy Town harbour became silted up and access to the sea had been moved to Overy Staithe. The stopping-up of the estuary protected farmland in the Burn valley from further marine inundation, and Faden's map of 1797 shows that the area of the estuary was already reclaimed marsh in his day (see Figure 3.5).

The Burnhams Inclosure Act of 1825 authorised the building of Telford's bank, which enclosed a large area of marsh between Burnham Deepdale and Norton. The visual impact on the landscape by this comparatively simple engineering solution has been considerable.

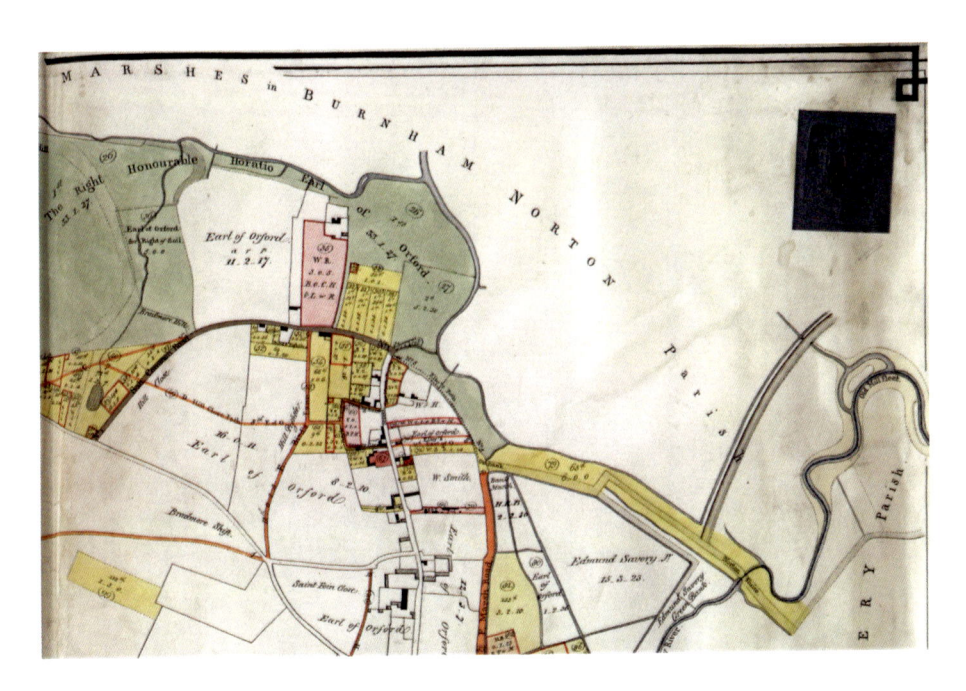

Figure 3.5 View of the coastal area at Inclosure.
[Norfolk Record Office, detail C/2FSca 2/2F060/3]

Disposition of routeways

A critical influence on how the medieval system of routeways developed in the area has been the existence of the coastal marshes and the estuarine landscape of the Burn. Very typically of such topography, the easiest routes to establish were those that ran with the grain of the country.[5] In the Burnham area this was north–south: that is, parallel with the valleys and along the higher ground. The more difficult direction in which to establish an effective route in North Norfolk was one aligned east-west. Running against the grain of the country, these routeways were hampered by such obstacles as the estuary of the Burn itself, and the nearer to the coast the more difficult it became. As a result, a coastal route that would create a land connection between seaports was directed farther inland, and was normally longer as a consequence.[6] Figure 3.6a depicts the area pre-Inclosure, showing indicatively how medieval routeways operated.

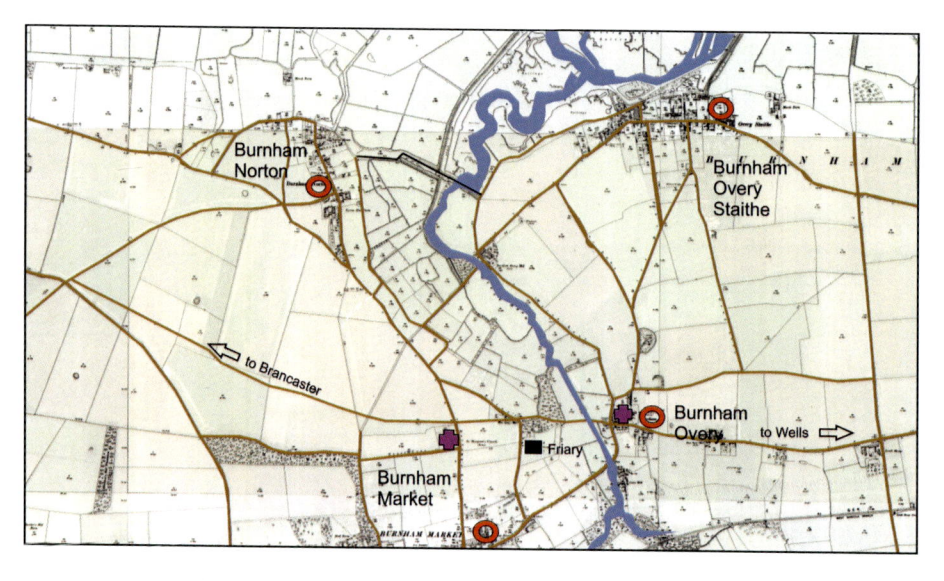

Figure 3.6a The public road system pre-Inclosure (1821).

The key routeway in the vicinity of the friary was the one that passed to the north of the friary precinct along an east–west alignment. There is now no evidence for it in the landscape in Norton parish to the west of the estuary, but it is still a public road eastwards from Overy.[7] In the Middle Ages this was the main route from Brancaster to Wells. After the Burn estuary was reclaimed this road continued on over the estuary to Overy and thence to Wells without interruption. Before this, there must have been a crossing of sorts to connect the two parts of the road, most obviously a ferry if the tides allowed for it. From the Wells road on the Overy side it would have been possible to travel in a south-easterly direction towards Walsingham, perhaps joining the more direct route at Burnham Thorpe. However, by turning south off the old Brancaster to Wells road before reaching the estuary and going along Friars Lane, the traveller could join the road from Burnham Market to Thorpe, which would not be dependent on the tides.[8] This arrangement would make more sense for the positioning of the friary gatehouse, and would also better accord with the siting and development of the friary as discussed below.

In the immediate vicinity of the Burn estuary, between Norton and Overy, it is obvious that the most numerous continuous routeways were those travelling in a north–south direction. Some of these, such as the Wells to Fakenham road, were main routes connecting coastal places with significant inland places. Others were local routes often associated with resource acquisition and typically, in coastal areas, aligned closely to the 5 m contour – the boundary between dry land and potentially inundated areas. Unlike in areas of ancient enclosed landscapes, where local lanes often persist over many centuries, it is often difficult in areas like the Burnhams to find this level of continuity for local routeways. It is necessary to try to infer earlier patterns of routeways from what happened when the open field systems were enclosed in the eighteenth and nineteenth centuries.

Post-medieval changes in routeway patterns

Figure 3.6b depicts the area post enclosure. In the Burnhams, at parliamentary Inclosure, many of these local routes (originally public ways) became byways and were either stopped up completely to vehicular traffic or became private roads. At Burnham Norton, the south end of Friars Lane probably originated as one of these byways to allow access to local resources, even though its present alignment may have been shifted slightly to the west by the establishment of the friary precinct. The northern section of Friars Lane joins the main thoroughfare from All Saints' church at Burnham Market to the village of Burnham Norton. This must always have been an important routeway as St Margaret's church is built along it, next to the cross roads with the Brancaster to Wells road. Additionally, there is the evidence in the road closure order and in Faden's map (1797) for a local resource routeway known as Marsh Road or Lane situated north of the friary site. This lane might once have connected to Friars Lane where it crossed the Brancaster to Wells road which passed just to the north of the friary, but it had ceased to do so by Faden's time. Going north, Marsh Lane closely skirted the western edge of the estuary, aligned either along the 5 m contour or in places just below it. This lane eventually led to the coastal marshes in the vicinity of what is now Norton Green, and from there to Bradmore Hill (the lane still exists in

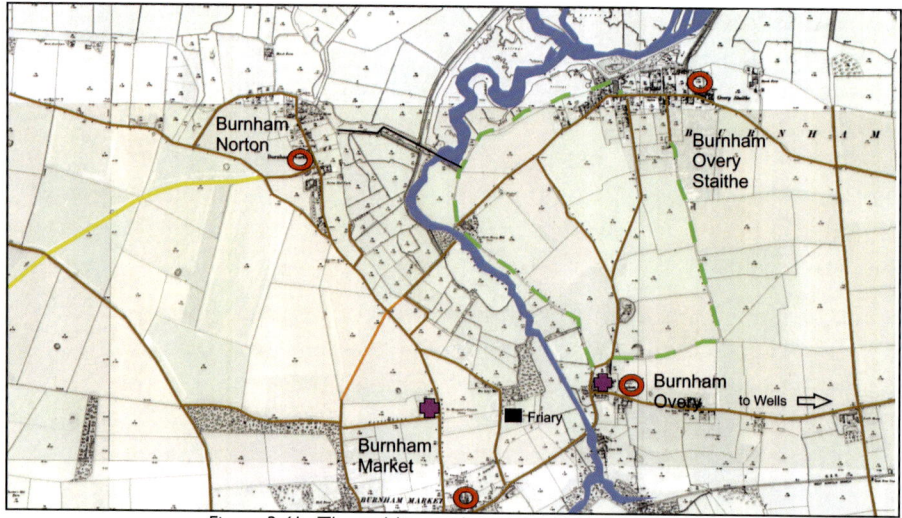

Figure 3.6b The public road system after enclosure.
[yellow = private road, green dashed = footpath only]

part). A similar routeway on the Overy side of the estuary still exists between Overy Town and the Staithe. Such lanes must normally have been passable most of the time, but other local routes, which lay lower in the landscape, may well have been inundated periodically, and perhaps in winter they were impassable.

Faden's map of the Burnham area shows a pattern of routeways in the process of change, but within which the medieval system of routeways was still discernible. By the time of the road closure Act of 1822 many of the older (mainly medieval) routeways had been pruned away. This applied to the King's Highway (older roads like the Brancaster to Wells road) and to many of the local lanes as well. Some of these defunct roads and lanes were closed altogether and have disappeared from the landscape, whilst others, even when stopped up to vehicular traffic, remained open to foot traffic. The erection of the sea wall at the mouth of the Burn estuary enabled a new river crossing to be created between Norton and Overy mill, replacing the previous lowest crossing between Norton Friary and Overy Town. This later crossing now forms part of the main coast road, but was still only a local route in Faden's time.

Settlement distribution

The centre of gravity for the Saxon settlement at Burnham (that is, that area later subdivided into separate parishes by the twelfth century or before) was around an inlet of the Burn estuary fed by the waters of Goose Beck to the east of today's Burnham Market (see Chapter 2). However, Saxon settlement was also present in the adjacent areas to the north, south and east where eventually the parish churches were built at Burnham Norton, Sutton, Thorpe and Overy. It is now generally agreed that the earlier Saxon 'port' at Goose Beck was superseded later in the Middle Ages by the one at Overy Town (see Chapters 1 and 2). Silting in the lower part of the estuary may well have initially driven this relocation, but no doubt the increase in the size of vessels made a difference too.

At some point, either during or soon after the eleventh century, settlement seems to have drifted away from the earlier centres of Saxon settlement: for example, towards the east and the creation of Burnham Market. At Burnham Norton settlement seems to have started to expand into areas nearer the coast to the north at the expense of settlement around the church of St Margaret. However, the archaeological evidence is slight, and the concentration of nucleated settlement at the site of the present-day Norton village might not have been completed until later in the sixteenth and early seventeenth centuries. The acquisition of an adjacent messuage and croft by the Carmelite Priory in 1350 suggests that there was still settlement in the vicinity of St Margaret's in the fourteenth century (see the Annex).

The evidence for thirteenth and fourteenth-century activity at Overy Staithe indicates that there was exploitation of resources along the coastal areas at this time (Chapter 2), and it would not be unreasonable to suppose that this also occurred on the Norton side of the estuary. Some of this evidence suggests resource exploitation along liminal areas, but it might also indicate some settlement dispersal, perhaps related to rising populations in the twelfth and thirteen centuries. It might be correct to assume that in an area of common agricultural management most settlement would be nucleated. However, it should also be borne in mind that the difference between nucleated and dispersed settlement is a relative judgement. The comparatively small populations in real terms in areas like the Burnhams often make the differences between what counts as nucleated or dispersed settlement fairly slight.

Post-medieval changes to settlement distribution

A feature of later medieval settlement was the apparent drift of the population northwards to the coast, particularly in Norton and Overy.[9] Settlement distribution in the post-medieval period changed little from about the seventeenth century, after the estuary of the Burn had been reclaimed: in the Burnham parishes it had largely stabilised into the pattern seen today. The enclosure of the common fields produced some additional farmsteads outside of the village context, but many of the farmsteads arising from enclosure were in fact already contained within nucleated settlements such as Burnham Norton.

Agriculture and land management

Despite the evidence for the exploitation of the marine environment, through activities such as fishing and trade, agriculture remained an extremely important element in the local economy. Most of the population must have been involved in agriculture, even if they worked at other occupations at times as well. The distribution of landed estates across a series of open fields in dispersed holdings produced a landscape alien to the one seen in the present day in the parishes of the Burnhams. The lands of individual manors were frequently dispersed throughout the open fields of several parishes, a practice that was still common up to the time of post-medieval enclosure.

In this respect the friars' holdings would have been no different from those of the lay lords. At the time of the dissolution the friary possessed 68 acres of land spread throughout the parishes of Norton, Sutton and Thorpe. However, it is not known how much of this land would have been open-field arable and how much permanent pasture or waste. However, names like

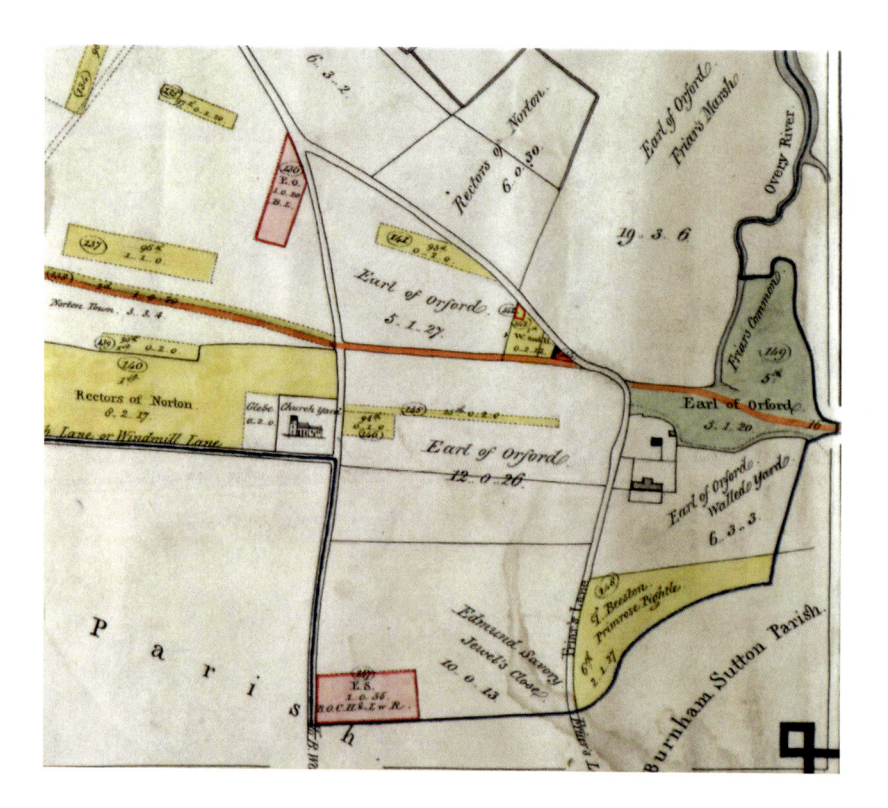

Figure 3.7 Land management post enclosure, 1825.
[Norfolk Record Office, detail NRO C/2FSca 2/2F060/3]

Friar's Marsh and Friar's Common on the inclosure and tithe maps might indicate that much of their land was in fact waste (that is, land that was neither arable nor had a 'taxable' value).

Post-medieval changes in land management practices

The medieval open field landscape of all of the Burnham parishes that would have been so familiar to the friars and the people of the Burnhams finally came to an end about 200 years ago with the passing of the Inclosure Acts in 1825. This was the final act of a process that had been gathering pace during the course of the eighteenth century, which was in many of the Burnham parishes largely a matter of enclosure by agreement. The result of this process can be glimpsed in a late eighteenth-century manorial map of lands in Westgate and Sutton (*c.* 1796) (NRO MC 1830/1, 852X7).

Piecemeal enclosure was certainly the case in Burnham Norton, for which parish the Inclosure Act was a mopping-up process, rather than a grand scheme. This can be seen clearly from a plan attached to the Inclosure Award, which shows that at the time of the Act most of the parish was already enclosed (Figure 3.7). Only a few isolated strips of land needed to be ironed out of the consolidated farmlands now forming the new agricultural units. The common fields in Norton were already enclosed and parcelled out. One reason for this is that much of the agricultural land had become part of the great estates, such as that of the earl of Orford, for whom the necessary amalgamation was a matter of locally negotiated agreements.

The situation in the surrounding parishes varied considerably. In Overy much of the enclosure had already taken place, but not perhaps to the same degree as at Norton (again, the great estates of the earl of Orford and Holkham Hall had facilitated that). Burnham Westgate and Sutton on the other hand still had their remnant common fields, although already in a partial state of enclosure. In these places the survival of a complex mix of medieval manorial estates seem to have impeded the rate of enclosure by agreement, so that more comprehensive Inclosure Acts were required.

Overview

The physical aspects of the landscape are a guide to the changes that have taken place between the time of the friars and the present day. Some of these changes have been very great, such as the reclamation of the estuary and its conversion to farmland. Others will have been subtler: for example changes in the routeways have less actual impact on the landscape, but by giving the observer a different viewpoint might radically alter their perspective of that landscape.

Viewpoint and perception are important: the way that people engaged with the landscape in the past was very different to how people engage with it now. A medieval landscape was probably both busier and quieter than today's countryside. The medieval population was smaller, but a larger proportion of them worked out of doors every day, either in the fields or on the waterways. Working the land with draught animals meant that it took longer to plough a field (so ploughmen would need to be in the fields for longer), but the process was much quieter than when, as now, post-industrial machines are used. The landscape might also have presented the viewer with more open aspects, partly because the large common fields had fewer hedgerows. Additionally, the management of trees was more intense in a society dependent on timber and wood products. Larger trees tended to be felled earlier in their life cycle, and the coppicing of woodland species restricted their growth. As a result the Burnhams generally must have appeared rather less wooded than they are today.

The greater use of waterways for transport and travelling would have meant that the friary site was accessible from all directions, not just from the north and south on the landward side as now. In fact the friary was placed in what must have been one of the busiest points on the Norton side of the estuary, which would suit a mendicant lifestyle very well. It also made sense of the fourteenth-century investment in a new gatehouse and preaching nave, as described below.[10]

Burnham Norton Friary, location and topography

The site of the Carmelite friary at Burnham Norton – as it is today – is widely recognised as the place at which an earlier foundation was re-established in 1253 from another location in the parish. This section explores the topography of this later foundation, but consideration is also given to the reputed earlier site.[11]

The first friary at Bradmer circa 1247

John Bale, the sixteenth-century Carmelite historian, is the main medieval source for the claim that the first Carmelite foundation was at a place called *Bradmer* in Norton parish.[12] However, despite Bale's account for the origins of the Norton house being at odds with other evidence in terms of its foundation date (see Chapter 6), it is generally accepted that the first Carmelite foundation at Norton was elsewhere than at the present friary site.

The site of the putative Carmelite house at Bradmer is unknown, and as yet no archaeological evidence has been found relating to it. Assumptions are made about the broad area in which it may have been located based

THE FRIARY SITE AND ITS LANDSCAPE CONTEXT

on the evidence of place names in the tithe survey (1839), the Inclosure Award (1825) and the road closure acts for Norton (1821). Faden does not mark Bradmer on his map of 1797, but the area known as Bradmore in early nineteenth-century parish maps is shown on Faden as common land. Figure 3.8 below shows a conjectural medieval landscape of the possible location of Bradmer.

The topography of this site is instructive. It lies on the stretch of coast protected by Scolt Head Island, an area of marsh, creeks and channels adjacent to the 5 m contour. The exact configuration of this liminal land in the thirteenth century is unknown, but probably in broad terms it was not too different from its form in Faden's day (see Chapter 1). The Bradmore of the early nineteenth-century maps is a shallow valley to the west of a detached parcel of land a little over 5 m above sea level close to the coastline, which before the encroachment of the marshland must once have been a small offshore island. On the eastern edge of this island of higher land is Marsh Farm, a post-medieval farmstead near Norton Staithe, which was Norton's access to the sea before the Telford sea wall was built. In the Middle

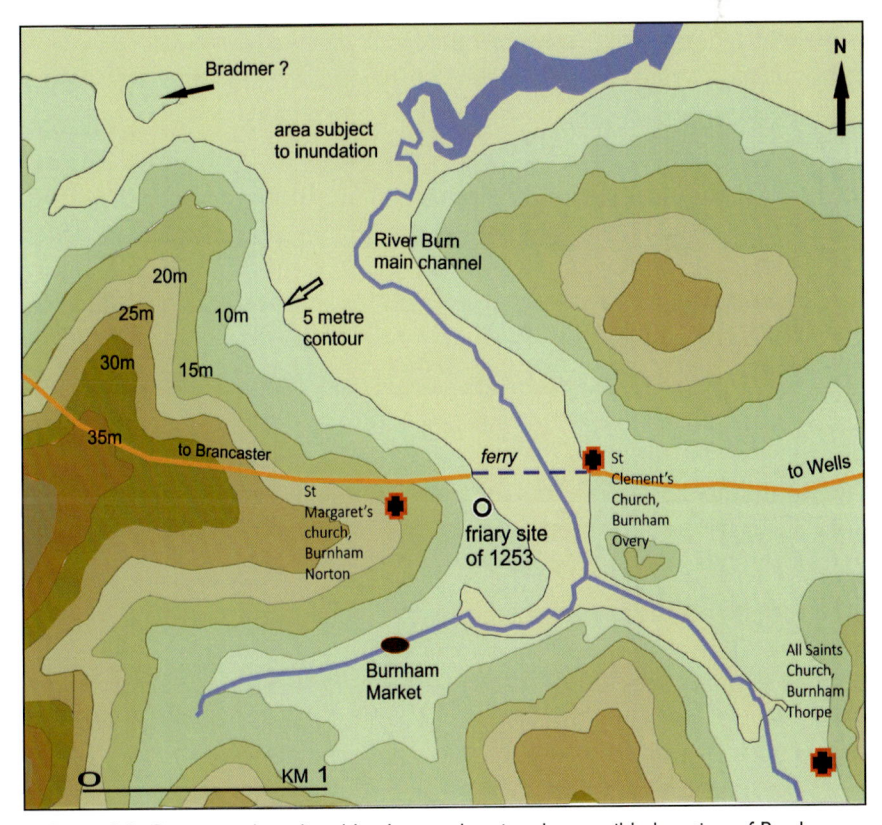

Figure 3.8 Conjectural medieval landscape showing the possible location of Bradmer.

Ages the area known as Bradmore Common most probably originated as a creek which would have given access to open water.

This 'island' between the medieval creek at Bradmer and Norton Broad (the seaward approach to Norton Staithe) would have been an ideal spot for a band of eremitic brothers seeking solitude.[13] However, it would have been very exposed to the elements, even on the landward side of the island at Bradmer. Whether this was the site claimed by John Bale must remain speculation, at least unless some clear archaeological evidence is forthcoming, and little more can be said of the Bradmer location with the present state of knowledge.

The topography of the 1253 friary site

The second site chosen for the re-founded Carmelite house was a little over a mile (c. 1.7 km) south-east of where Bradmer is estimated to have been. Situated on the left bank of the Burn estuary, it was directly opposite Overy Town, below the Norton parish church of St Margaret to the west. In the thirteenth century the estuary would have been up to about 400 m wide, but the width of the tidal stream would have varied greatly according to the conditions of the tide and the volume of the outflow of fresh water through the river valley. Figure 3.9 illustrates a conjectural medieval landscape with contours showing the situation of the friary site after 1253.

The friary was close to the estuary on the southern side of the Brancaster to Wells road, a major thoroughfare in the thirteenth century. The estuary here was too wide to bridge without seriously impeding the usefulness of Overy Town as a port, so a ferry must have linked the western and eastern sections of the road.[14]

The parish churches of Norton, Overy, Holkham, and indeed the friary church itself, all lay close to the Brancaster to Wells road on a broad alignment with each other. Their occasional intervisibility gave a special character to this landscape, and in particular the intervisibility between the site of the friary church and that of St Clement's (the Overy parish church) is particularly striking even today.[15]

The topography of the friary is best understood in its relationship to St Margaret's Church to the west and the estuary of the Burn to the east. St Margaret's church was built just above the 20 m contour on a spur running eastwards from Hawker's Hill (47 m in height). Friars Lane, which forms the western edge of the friary precinct, is approximately on the 8 m contour below the church site. The principal buildings of the friary stand between Friars Lane and the 5 m contour – the boundary between the dry land and that prone to inundation. The friary church is slightly higher than the

THE FRIARY SITE AND ITS LANDSCAPE CONTEXT

areas to the south and north, being built upon the highest point of the spur, although the differences in height at this point are minimal.

Looking in close-up at the site's topography the positioning of the main conventual buildings starts to make more sense. A shallow terrace follows the 5 m contour, marking the eastern boundary of the area of land available for building without running the risk of periodic inundation. The church, the most important building on the site therefore not only lies on the highest portion of the land available, but also more or less occupies the total width of the buildable land available along an east–west alignment.

The head of a stream that flows into the Burn marks the northern edge of the late medieval site, and together with a shallow basin to the east of the present-day Friary Cottage, even though they both lay outside the fourteenth-century precinct wall, were clearly associated with the friary. In this area there are a number of natural springs, one of which was identified in the nineteenth century as a Holy Well. This body of water is to the south of the line of the old Brancaster to Wells road, and may well have been more substantial in the past at a time when the water table was generally higher. Towards the eastern boundary of the fourteenth-century precinct, and just inside it, there is a drain that might date from the medieval friary.

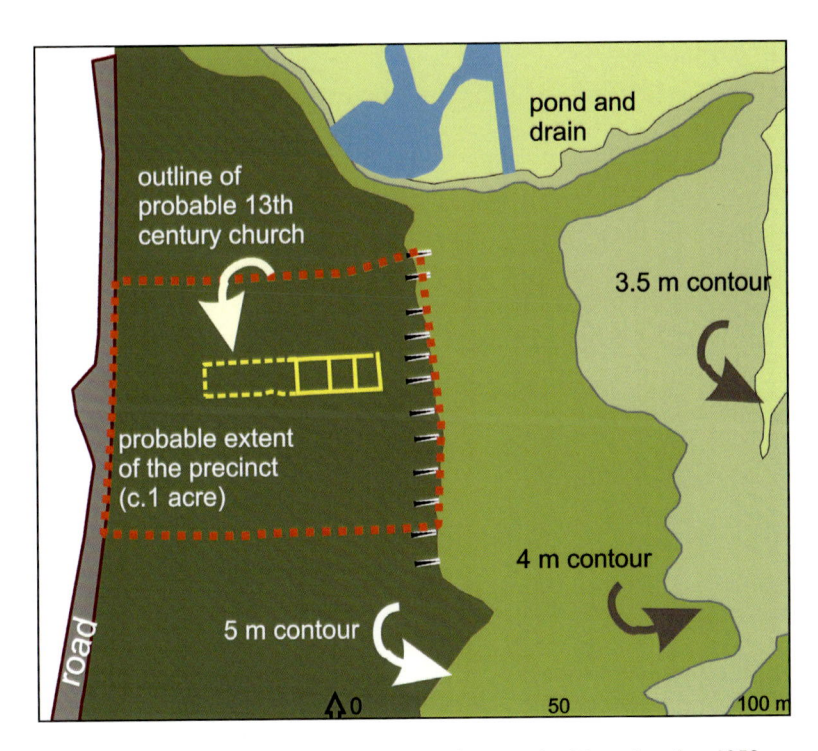

Figure 3.9 Conjectural medieval landscape showing the friary site after 1253.

The development of the friary site after 1253

The area of the friary site that the Carmelite brothers first settled in the thirteenth century was considerably smaller than it was to become by the second half of the fourteenth century. Many Carmelite establishments contemporary to the one at Burnham Norton had fairly humble origins. Only later, after they had the opportunity to either move to another site or acquire greater wealth, did their houses expand.[16] The development of the friary site at Norton followed this pattern.

Expansion of the friary site in the thirteenth and fourteenth centuries

According to Bale, local landowners Ralph Hempnale and William Calthorpe had founded the Carmelite house at Bradmer, and they may also have been the patrons associated with the relocation of the friary to its present site in 1253. The site today, still partly enclosed by its fourteenth-century precinct wall, has an area of approximately 2.25 hectares.[17] However, to gauge the size of the original precinct the area of a series of land acquisitions, made between 1298 and 1353, should be subtracted from the approximate figure of 2.25 hectares.

The first acquisition was a grant of land made in 1298 by Walter de Calthorpe of a rood of meadow for the 'enlargement of their place'. It is not known exactly where this land was situated, except to say that it must have been adjacent to the existing precinct if it were to enlarge 'their place'. A second acquisition is recorded in 1350 when a licence was issued for *'the alienation in mortmain by William de Denton, chaplain, to the prior and Carmelite Friars of Brunham Norton of a messuage and a croft for the enlargement of their dwelling place'* (CPR 1348–50: 497). The area of the messuage and croft is not recorded, but again it must have lain adjacent to the existing precinct, and the use of the term 'dwelling place' suggests that it was close to the then existing buildings. The final acquisition was in 1353, when the King Edward III issued a licence for the alienation in mortmain by Ralph de Fermenhale and Richard Ferman of Burnham Sutton of 3 acres of land in Burnham Norton for the enlargement of the Carmelites' 'manse'.[18] Again this suggests a parcel of land adjacent to the existing precinct, but the measured land area of the donation allows further investigation that might help to locate it.

It has been argued that the part of the site amenable for building the principal buildings was that which lay above the 5 m contour, where in fact the visible foundations of the surviving remains are situated. It is reasonable to suggest that this represented the core of the original thirteenth-century precinct, which fronted Friars Lane but was not at this period necessarily

THE FRIARY SITE AND ITS LANDSCAPE CONTEXT

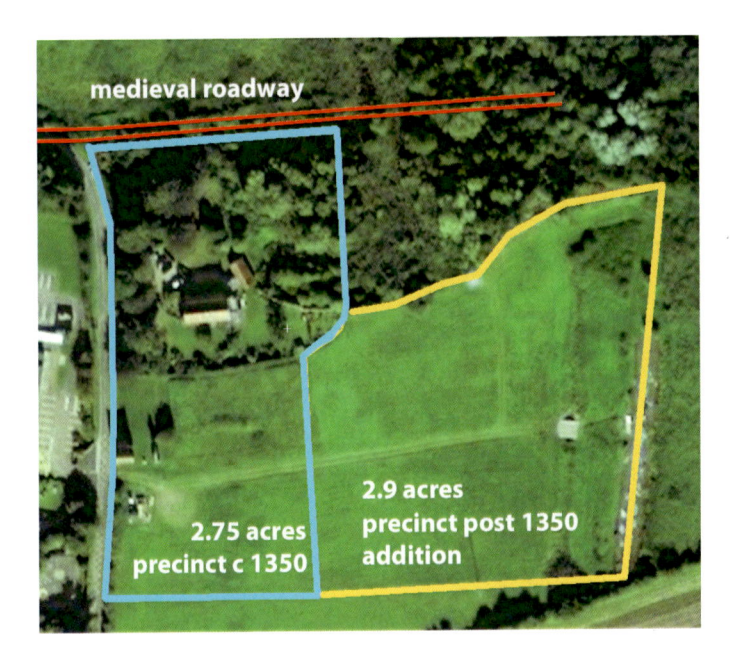

Figure 3.10 Friary site precinct landscape with gauged measurements.

immediately adjacent to the Brancaster to Wells road. The challenge is to see whether more precise details about the locations of the later thirteenth and fourteenth century acquisitions can be ascertained.

The total area of the fourteenth-century precinct, including some of the water features that are closely associated with the friary, is approximately 5.65 acres (2.25 hectares). The area above the 5 m contour is about 2.75 acres, leaving the area below 5 m at 2.9 acres (see figure 3.10). This is close to the 3 acres of land donated to the friary in 1353 and may well represent this gift. If this is correct, then the earlier gifts must be included in what remains, and this is the area also wherein lies the main conventual buildings. The first gift of a quarter of an acre (the rood of meadow in 1298) may well have been situated south of the friary church, as this area seems more likely to have been open land suitable for meadow. If this is the case it might also account for the apparent position of the cloistral range being north of the church, as there would not have been sufficient room for the cloister to have been built in the usual place to the south, before this gift was made. The messuage and croft gifted in 1350, therefore, should be approximately where Friary Cottage is today – an extension of the *manse*. Whilst this intuitive reading of the site is speculative it does suggest a realistic interpretation of how the site might have developed over this critical period.[19]

The remodelling of the friary in the fourteenth century

All the upstanding remains suggest that a major remodelling of the friary took place during the course of the fourteenth century. However, the developments that were necessary to ensure that the brethren at Burnham Norton could continue their mission successfully would not have been possible without the acquisition of extra land as described above.

The precinct

The precinct at Burnham Norton was of a generous size, as can still be seen today. The northern and eastern boundaries still retain much of their integrity as standing structures, although parts of the northern wall have fallen in recent times (see Chapter 5). Where the western end of the standing section of the northern boundary wall now finishes, it would originally have continued until it met the 5 m terrace. From that point it turned towards the north-west, following approximately the 5 m contour through the outbuilding east of Friary Cottage before appearing to turn sharply to the west between the cottage and the stream containing the putative site of the Holy Well. The southern boundary is now visible only by an embankment, and the line of the precinct wall between the southern boundary and the fourteenth-century gatehouse is also lost. North of the gatehouse the wall continues for a short way along Friars Lane before coming to an end. However, it almost certainly went farther in that direction, meeting up with the northern boundary behind Friary Cottage.

It is highly probable that the 5 m terrace formed the eastern boundary of the original thirteenth-century precinct. The eastern area of the later precinct, which it has been suggested is formed by the 3 acre donation to the friary made in 1352, swept down towards the estuary in medieval times and would have been prone to inundation from time to time.

There are two features in the present-day landscape that may represent attempts by the friary community to manage this area. The first is a second terrace that broadly follows the 4 m contour. The second is the drain that runs parallel to, but on an alignment a little to the west of, the eastern precinct wall. This drain follows along the western edge of a shallow depression between the 3.5 m and 3 m contours. The eastern precinct wall, it might be noted, stands on a strip of land above the 3.5 m contour which might have been artificially built up to carry it. There is archaeological evidence for a blocked-in culvert near the north-eastern corner of the precinct wall where the water from the drain made its way out into the estuary (see Chapter 4). The fact that it was possible to build the precinct wall well below the 5 m contour might also suggest that the later fourteenth century was a period when the area of inundation had receded to some extent. Figure 3.11 shows how the fourteenth-century precinct may well have looked, and how it has been interpreted.

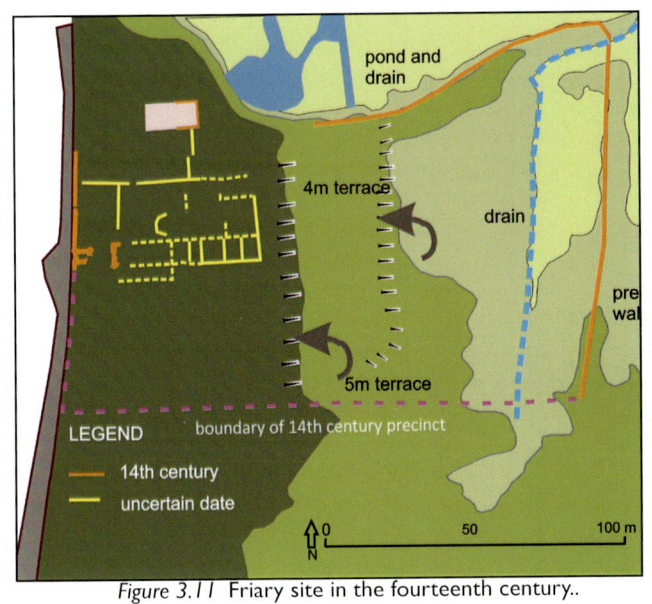

Figure 3.11 Friary site in the fourteenth century..
Outline of conventual buildings as per OS First Edition/Cushion.

Entrances to the precinct

The gatehouse is the one complete structure on the site that has been largely restored to something of its former fourteenth-century state. Stephen Heywood gives a detailed description of it in Chapter 5. One significant insight of his is that the passageway through the gatehouse is suitable only for pedestrians as the arch is too narrow for carts. This begs the question about access in the context of the precinct as a whole. It is possible that goods were brought into the precinct by boat rather than road, which would make sense for a site that was so well served by water. There is evidence for a gateway in the eastern precinct wall, which may be the water gate (see Chapter 4). Alternatively, there may have been a carriageway gate somewhere else, but if so the evidence for this has not yet been forthcoming. The siting of the gatehouse along Friars Lane makes sense in terms of the structure of the medieval road network as discussed earlier.

The church

The plan of the fourteenth-century church at Norton corresponds to other friary church plans of that date, with a choir at the east end and a passage or walking place separating it from the nave (see Chapter 5). The proximity of the gatehouse to the west end of the church has in the past caused comment, and in its listing English Heritage claimed that this precludes the gable wall from being that of the church.[20] However, in this English Heritage is now considered to have been wrong. A further examination of the remaining earthworks and the landscape setting will help to better explain the probable form of the church and why it came to be built so close to the gatehouse. The reason may simply be that the nave of the thirteenth-century church was shorter than the one rebuilt in the fourteenth century. The restrictions presented by the nature of the site made it unrealistic to relocate the church from its original position, and the only way to accommodate a longer preaching nave was to build the west end nearer to the gatehouse. The longer preaching nave eventually became a necessity for the Carmelites as they further developed this aspect of their ministry (see Chapter 9). It may be noted that when the first church was constructed on this site the laity were not yet permitted to frequent Carmelite churches, so that extensive naves were not considered a necessity in early Carmelite friaries (Andrews 2015: 17).

Figure 3.12 illustrates the topography at the site of the friary buildings and helps to explain by how much the site needed to be levelled by the construction of an undercroft. To understand the nature of the site it is useful to explore the gradient between the gatehouse and the east end of the church remains. The gatehouse stands at about the 7.5 m contour, the west

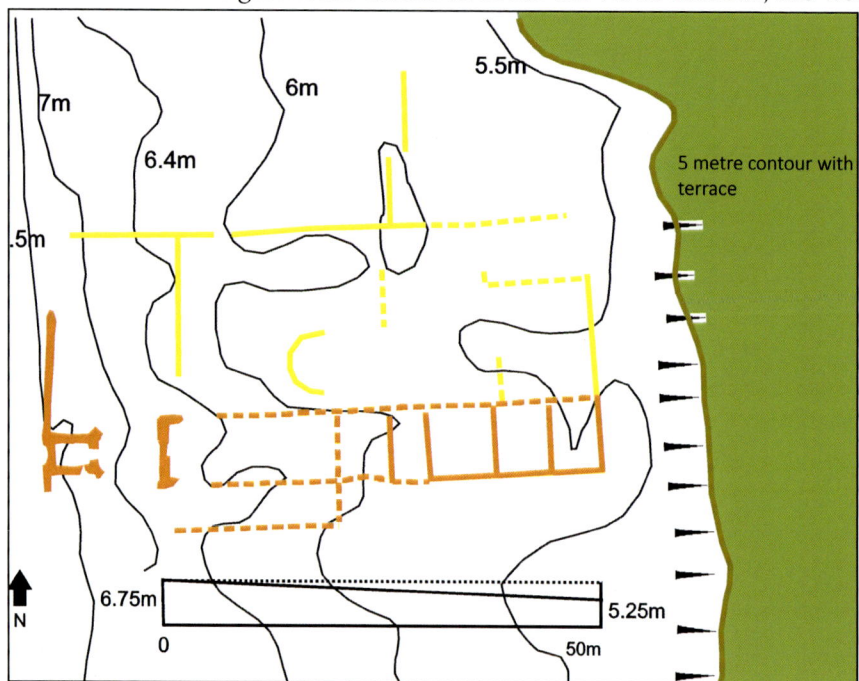

Figure 3.12 Site of the conventual buildings showing gradients. Outline of conventual buildings as per OS First Edition/Cushion.

end of the fourteenth-century church approximately at the 6.75 m contour, and the ground falls away to the east so that the east end of the choir is approximately on the 5.25 m contour. It will also be noted that the east end of the church was close to the 5 m terrace, which delimits the practical area for major structures. From this it can be seen that the desired length of the church itself determined the distance between the west end of the church and the gatehouse, because it was not feasible to built the church elsewhere on the site.

Figure 3.13 shows diagrammatically the dimensions of the church building as can be approximately estimated from the remaining footings.[21] The choir was 18.5 x 8 m, the walking place 4 x 7.5 m, and the nave 27 x 7.5 m. The choir at 18.5 m in length was typical for early Carmelite choirs: for example, Hulne was 18.29 m (O'Sullivan 2013: 166); Aylesford 19 m (Rigold 1963: 9); Norwich may have been about 17 m, if the choir occupied half of the total length of the 1256 church (see Chapter 7). This may suggest that the choir at Burnham Norton was either retained from the earlier church or at least rebuilt in the fourteenth century on its original footprint when the nave was rebuilt.

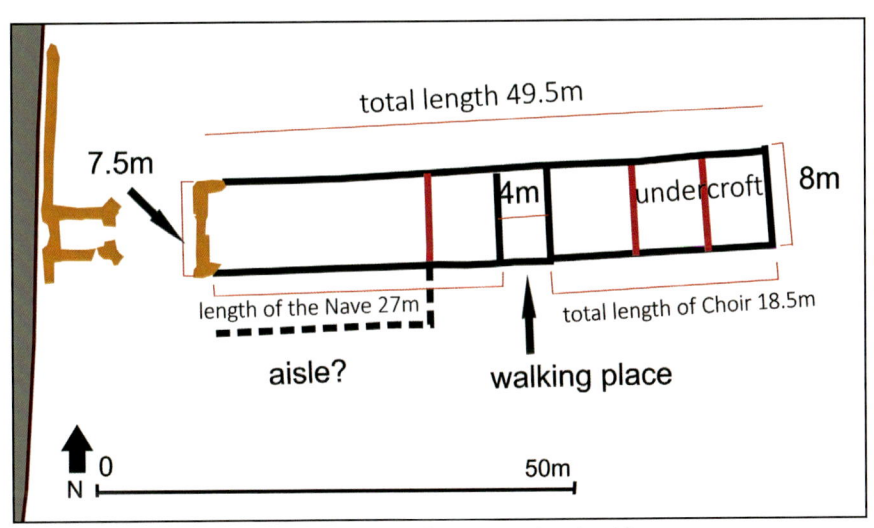

Figure 3.13 Plan of the fourteenth-century church with measurements.

Figure 3.14 shows the probable layout of the thirteenth-century church at Burnham Norton. The thirteenth-century plan for early Carmelite churches were often simple aisle-less structures, usually with no walking place between the nave and the choir (notable exceptions being Hulne and London, both of which had walking places from the beginning). For example, of the first ten Carmelite houses in England, founded either before Norton or very soon after (between 1242 and 1256) and for which the original plan is known, most conform to this simple plan.

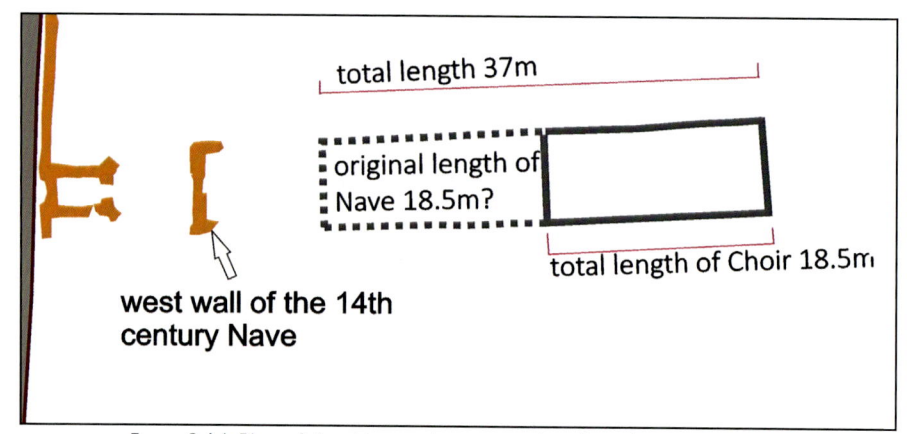

Figure 3.14 Plan of the thirteenth-century church with measurements.

Conclusions

Knowing the landscape context of the friary site in the Middle Ages is important to understanding why the friary was situated as it was and how it engaged with other places within the medieval topography. The modern landscape is radically different in many respects, because of the very dynamic nature of this part of the North Norfolk coast. The transformation of the open field system of agricultural management to that of discrete farmsteads of enclosed fields has also altered the nature of the landscape visually. Knowing the changes that have occurred since the dissolution of the friary in 1538 can help to re-envision the realities concerning the earlier landscape.

The topography of the site on which the friary was settled has determined how it developed over the nearly 300 years that it was maintained as an active inhabited location. The key to understanding the site, it is suggested, is the 5 m contour and what this signified in topographical terms: that it was the boundary between land that would take built structures such as the church, and land that was prone to permanent or periodic inundation.

The second factor that influenced how the site developed was the size of the plot owned by the friars. For example, the issue of where the cloister and other conventual buildings were situated was clearly influenced by the availability of land. There is little firm archaeological evidence for the exact layout, but the most probable plan puts the cloister on the north side of the church – unusual for a rural site. The additional 3 acres gifted to the friars in 1353 greatly enlarged the precinct, but did not provide many more opportunities to redesign the plan of the friary. It is hoped that future archaeological investigation will allow more of the plan to be uncovered and enhance an understanding of the site.

THE FRIARY SITE AND ITS LANDSCAPE CONTEXT

Notes

1 The history of early church foundations in the Burnhams was complex – for more information on the early churches in the Burnhams see Andrew Rogerson's contribution, Chapter 2.

2 A detailed explanation of the mechanism for coastal formation at Burnham is given in Jonathan Hooton's contribution, Chapter 1.

3 The 5 m contour has been taken as the limit of inundation as this fits well with the evidence, such as that for the tidal and high water data for South-East England in surviving historical map evidence. Examples of similar areas include the Broads west of Yarmouth and Lowestoft, the Isle of Thanet in North Kent, the upper levels of the Rother on the Kent and Sussex border, and at Pevensey Bay in Sussex (Chester-Kadwell 2017: 234).

4 In reality the distinction between dry land (the areas not prone to inundation) and the marshes and tidal channels was more clearly defined than today. That is because land above 5 m would – in terms of the nature of its vegetation, the presence of permanent habitation and established routeways – have presented an even sharper distinction to the lower, wetter and less well-developed land running up against it. The extensive areas of reclaimed agricultural land and the formation of fresh marsh by the construction of protective sea walls have created a different form of landscape.

5 This was shared by most medieval estuarine landscapes. For example, around the tidal estuary of the upper levels of the Rother between Kent and Sussex the same phenomenon is observed (Chester-Kadwell 2017: 245–51).

6 While ferries were common and could significantly shorten the journey time over the land route, they could be very dependent on the tides and were particularly problematic at times of very low water.

7 The road enclosure order of 1822 clearly shows the line of the road, parts of which were still in use in Faden's day.

8 The present causeway and bridge between Burnham Market and Overy were not constructed until 1421–2 (see note 14 to Chapter 2), so before that date the crossing of the Burn at Thorpe was the lowest road crossing available.

9 Andrew Rogerson sets out the development of the medieval settlement pattern in the Burnhams in Chapter 2. Saxon settlement in Burnham Norton, it seems, was mostly around the parish church.

10 The relationship between the religious community and the secular community that this last point suggests is looked at in more detail in Chapter 9.

11 Events and dates relating to the history of the medieval friary are taken from Richard Copsey's Chronology unless otherwise stated (Annex to this volume); manuscript references are contained in the Chronology under each entry.

12 The name of the first place for the foundation of the friary is spelt in a variety of different forms. Here, the name is spelt as *Bradmer* for consistency. Variations in the spelling of names such as Bradmer or Burnham were often influenced by what is known as the great vowel shift that occurred between the thirteenth and sixteenth centuries. Thus Brad/Bard and Burn/Brun represent different pronunciations of the same word.

13 In some respects it is similar to the site chosen for Mulcheney Abbey in the Yeo Valley,

Somerset. Although on an inland site and therefore less exposed to the elements, Mulcheney is on a low peninsula in an area prone to flooding.

14 Tidal estuaries of this width were bridged in medieval times with causeways and bridges, such as at Newenden between Kent and Sussex. However, although that valley was in fact wider, it was farther from the sea and the tidal range and strength were much less (Chester-Kadwell 2017: 239–42).

15 Apart from the friary church, now gone, the three parish churches can be seen in this alignment from St Margaret's, Norton. With the more open aspects of the landscape in the past the church of St Clement at Burnham Overy, viewed from the friary across the estuary of the Burn, must have been quite stunning – enhanced by the greater height of its tower at that time.

16 For example at Norwich (see Chapter 7) and Cambridge where the later Whitefriars moved to a more favourable site in the city – as also happened at York (O'Sullivan 2013).

17 This includes an area to the north and east of Friary Cottage that contains the putative 'holy well' and the head of the stream that connects to the River Burn.

18 'Manse' from Latin *mansia* suggests a chief dwelling place, the friars' home (Latham 1999).

19 There is an argument for an alternative site for the 'messuage and croft' gifted to the friary in 1350. Giles Emery (in Chapter 4) cites archaeological evidence that suggests that there may have been medieval settlement to the west of Friary Lane opposite the gatehouse. Conceivably, then, the 1350 gift was next to the thirteenth-century precinct but on the other side of Friary Lane (a good site for a guesthouse?). However, this evidence was destroyed by the building of the school. If Friary Cottage broadly marks the site of the 1350 gift, then it follows that the putative Holy Well was not immediately associated with the earlier precinct, and there could not have been an entrance way directly to the friary from the Brancaster to Wells road earlier than the middle of the fourteenth century.

20 'Detached gable wall. C14, Decorated flint with cut-stone dressings. Central doorway with 2 continuous hollow chamfers, outer label and string course continued across facade. Arch filled in with brick. 2 cusped niches north and south. Outline of large west window embrasure. Set of buttress at north east. Built up to form gable of demolished later building with clunch and brick. Proximity to gatehouse (q.v.) precludes suggestion of west gable of church.'

21 The measurements of the friary church footings at Burnham Norton were checked by the author using a measuring wheel, and are as accurate as possible given the condition of the earthworks that now mark the location of the building.

4

Results of recent archaeological surveys of the Burnham Norton site

Giles Emery

Introduction

As the array of contributions in this volume attests, the site of Burnham Norton Friary has captured the interest and imagination of historians and local people in recent years. The friary has never been subject to a complementary programme of archaeological investigation, and aside from the excavation of several skeletons during restoration of the friary gatehouse in 1840, little physical subsurface evidence of the friary beyond that of the gatehouse and church ruins has been investigated archaeologically. More recently earthwork surveys, such as those in 1995, and examination of aerial photographs have provided the basis for some interpretation of the layout of the overall friary, while a magnetometry survey in 2017 has provided evidence for previously unknown subsurface features.

This chapter presents a chronological synthesis of recent archaeological surveys and excavations at the Burnham Norton Friary site, including archaeological work arising from a programme of repair work to the precinct wall remains from 2016 to 2018. It is intended that this summary of work will provide a useful resource for consideration in the long-term preservation and management of the site, and inform any potential future archaeological investigations.

The site

The ruins of the Carmelite Friary of St Mary at Burnham Norton occupy a well-sloping meadow on the west side of the valley of the Burn River. The first Carmelite friary to be established in Norfolk was founded at Bradmer in Burnham Norton parish some time after 1242, but relocated in 1253 to the present, more accessible site in this parish. The site was expanded on more than one occasion before its eventual dissolution in 1538.

The friary site is considered to be of national importance, and is scheduled as St Mary's Carmelite Friary and Holy Well (National Heritage List: Scheduled Monument 1013095/SM 21389, NHER 1738, Historic England scheduling notes 2015). The 2.1 hectare area contains remains of the west, north and east precinct walls, with the restored fourteenth-century gatehouse on its west side on Friars Lane. Close to the gatehouse is the west gable wall of the church, with various earthworks associated with the church ruins and possible conventual buildings to the east and north of the church.

In the meadow to the south and east of the church are earthworks representing subdivision/terracing of the friary precinct. The site is managed under a Higher Level Stewardship (HLS) Agreement with Natural England by the Norfolk Archaeological Trust.

Archaeological investigations and surveys – 1995 to present

Each investigation summarised below includes references to the source material whether printed or digital. For more detail on any of the individual investigations, readers are directed to the original publication (see bibliography).

Cushion's 1995 Earthwork Survey (Figure 4.1)

The friary monument and its earthworks were comprehensively surveyed and described by Brian Cushion in 1995, and the results of this were published in *Earthworks of Norfolk* (Cushion and Davison 2003). Cushion also reported on the standing remains and their condition. The main observations were:

- The line of the missing southern precinct wall was recorded as indistinct, marked by either the current field boundary or a low bank to its north.
- Earthworks internal to the precinct walls were visible, and interpreted as perhaps representing terracing.
- To the east of the gatehouse and extending east from the surviving gable end of the church are the much-subdivided outlines of buildings. Cushion suggested that parchmarks along part of the south side of the church indicate a possible south aisle.[1]
- On the northern side of the church, fragmentary lengths of walling may relate to a cloister and adjacent buildings, while the purpose of a large C-shaped flint wall is unknown.
- A small courtyard is formed by the wall of Friary Cottage's garden and another extending southwards.

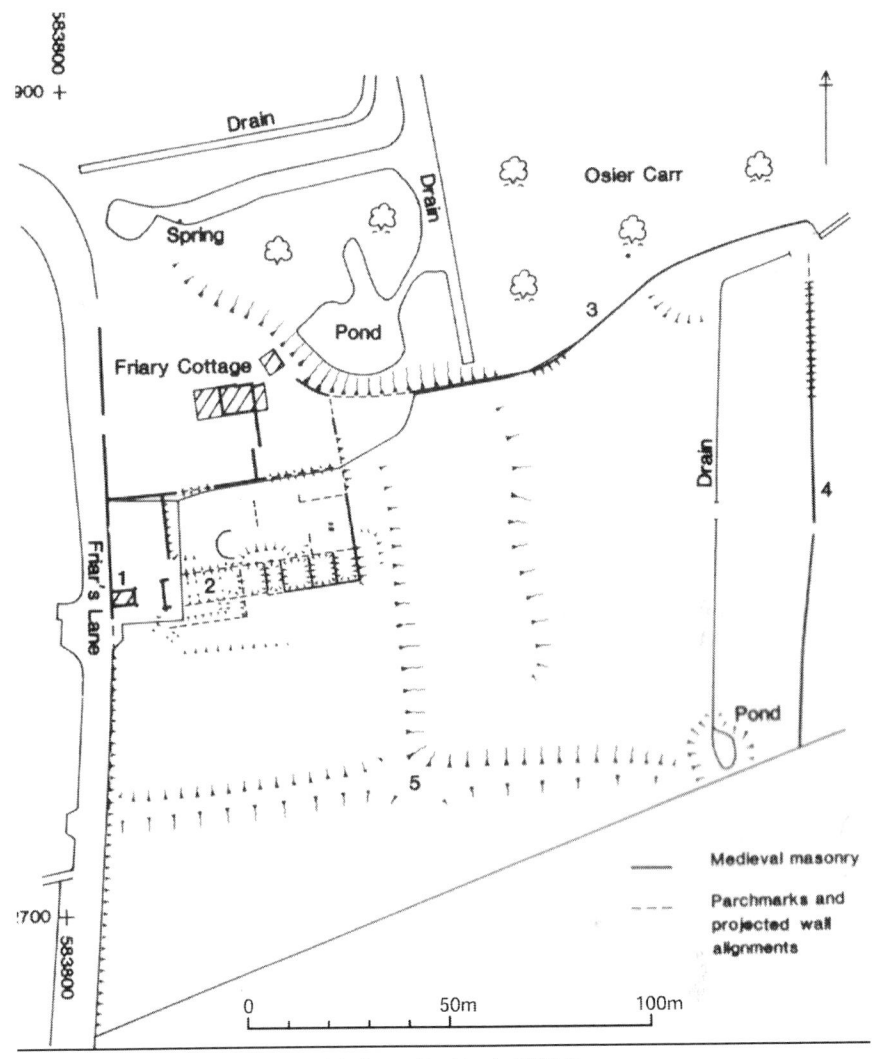

Figure 4.1 Brian Cushion's 1995 Survey.
Reproduced with permission from East Anglian Archaeology, 2003, vol. 104.

Norfolk Mapping Programme (NMP) 2002: aerial photography

The friary remains were digitally mapped in 2002 as part of the Norfolk Mapping Programme from 1946 RAF aerial photographs. The NMP mapping exercise provides much the same data as Brian Cushion's survey of 1995, with the exception of offering new insights into the earthworks to the east of the church, where two platforms or terraces are suggested. A slight causeway or hollow leading up between them, towards the church, was also recognised, which may now tie in with recent evidence for a trackway extending down toward an eastern gate (see below).

The Norfolk Historic Environment Record details evidence drawn from a Cambridge University Collection of Aerial Photography (CUCAP) oblique aerial photograph taken in 1951, prior to construction of the Burnham Market Primary School in 1953, directly opposite the friary site.[2] The image suggests the position of possible buildings contemporary to the friary on the west side of Friars Lane. Three angular parchmarks may indicate subsurface building remains. In particular, a rectangular parched area is noted on a roughly east-to-west orientation, running from TF 8380 4277 to TF 8377 4277, and measuring 25 × 6 m (the approximate location of which is marked on Figure 4.2). This places the parchmark within the footprint of the school buildings. Unfortunately, the construction of the school included significant terracing into the sloping ground here, along with the creation of a subsurface basement, obliterating any traces of whatever may have caused these parchmarks.

Whether any such structures here were associated directly with the friary in the form of a guest house or localised settlement of a more secular nature remains unknown. There was certainly medieval settlement in the area, as attested by the adjacent 'messuage and croft' gifted to the friary in 1350 (see Chapter 3).

Archaeological work at the Gatehouse and Friar's Cottage (1995)

A small excavation on the north side of the gatehouse, prior to the installation of the external stairs in 1995 (Heywood and Rogerson 1995) identified a possible medieval doorway to a room built against the precinct wall. It measured c.3.5 m wide from east to west, and might have contained a stairway to the upper floor of the gatehouse. Their report references an etching from 1794 which, when reversed, shows a building in this position, but whether this was a surviving medieval structure or a post-medieval successor is unknown.

Archaeological work at Friary Cottage (2010–12)

Friary Cottage borders the north-west corner of the managed site but is located partly within the area formerly occupied by the friary. The cottage grounds include a spring and running water outside the precinct wall, generally thought to be a possible candidate for the site of the medieval holy well associated with the friary.[3] The cottage has seen several phases of late medieval to modern redevelopment, most notably having been shortened and renovated in the late sixteenth century. The fabric includes many examples of reused medieval masonry. The building was subject to a Historic

Building Survey in 2012 which confirmed that the core of the building has medieval origins and contains some surviving masonry, including in situ ashlar quoins. It has been suggested that the original building served as an infirmary, guest house or prior's lodgings (Heywood 2012).

The adjacent cottage grounds have been subject to minor excavation and archaeological monitoring in mitigation of modern development works. An excavation in 2010, around an outbuilding to the north-east of the cottage, revealed the probable north precinct wall following the edge of the dry land on a north-west–south-east alignment, with a number of smaller walls parallel or perpendicular to it, perhaps representing small buildings aligned upon it. Subsequent monitoring of groundworks identified three more walls aligned with Friary Cottage and the church buildings to the south, along with a well (Crawley 2011). Monitoring of further groundworks in 2012 revealed two possible medieval walls, one parallel to the west precinct wall and one perpendicular to it. These probably represent buildings against the inside of the precinct wall. Medieval demolition rubble and a shell midden were also identified (Hickling and Crowson 2015).

Summary of the 2017 magnetometry survey results

A geophysical survey of the open ground enclosed by the precinct walls was undertaken by Dr David Bescoby in March 2017, commissioned by the Norfolk Archaeological Trust and funded by the Heritage Lottery Fund as part of the Imagined Land Project (Bescoby 2017). Some areas close to the site entrance could not be surveyed owing to the presence of a contractor's compound, and the survey did not extend into the rough ground of earthworks in the north-west corner of the site.

The aim of the work was to assess the potential for subsurface remains within the meadow area, to assist in increasing an understanding of the layout and development of the friary. Evidence was previously limited to scant documentary sources, cropmark data and the extensive earthwork survey by Brian Cushion summarised above (Cushion and Davison 2003). Beyond the earthworks associated with the area of the church, very few details were recorded within the enclosed precinct other than internal linear earthworks, interpreted as medieval terracing.

The magnetometry survey method employed proved effective in re-examining this open area. It also revealed a number of previously unknown surviving subsurface features relating to former masonry structures, possible routeways and divisions within the precinct. The full report is available as a digital archive through the Archaeological Data Service online library of grey literature reports (OASIS id: dbescoby1-283340).

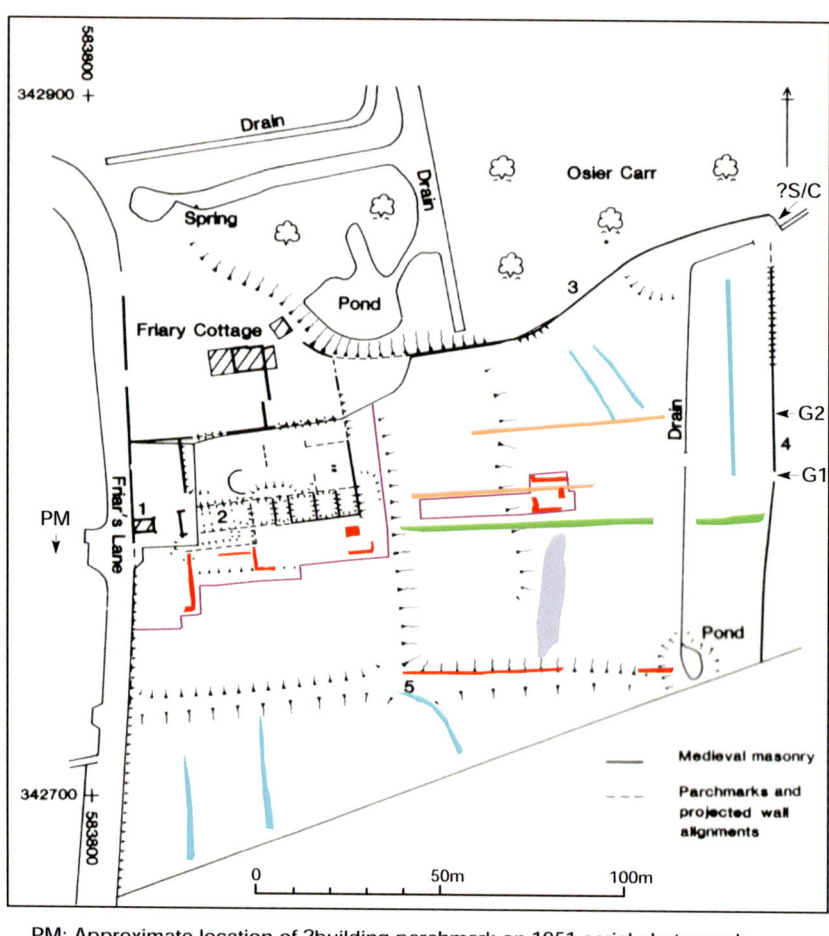

Figure 4.2 Brian Cushion's 1995 Survey with additional features identified by magnetometry. Source: EAA, 2003, vol.104 with additions

RECENT ARCHAEOLOGICAL SURVEYS

The main conclusions of the report are illustrated in Figure 4.2 and briefly summarised here:

- The survey identified evidence for a masonry wall which runs north to south parallel to Friar's Lane. This wall could represent the eastern extent of a building extending southwards from the gatehouse, fronting the lane. To its east, several clear wall/masonry elements were detected, indicating a further range of buildings extending south from the church by c. 15 m.

- In addition to discrete wall elements, the survey revealed associated spreads of enhanced magnetic responses indicating areas of building rubble. This clearly delineates the maximum southern and eastern extent of the main complex of buildings occupying the north-west corner of the site, which coincides with an area of higher relief.

- Demolition spreads with surviving masonry elements detected at its eastern limit indicate the presence for a further building or building range c. 50 m to the east of the friary church, but aligned with it. This sizeable footprint might have measured as much as 40 m along its east–west axis, and appears to be associated with the east-to-west line of a track or thoroughfare linking the friary church to a gateway in the extant eastern section of the precinct wall.

- Away from the focus of building remains and associated demolition rubble, the nature of the magnetic responses within the enclosed area of the precinct is indicative of multiple phases of agricultural activities.

- Two probable trackways on parallel east-to-west orientations appear to head toward lost gateways in the east precinct wall, the locations of which were suggested during recent recording of the surviving precinct walls from 2016 to 2018 (see below).

- Within the southern portion of the surveyed area, the remains of a possible masonry wall were detected running for 73 m along the top of a low earthwork bank. Projecting the alignment of this wall to the east connects it with the remains of the eastern wall to form a south-east corner, and it is likely that this represents the remains of the southern return of the precinct wall or alternatively a walled subdivision within the precinct.

- Faint traces of an internal division were recorded c.30 m to the north of the possible southern precinct wall line and running adjacent to the possible long building/building range.

- Several ditch-like cut features on variable alignments were recorded within the area of the precinct, which have the potential to pre-date the layout of the friary.

- A large but fairly shallow feature of uncertain date running roughly north to south on the southern side of the possible gatehouse (shown in grey on Figure 4.2) does not appear to be of modern date, and its origin remains unclear.

BURNHAM NORTON FRIARY

Figure 4.3 The east wall during repair work.

Figure 4.4 The eastern gateway.

RECENT ARCHAEOLOGICAL SURVEYS

Survey, monitoring and minor investigation of the precinct walls (2016–18)

Prior to a lengthy programme of repair and consolidation work to the precinct walls, an initial photographic and digital survey of all standing elements was carried out in January and February 2016 by NPS Archaeology (Report No. 2016/1231/Crowson et al. 2017). This was followed in 2017 by a programme of archaeological monitoring during the works by Norvic Archaeology (Emery 2019b), which included targeted investigation of subsurface masonry in the north-east corner of the precinct.

The NPS Archaeology survey recorded the fabric and forms of the walls along with a record of the repair work, and provides a detailed resource for any future conservation work to the monument. The main fabric requiring repair was the surviving stretches of the east precinct wall, which had suffered greatly from weathering and vegetation damage. This is the longest extent of standing precinct wall, although several stretches of it are intermittent, particularly where it runs to the north-east corner. See Figure 4.3.

In addition, a 5 m stretch of severely leaning north wall which runs to the very north-east corner of the precinct was leaning heavily and in danger of toppling without urgent attention. This is almost all that has remained of the north wall since January 1998, when about 50 m of masonry overturned to rest on its outer face. The surviving stretch of masonry was buttressed with brickwork and has now been stabilised.

The date of the walls remains open to some interpretation, although given the likely development of the friary a fourteenth-century date is currently supposed for much of the circuit (see Chapter 5).

General observations made of the precinct wall

The initial wall survey concluded that the flint and mortar precinct walls were unlikely to have been especially formidable. The ruins of the north and east precinct walls measure no more than 1.3 to 1.5 m in height, and possibly stood just over 2 m in total. They measured c. 0.65 m wide, and have the appearance of a single phase of construction with local vernacular techniques present.

Historic repairs were evident only in specific areas, notably close to the extant gatehouse, employing some reused examples of limestone and chalk masonry (believed to have been sourced from demolished friary buildings) with erratics collected from local gravels. Similar materials were also present within the surviving most northern part of the east wall. The much-repaired west precinct wall to the north of the extant gatehouse comprises multiple fragments of medieval building rubble in the form of reused limestone ashlar fragments, with large numbers of chalk block fragments and a few fragments of medieval brick. A well-weathered reused Barnack limestone window or door jamb was also incorporated into the fabric. Given the form of the architectural stone and presence of medieval brick, this reused material appears to be waste from a demolished medieval structure of possible thirteenth to fourteenth-century date. The most obvious source for such material is from within the friary complex itself, generated during either a fourteenth-century remodelling of the site or later demolition work.

The curious shape and narrower thickness of this short curving wall section suggests that it was created to close or repair a gap between the northern and eastern walls. Although another gateway is one possibility, the low-lying marshy ground here makes this unlikely, and the presence of the modern drainage dyke allows for a medieval antecedent to be considered, perhaps with a sluice or culvert set within the low far corner of the precinct wall here. The 2017 magnetometry survey shows an internal ditch-like feature of unknown date running roughly south to north between the modern dyke and the precinct wall. If this lost ditch was contemporary to the friary, it could also relate to an internal drainage dyke running out through this north-east corner.

Imagined Land Project archaeological test-pits at Burnham Market Primary School (2018)

The Burnham Norton test-pitting project was part of the Imagined Land project, a Heritage Lottery Funded (HLF) project managed by Simon Floyd on behalf of the Norfolk Archaeological Trust. This was the second part of a two-year project, based at two of the Trust's sites, the Scheduled Monuments of Tasburgh Enclosure (2017) and Burnham Norton Friary (2018). The project was created to offer local people the chance to explore and celebrate the heritage of sites at the heart of their communities, through practical research and creative activities.

The project was highly successful in engaging with the local community at Burnham Norton and raising interest in the friary site, where volunteers included local residents, family groups and all the year groups of the Burnham Market Primary School. The test-pitting project was overseen by Norvic Archaeology. An impressive eight test-pits were excavated over the course of eight days in May 2018, which have served to both enhance the local Historic Environment Record for the area of the school and St Margaret's Church, and increase our understanding of the archaeological potential of the setting of the friary.

Test-pitting at Burnham Market Primary School

The finds retrieved during the test-pitting and localised metal detection include evidence of several thousand years of human activity, ranging from the prehistoric to the modern day. A total of 870 individual finds of a wide range of material types were collected, including artefacts such as worked prehistoric flints, pottery sherds, butchered animal bone, marine shells, clay tobacco pipe, coins, buttons, ceramic building materials and iron smelting slag. The full report (Emery 2019a) has been submitted to the county's Historic Environment Record, and is also available as a digital archive through the Archaeological Data Service online library of grey literature reports (OASIS id: norvicar1 -342594).

Figure 4.5 Test-pitting at Burnham Market Primary School.

Three test-pits were excavated by pupils and volunteers within the grounds of Burnham Market Primary School, opposite the friary. They produced a pottery assemblage from mixed ploughsoils which included prehistoric, Iron Age, Roman and medieval sherds along with small quantities of Late Neolithic to Bronze Age flints. Fragmentary butchered animal bone and marine shell may be attributed to midden-spreading activities associated with the friary or localised occupation (previously indicated by parchmarks for a possible building identified opposite the friary gatehouse in 1951). A small number of medieval brick/tile pieces were collected, which included a fragment of medieval floor tile. This corner piece is of Flemish type of fourteenth to fifteenth-century date, with traces of a dark green glaze. Such floor tiles are common in the region, and were widely used in geometric and chequerboard patterns in high-status and ecclesiastical buildings. Given the context of the find, the tile may well have come from the friary site or an associated high-status building. A concentration of burnt daub was encountered by a test-pit at the rear of the school playing field, which might be attributable to an oven or fired structure of uncertain date.

Figure 4.6 Metal detecting at Burnham Market Primary School.

Metal detected finds included two Anglo-Saxon objects: a sixth-century iron wrist clasp and an unusual ninth-century copper-alloy zoomorphic belt fitting with gold gilding and decorative silver rivets (illustrated in Emery 2019a; Norvic Archaeology Report 120). These finds augment various finds of Anglo-Saxon date collected from the fields surrounding the friary site, where several decades of surface finds collected through field walking and metal detection have reported finds scatters of multiple periods, demonstrating a longevity of human activity in the immediate area, with evidence for prehistoric, Roman, Saxon and medieval land use. Detailed information of such finds scatters and cropmarks for monuments within the wider landscape are recorded as part of the Norfolk Historic Environment Record, with the Anglo-Saxon development of the Burnhams discussed in Chapter 2 of this volume.

Test-pitting at Friar's Acre, Friars Lane

A single test-pit was excavated in the garden of Friar's Acre, located *c.* 250 m north-west of the friary site. This revealed modern make-up associated with the construction of the house above a deep layer of waterlogged colluvial silty subsoil. The plot backs onto the marshier ground that forms part of the

River Burn floodplain, and was formerly part of an open field with drainage dykes, depicted on the First Edition OS plan of 1886. This area of land can be considered to be relatively marginal until post-medieval drainage work and the construction of modern housing on the higher land immediately adjacent to the lane. Residual finds of note include two pieces of iron smelting slag, a single sherd of medieval pottery and a small number of prehistoric flints.

Summary

The information summarised above provides a valuable resource for future research and interpretation of the friary site, with the potential to be tested through further historical and archaeological research or excavation.

Results from the magnetometry survey are particularly significant, and have added valuable detail beyond the limitations of the 1995 earthwork survey (Cushion and Davison 2003). The demarcation between zones of building activity and agricultural activity allows for a greater understanding of the friary layout, with masonry traces of several hitherto unknown buildings along the western precinct wall and to the east of the main complex being of particular interest. Combining the magnetometry results with observations of the precinct walls has also confirmed the presence of an east gate leading out to the riverside, paired with a subsidiary gate by the presence of trackways leading towards each. The survival of subsurface walling that appears to relate to the lost south precinct wall is also useful in terms of an appraisal of the exact limits of the enclosure.

The magnetometry survey work has provided several new potential targets worthy of archaeological ground testing beyond the obvious complex of earthworks. There is still significant scope for further non-invasive survey work to refine our interpretation of the main building complex, where resistivity or ground penetration radar methods have the potential to add new dimensions of detail and highlight the preservation of any subsurface remains. For example, the arrangement of buildings is yet to be more clearly defined, including the exact siting and dimensions of what appears to be a northerly-located cloister - the possible rationale for which is mentioned by Chester-Kadwell in Chapter 3. The assumption that the majority of features identified have either a pre-friary or friary-dated origin is worthy of further research and possible ground testing.[4]

Future investigations at the friary may also offer the potential to understand a hitherto under-represented aspect of the site, namely the practical and cultural life of the people who lived and worked within the precinct walls. Currently no significant finds assemblages have been collected through the work outlined above. The friary was occupied for 285 years, a significant period of time for the accumulation and dispersal of large volumes of material. Although limited in scope, the test-pitting at Burnham Market Primary School, on land immediately west of the friary, demonstrated that soils there were laden with residual medieval finds in the form of food refuse (bone and shell) and pottery sherds. Any future investigations that result in the recovery of a meaningful assemblage could provide valuable data to allow the nature of the life at the friary to be explored.

Scant evidence has come to light to provide details on the appearance of former structures, such as painted glass, lead work, roof tiles or decorative floor tiles. Environmental evidence might also be preserved across the site within buried soils or features, which could allow for a greater understanding of land use within the walls.

Although many questions remain regarding the nature of the site, what is certain is that any future archaeological investigations have a very high potential to uncover evidence that may allow for a fresh interpretation on the origins, development and spatial organisation of the friary, and perhaps provide evidence of everyday life behind the precinct walls.

Acknowledgements

Many thanks are given to Natural England, in collaboration with the Higher-Level Stewardship scheme, which together funded the wall conservation and repair project. The author is grateful to David Adams of NPS Archaeology and Dr David Bescoby for the supply of relevant survey data, and to Caroline Davison of the Norfolk Archaeological Trust who instigated the overall conservation project. The author extends his thanks and appreciation to the staff and pupils of Burnham Market Primary School for hosting and facilitating the school test-pitting event, and the wider community for engaging so enthusiastically with the Imagined Land project.

Notes

1. Since Cushion's survey further work has been done on interpreting the earthworks. For example, it is suggested in this volume that they represent the foundations of the church Chester-Kadwell (Chapter 3) and Heywood (Chapter 4) have cast doubt on whether the church actually had a south aisle; arguably these earthworks are actually later disturbances.
2. Oblique Aerial Photograph: CUCAP. 1951. NHER TF 8342ABK (CUCAP FQ20) 15-JUN-1951.
3. Both Heywood (Chapter 5) and Chester-Kadwell (Chapter 3) discuss this feature.
4. Subsequent to the dissolution of the friary in 1538 the site has had a number of reuses, any of which might have left their mark.

5

The existing remains including Friary Cottage and Our Lady's Well

Stephen Heywood

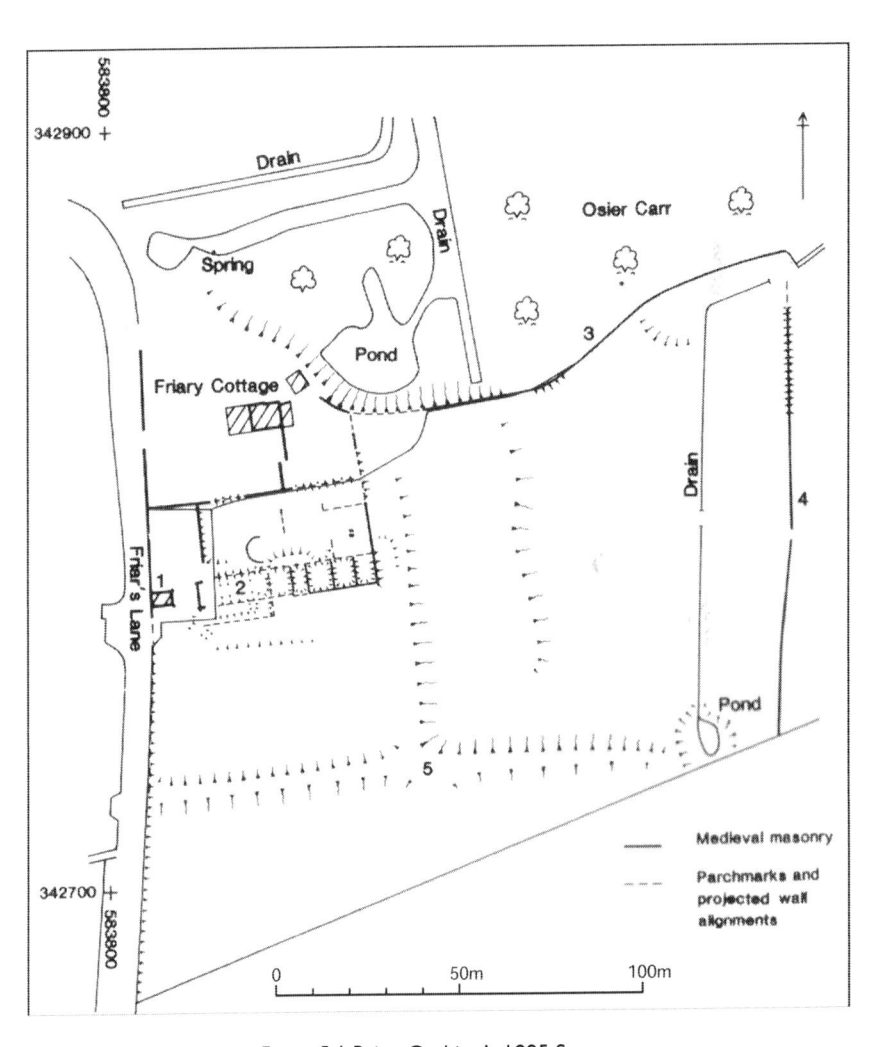

Figure 5.1 Brian Cushion's 1995 Survey.
Reproduced with permission from East Anglian Archaeology, 2003, vol. 104

Summary

The principal upstanding masonry remains of the friary buildings at Burnham Norton consisting of the gatehouse and the west wall of the friary church immediately east of it, belong to the first half of the fourteenth century (Figure 5.1). The cottage to the north with a modern outhouse beside it might be later. The surviving parts of boundary wall to the east and north are or were of fourteenth-century date, belonging perhaps to the enlargement of the site in 1353 (*Cox 1906: 425-6*). The spring at the north-west corner of the site and the stream which flows from it have no identified medieval structures directly associated with them. However, the proximity of Friary Cottage reinforces the traditional view that it was a focus of devotion. The information is enhanced by extensive earthworks marking the buried walls of the church, which was still standing in the mid-nineteenth century, although by then it had been converted into a barn. A magnetometer survey has added further valuable information on possible former buildings on the site. Chapter 4 provides an analysis of this material. Minor archaeological excavations uncovering walls have also taken place.

The gatehouse

The gatehouse is the most impressive surviving building on the site (Figure 5.2). 'Gatehouse' gives slightly the wrong impression, as it has more in common with a two-storey church porch because it is too narrow to have allowed the passage of carts. It is oriented with the west gable-end to the road side, with the arched entrance stepping down to the floor level. Above the doorway are three pedestals in a recess for statues of saints, long gone. The glazed west window above, with modern moulded brick tracery, lights the upper room which may have contained an altar. The window is flanked by panels of blind tracery, the limestone contrasting with the carefully knapped flint. The stone coping of buttresses can be seen to each side of the west façade. The buttressing was originally the precinct wall itself, the remains of which are directly beneath the copings and the surviving low walls stretching to the north. The height of the original precinct wall can be seen most clearly on the north side of the gatehouse where the linking flints project. On the south side the precinct wall diminishes to ground level in steps.

The east façade of the gatehouse has diagonal buttresses flanking an open arch of two orders on responds of engaged shafts with bell capitals. There are niches to each side of the opening, and panels of blind cusped Y tracery flank another niche above. The upper level is plain, with ashlar quoins and a gable parapet. A modern metal stair leads up to the doorway on the north side.

Figure 5.2 The gatehouse from the north-west.

The ground floor is covered by two bays of a fine rib vault with longitudinal and transverse ridge ribs and carved bosses at the intersections of the ribs (Figures 5.3 and 5.4). The ribs are laid in *tas-de-charge*,[1] and the elaborate carved bosses have been mutilated, but the eastern boss has a surviving human laughing head with its tongue protruding, and a lion can be detected on the western boss. The open arch to the east of the two vaulted bays is directly in line with the doorway in the west wall of the church (Figure 5.5).

Figure 5.3 The gatehouse interior looking west.

Figure 5.4 A boss in the west bay.

THE EXISTING REMAINS

Figure 5.5 View of the Gatehouse from the east through the church doorway.

The excellent condition of the building is owing to it having been saved from dereliction by the earl of Orford. An engraving of 1795 shows its state at the time (Figures 5.6 and 5.7).[2] The side (north and south) walls and the east gable were missing down to the upper floor level, with the west gable-end damaged but still standing, and according to another drawing formerly in the Wolterton Hall library, the tracery of the west window of paired mouchettes was still intact and remained until *c.* 1940 (Figure 5.8). The upper side walls and the east gable were rebuilt and a new roof erected before 1886 (when the Ordnance Survey map shows the building as roofed),[3] and the buttresses and gable parapets were reconstructed. In the late twentieth century Norfolk County Council undertook works which included the installation of tracery made of moulded brick, glazing, the erection of the metal winding stair and the flooring with tiles of the upper room.

Figure 5.6 The priory ruins from a 1795 etching by Jane C Hayles from a drawing by the Rev. Thomas Kerrich.

Figure 5.7 The priory ruins from a 1795 engraving (reversed).

Figure 5.8 Detail from a repair specification for the Gatehouse.
Source: Wolterton Hall Estate papers.

Figure 5.9 The church façade

The church façade

The remains of the west front of the friary church consist of a fully dressed west doorway with two orders of simple hollow chamfers, angle buttresses, a pair of small cusped niches (the southern one with its dressings robbed) and the north side and sill of a former very large traceried west window (Figure 5.9). The angle buttresses (two buttresses to each corner) survive, with dressings robbed on the western side of the façade, while those to the north and south are less distinct. The north side has lost its buttress altogether, and there are only slight indications of where it stood, and on the south side it is more clear but without dressings. Both sides have the stumps of the nave walls with putlog holes, and on the south side the remains stand to full height. The masonry is of quite tightly jointed random flint rubble with significant amounts of clunch incorporated. The window was blocked and the gable rebuilt at a lower pitch when the building was brought back into use and converted into a barn.

The earthworks show an aisleless nave, as is to be expected in friary churches. In the eastern half the earthworks suggest four transverse walls, of which two form a narrow bay in the right position for the walking space, so typical of mendicant order churches, and the two in the choir may have had something to do with stalls for the clergy. Another transverse feature crossing the nave further west is probably post-medieval.

Precinct walls

The walls of the site are fragmentary, and no sections standing to full height remain. However, it has been noted that the height of the wall at least on the road side can be established from the provision for it on the gatehouse (Figure 5.2). Sections of wall survive on the west side of the precinct north of the gatehouse, extending farther north to form part of the west boundary of Friary Cottage. The fence between Friary Cottage and the western half of the friary enclosure appears not to replace a former wall: an excavation that took place on the east side of the Friary Cottage garden just north of the outbuilding (Crawley 2011) identified another section of the boundary wall going towards the well, indicating that the cottage and the land up to and possibly including Our Lady's Well was within the friary enclosure. The roadside section of wall has been recently repaired and consolidated by the County Council, and reveals the dressings of a former entrance to the site of uncertain date. The eastern section has been repaired, consolidated and partially rebuilt by the Norfolk Archaeological Trust.

The north wall survived almost to full height until 1992/3. The wall was completely shrouded in ivy and hidden in thickets until this was cleared away in 1992. Shortly afterwards it fell over, and is now lying largely intact yet flat on its back face. Figure 5.10 is a photograph of 1992 after clearance and before it fell. The horizontal lift lines can be seen, very similar to the fourteenth-century priory precinct wall at Castle Acre (Heywood 2014b: fig. 12). The wall closer to Friary Cottage still stands, curving northwards towards the stream. The walls are constructed of small broken flints laid in courses rather than the more sophisticated random work on the gatehouse, the church and Friary Cottage.

Figure 5.10 The boundary wall on the north side of precinct photographed in 1992 before it fell.

Friary Cottage

This building is in large part made up of stone from the friary after its closure in 1538 (Figures 5.11 and 5.12). However, this stonework relates mainly to added parapets, the construction of a massive buttress to the north-eastern corner and the jambs of the added central hearth. The reconstructed arches at the present main entrance to the house and at the south-east corner are clearly relatively modern additions. Therefore, the main fabric of the original house is free of reused materials and enough to indicate medieval date. The clearest sign of this is the north-east corner, which has tightly jointed rounded quoins in situ bonded into contemporary well-laid random flint work (Figure 5.13). Patches of this original facing can be seen elsewhere in the building, but large areas are refaced. Some in situ ashlar quoins also survive at the south-east corner. There is an area of original flint facing on the east gable-end (now on the interior of the new extension) which has a putlog hole with a medieval brick lintel (Figure 5.14). The internal faces and core work contain large quantities of clunch, and the spiral stair is contained within an adjunct with two sides entirely of roughly squared clunch.

The building has a long mid-twentieth century extension to the west, faced with flint. Before this, probably during the eighteenth century, the side walls of the building were heightened with brick work. The same bricks were used to build new quoins at the west end of the small cottage (Figures 5.11 and 5.15). There is no indication of original stone quoins as at the eastern gable-end, which would be expected. This suggests that the original house was longer, and that at the time of the cottage heightening or a little beforehand, it was also reduced in length, continuing the brick work to form new corners. Along with this work the gables were rebuilt with reused stone from the friary, and the new gable-end with chimney stack was built.

On the south elevation it can be seen that the brick work heightening is not carried to full length because at the eastern end of the building the original masonry already rises to the new level. The reason is to accommodate a former extension to the south. The staircase which had its access from the exterior was in fact within this extension, and led not only to the existing upper floor but also to the upper storey of the extension. Further evidence of this extension is the survival of some masonry emerging from the wall at the junction with the brick work heightening (Figures 5.12 and 5.15). In line with the east and west walls of the extension towards the friary church there are some walls surviving just above ground level, and more that were picked up by the magnetometer survey: this lends support to the hypothesis that there was a two-storey covered link to the main friary buildings.

THE EXISTING REMAINS

Figure 5.11 (above) The north façade of Friary Cottage before the works of 2011/12.

Figure 5.12 (below) Friary Cottage, interpretive plan.

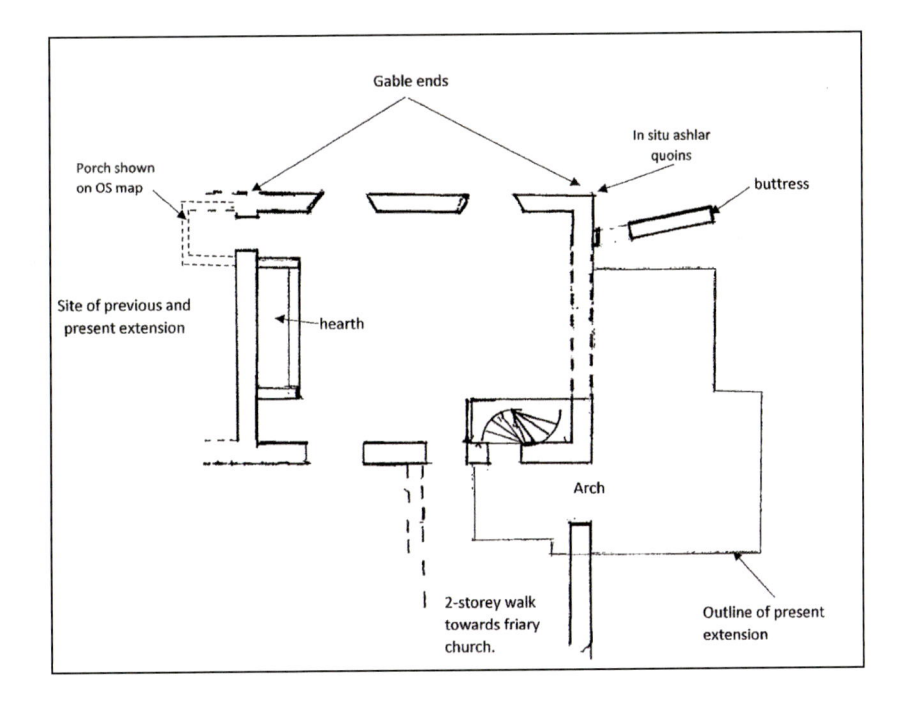

95

Figure 5.13 Friary Cottage, the north-east quoins.

Figure 5.14 Friary Cottage, a blocked puthole in the south section of the east gable-end.

Figure 5.15 Friary Cottage, the south elevation before alterations.

Our Lady's Well

At the north-west corner of the site is the spring. The use of the word 'well' commonly refers to springs, and they often acquire sacred association: most famously for example the holy well at the eponymous town in Clwyd. St Walstan's well at Bawburgh must have been a spring also, as indeed the holy well at Appleton near King's Lynn still is. The latter has a structure around it and niches for people seeking cures wishing to immerse themselves. The Appleton holy well is mentioned in Blomefield (1805–10 vol. 8: 331) but Our Lady's Well at Burnham is not, and the first documentary evidence seems to be the Ordnance Survey map of 1886/7. There is evidence of a pool having been made around the spring at Burnham, and Friary Cottage may have been built close to it in order to oversee the well and to accommodate pilgrims.

Its dedication to Our Lady and the presence of the religious community, also dedicated to St Mary, strengthen the view that it was a good stopping-off place for pilgrims on the coastal route to Little Walsingham and the famous Virgin Mary's well and holy house. Pilgrims to Little Walsingham may well have arrived at Burnham by boat, and the river – at least up to the friary – was navigable during the Middle Ages. There are no identifiable masonry remains around the spring, but the site was clearly made up to be accessible, and a detailed investigation around the immediate vicinity might reveal evidence of its medieval origins as a devotional subject.

Discussion

From the surviving fragmentary buildings and earthworks on this rural site we might expect to find some more evidence of the monastic layout, in a form typical of friaries. The cloister is common to all monasteries, but the rigidly adhered-to plan types of the older monastic foundations were often less strictly followed in friaries. However they had particularities of their own, stemming no doubt from the very constricted urban sites which were the favoured places for their ministry.

A comparison with other Carmelite friary sites might provide a useful aid to interpreting the site at Burnham. The friary ruin at Hulne near Alnwick in Northumberland is one of the four early, rural sites in Britain. It is the best-preserved and the best-documented medieval Carmelite friary, and was founded a decade earlier than Burnham in 1242 (O'Sullivan 2013: 166). The church is long, narrow and aisleless, with a choir of the same width yet divided from it by a walking space, leading from the open area directly to the cloister in true friary manner (Figures 5.16 and 5.17). There was no tower over the walking space.[4] The cloister itself had glazed arcades, and the west walk was undershot[5] – again a typical friary technique. The dormitory,

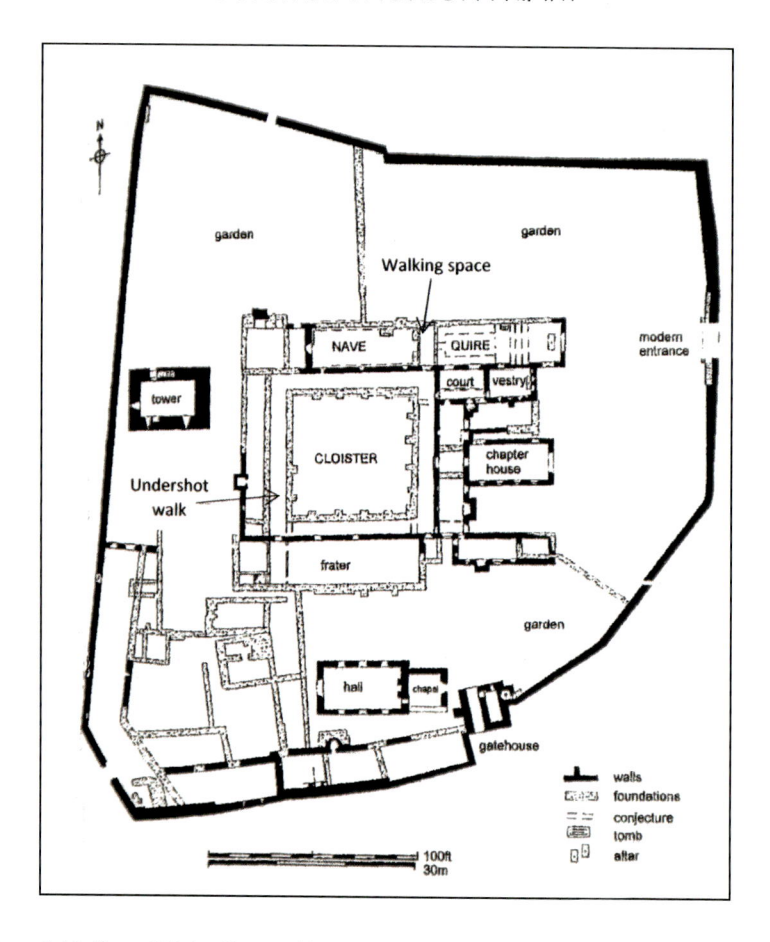

Figure 5.16 Plan of Hulne Friary, Alnwick. Used with permission from O'Sullivan (2013)..

Figure 5.17 Aerial view of Hulne Friary, Alnwick, looking south-east, with the remains of the church in the foreground. © Historic England Archive

instead of carrying on the east range past the refectory to the reredorter at the end, projects at right angles eastwards from the south end of the east walk. Connected to the choir and occupying the east range is an exceptionally large vestry. There is also another building followed by an open slype next to the chapter house, which is in a conventional position. The frater is also in the normal position, with the freestanding kitchen and services further west. It is interesting that Hulne, like Burnham, is rural yet still uses a space-saving undershot cloister walk.

At Burnham there is the long aisleless nave with a good case for a walking space. The aisle-like addition at the west end shown on maps and identified by the geophysical survey is a later, possibly post-medieval, addition during its barn/byre phase. The cloister probably stood to the north of the church, unusual but not very uncommon. The curved feature could represent the friary *lavatorium* with a structure around a well. The typical position would be in the cloister garth. At Hulne the cloister is in a normal position, but it is fairly common with mendicant orders to have irregular cloisters, and sometimes more than one. The walks could have been undershot, especially to the east, with the frater and kitchens closest to Friary Cottage, which was then longer, of course. The walkway from Friary Cottage would have joined onto the east walk and the upper storey of the east range, which when undershot would have been immediately above the walk.

On the question of two-storey walkways, which are unusual, the prior's lodge at Much Wenlock (Pevsner 1958: 425–6) has a two-storey gallery with a similar function, and the bishop of Norwich had a raised walkway from his palace to the cathedral (Heywood 1996). The association of the friary with Our Lady's Well is unusual and an interesting additional aspect to the site, and provides a reason for Friary Cottage being built as a pilgrims' hostel.

There is much scope for further study on this site, which stands alongside research undertaken recently on the Greyfriars at Little Walsingham and the Carmelites in Norwich.

Notes

1. The lower courses of a vault or arch which are laid horizontally.
2. The reversed image relates better to the remains, as the early maps show the ruined building to the north of the gatehouse not the south. Both images are reproduced here.
3. OS 6-inch England and Wales 1842/1952, surveyed 1886, published 1886.
4. The lack of a bell tower for such a well-endowed house is remarkable.
5. An undershot cloister walk is found when the walk instead of being a lean-to structure is incorporated into the building flanking the cloister. See for example the east walk of the Blackfriars cloister in Norwich.

Part II

The Norfolk Carmelites and their cultural context

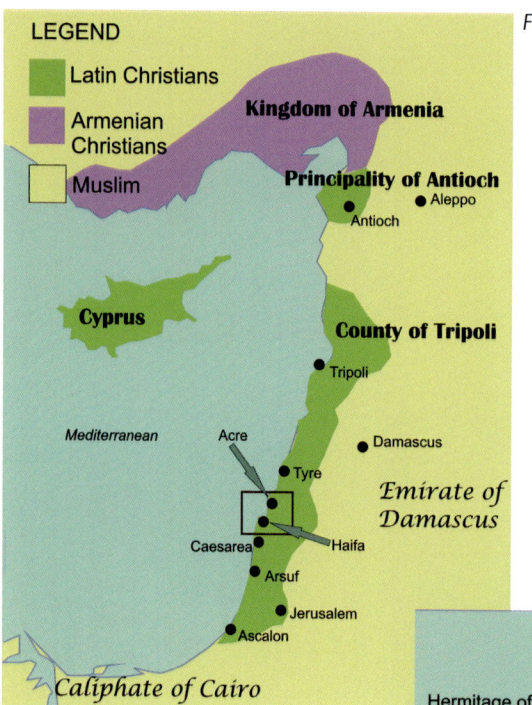

Figure 6.1a (left) The Christian states of the Levant c. 1241. Source: based on Runciman vol 3 1955.

Figure 6.1b (below) Location of the Hermitage of St Mary of Carmel. Source: based on OpenStreetMap from topographic-map.com (indicative contours).

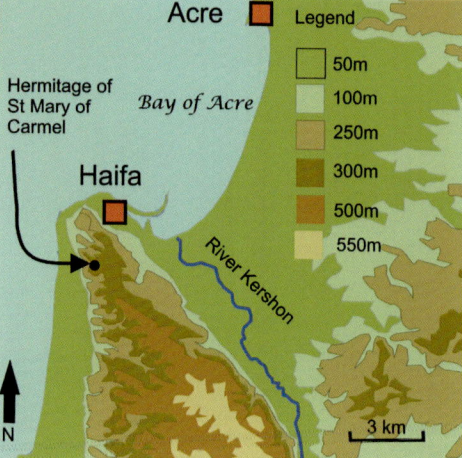

Figure 6.1c (left) Hermitage of St Mary of Carmel, looking west to the coast and Haifa peninsular. Source: © biblewalks.com with permission

6

From hermits of Mount Carmel to Whitefriars in England *c.* 1200–50

Helen Clarke

Introduction

This chapter follows the story of the Carmelites, from their beginnings around 1200 in a hermitage on Mount Carmel in the Holy Land to their arrival in England, where they settled in 'desert' places, including Burnham Norton. The first hermitage was established near the so-called 'Elijah Spring' in *Wadi 'Ain as-Siyah*, a narrow valley on the western slopes of Mount Carmel. The hermitage is located on a hillside terrace on the southern side of the valley about a mile from the sea south of Haifa (Figures 6.1a, b and c).[1] There they followed an eremitical life of silent prayer and contemplation, each in his own cell.

By the 1230s the hermits had increased in numbers, being augmented by other Christians, both religious and secular, who were escaping from the turbulence of life in a country beset by warring Crusaders and Muslims. Finally, the hermits themselves began to leave for the safety of Europe, establishing new hermitages in Cyprus, Sicily, and as far away as England. Those who arrived in England maintained their eremitical traditions and settled in remote locations in the countryside. Soon some of them acknowledged that the 'form of life' which the hermits of Mount Carmel had followed since the early thirteenth century needed to be modified to fit the new conditions in Western Europe. Two hermits were sent to Pope Innocent IV to ask him to revise, or mitigate, some parts of the Carmelites' strict eremitical rules.[2] The revision received papal approved on 1 October 1247, and was adopted by the Carmelite General Chapter at Aylesford later in the autumn of that year.

The paucity of contemporary evidence has led to many modern researchers into early Carmelite history disagreeing about what lay behind the request to Innocent IV. Some have seen the Carmelites' desire to become associated with the mendicant friars as an acknowledgement on their part that they could not continue their austere lifestyle in the West. They may have found it difficult to attract converts to their rural hermitages when the urban friars appeared to be offering a much more fulfilling way of life. Others have suggested that the mendicant connection was 'accidental': the Dominicans, appointed by the Pope to formulate the revision, would naturally tend towards recommending changes to the existing Rule along the lines of that with which they were familiar (Andrews 2006: 16–17).

Whatever the reason, the Rule was revised and the strictness of the Carmelites' life somewhat alleviated. For example, the hermits' isolation within their cells was to be broken by communal meals in a refectory, and the length of the 'great silence' overnight was shortened, but vows of chastity and poverty (no holding of private property) were added to the original vow of obedience. Of less immediate interest to the hermits may have been the abandonment of the rule that Carmelites could only accept gifts of land in isolated spots, but this had far-reaching consequences as it enabled the Carmelites to expand into urban sites and set up their houses alongside the Franciscans and Dominicans. Another of these mitigations was the relaxation of dietary observances to allow brethren who were begging for alms in towns to eat food that had been cooked together with meat, and for those of them who travelled by sea to eat meat on board (Egan 1992a: 110–11).

Before the Mitigation, the Carmelites had four houses in England: Hulne in Northumberland, Aylesford and Lossenham in Kent, and Bradmer (later Burnham Norton) in Norfolk (Figure 6.2). All of these houses attempted in their own ways to replicate their mother house in the Holy Land, the remains of which are discussed in the next section. The foundation and early development of all four is then briefly outlined, with the later history of Hulne, Aylesford and Lossenham also explored in as far as it is relevant to that of Burnham Norton.

The hermits of Mount Carmel

The Carmelites took their name from the mother house in the Holy Land, at first being called simply 'hermits of Mount Carmel', but after the revision they took the name 'Brothers of the Blessed Virgin Mary of Mount Carmel' (Copsey 2004: 3), keeping the reference to the original hermitage. The first hermits who lived there may have followed the Greek Orthodox branch of Christianity but by the first decade of the thirteenth century they were brought into the Latin Church and began to live according to a Rule or a 'form of life' (*vite seu conversationis formula*) drawn up for them by Albert of Vercelli, Patriarch of Jerusalem 1205–14. Albert's 'form of life' confirmed that the hermitage was a religious house under the direction of a prior elected by the community. The prior's cell had to be near the main entrance so that he could welcome visitors, but otherwise there was to be little interaction between the hermits and the outside world, or even between individual

THE CARMELITES IN THE HOLY LAND AND ENGLAND

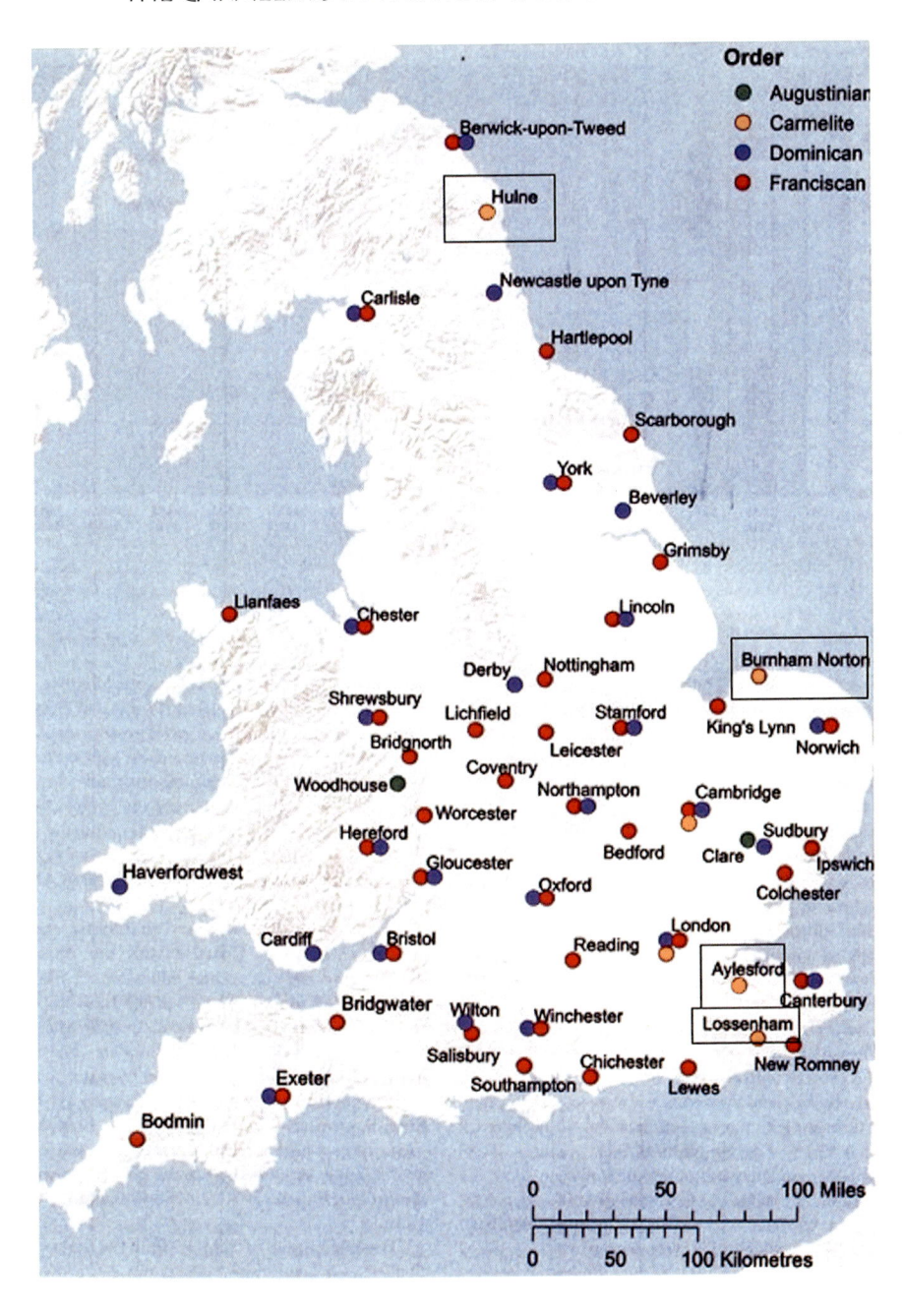

Figure 6.2 Distribution of friaries in England c.1250, with the Carmelite hermitages marked.
Source: based on O'Sullivan (2013, fig. 1.2) with the kind permission of the author.

brethren, who were to live in their solitary cells and devote themselves to prayer and silent contemplation. The exception was that once a day they met together to celebrate Mass in the oratory or chapel (Pringle 1998: 249).

The foundation of the hermitage on Mount Carmel might date from the end of the twelfth century, when the Third Crusade – led by Richard I (the Lionheart) of England and Philip II of France against the Saracen leader Saladin – had been ended with the Crusaders' successful siege of Acre and the peace treaty between Richard and Saladin in 1192. However, this and subsequent treaties were frequently broken by Saracen raids, the resultant unrest leading to more Christians seeking refuge in *Wadi 'Ain as-Siyah* and even leaving there for the greater safety of Cyprus (1235) and Sicily (1238). Finally, in 1239 Pope Gregory IX instigated another short-lived Crusade. The English forces, led by Richard of Cornwall (brother of King Henry III), included William de Vescy, lord of Alnwick in Northumberland; Richard de Grey, Lord Codnor and lord of the manor of Aylesford, Kent; Thomas Aucher, lord of the manor of Lossenham, also in Kent; and other noblemen whose names we do not know as 'they would run to too long a list' (Egan 1992a: 88). These noblemen may have included Ralph Hempnale and Walter Calthorp of Norfolk (*viri nobiles et aurati equites*: 'noblemen and distinguished knights'; Egan 1992b: 19) who were instrumental in founding Bradmer, forerunner to Burnham Norton. After arriving in the Holy Land in 1240 the Crusaders negotiated a peace treaty involving the return of the lands west of the River Jordan to Christian hands. This success enabled Richard of Cornwall to set out for England in 1241 taking his noblemen and some hermits from Carmel with him.[3] Between 1242 and 1247 four new houses were provided for the hermits, each with a founding core of five or six individuals: one in Northumberland, two in Kent and one in Norfolk (Egan 1992a: 87–92; Figure 6.2). Even in their new surroundings, the 'hermits of Mount Carmel' at first tried to emulate life in their homeland. They probably laid out their churches along the lines of that at the Mount Carmel hermitage.

The Hermitage of St Mary at Carmel

The Hermitage of St Mary at Carmel is situated in a narrow valley orientated to the southwest, about a mile from the sea south of Haifa (grid reference: 32 48 06.4N/ 34 58 22.0E). The surviving remains of the hermitage have been excavated (Nitowski 1987a, 1987b, 1989; Nitowski and Qualls 1991), and two phases of construction were discerned there (Figure 6.3). The earlier phase dates from the first half of the thirteenth century, most likely to have been built shortly after Albert of Vercelli's new 'form of life' specified the buildings that were needed if the 'form' were to be pursued satisfactorily. This would have been the layout familiar to the hermits who settled in England in 1242,

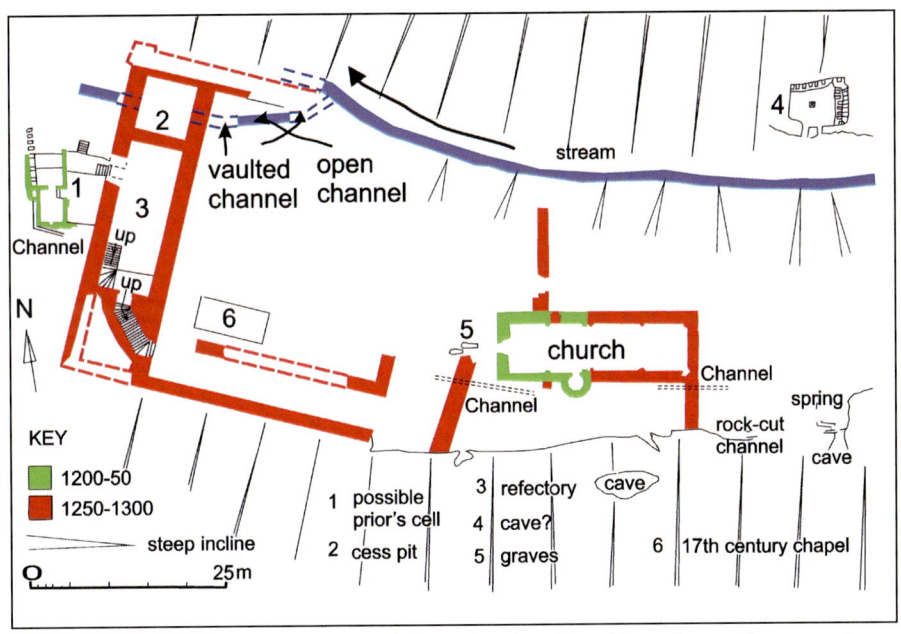

Figure 6.3 The hermitage of St Mary of Carmel with early and late phases of construction outlined in green and red respectively.
Source: based on fig 67, 'Monastery of St Mary of Carmel: plan showing the location of the church' (No 213) in Pringle, D 1998 'St Mary of Carmel' pp 249-57 in *The Churches of the Crusader Kingdom of Jerusalem,* vol 2. Cambridge: CUP.
Reproduced with permission of the The Licensor through PLSClear.

consisting of the prior's cell near the entrance to the precinct, individual cells for the hermits, and a church as the only communal structure.

The remains from the earlier phase at Mount Carmel consisted of the west end of the chapel with a bell-tower in its south wall, a west doorway,

Figure 6.4 Remains of the church of St Mary of Carmel, from the north west.
Source: © biblewalks.com - with permission

and a door in the north wall which was blocked in the later phase. A small structure of three rooms on the far western edge of the hermitage could have been the prior's cell, but Pringle (1998: 255) states that 'the function of the rooms is uncertain'. Its masonry walls were built in the same style as the west end of the chapel, so it was probably put up at the same time. Caves in the cliffs lining the sides of the valley were used for cells, thus obviating need for constructions. Habitable caves are unlikely to have been available in the English foundations, and stone buildings of any sort are equally doubtful. The initial layout of the four English foundations was probably a scatter of small, simple timber buildings providing cells for the hermits, and perhaps a more substantial, but probably still timber, chapel. The buildings were essentially temporary, and they would have been replaced by masonry structures when the means became available. Figure 6.5 depicts a fourteenth-century imagining of the hermits on Mount Carmel.

Figure 6.5 The hermits gathered around the Well of Elijah on Mount Carmel, painted by Pietro Lorenzetti between 1328-29 as part of an altarpiece for the Carmelite Church in Siena, Italy, now at the Pinacoteca in Siena.

By permission of the Ministry of Cultural Heritage and Activities and Tourism, Museum complex of Tuscany. National Picture Gallery of Siena.
"*Su concessione del Ministero dei Beni e delle Attivita culturali e Turismo. Polo museale della Toscana. Pinacoteca Nazionale di Siena.*"

At Mount Carmel the later phase of construction, dating from the second half of the thirteenth century, consisted of an eastern extension to the chapel, keeping the same width and more than doubling its length to 26 x 6.35 m. To its west there were the foundations of a cloister with a two-storey west range perhaps incorporating a first-floor refectory, and with a cesspit tower flushed by a canalised stream at its northern end. This phase of the hermitage conformed much more to a standard West European monastic plan, and it was occupied as such until 1291 when Acre was lost to the Saracen forces and the Seventh Crusade came to an end. According to legend the hermitage was demolished by a savage attack and looting, but excavated ceramic evidence suggests that it was gradually deserted and taken over by *fallahin* (local civilians) who occupied it through the fourteenth and fifteenth centuries (Pringle 1984; 1998: 57). Andrews (2006: 23) suggests that those hermits who survived the 1291 destruction of Mount Carmel moved over to Cyprus, where the Carmelite house in Famia, already founded in the 1230s, continued until 1571.

The first four Carmelite houses in England

These four Carmelite houses were all founded between 1242 and the revision of the Rule in 1247. They therefore started out as hermitages in which the brethren dedicated their whole lives to prayer and contemplation within the confines of their cells. They had little contact with the outside world, belonging to what is known as an 'enclosed Order'. As outlined above, the revision changed all that (Egan 1992a: 108–11).

One of the consequences of the change was that in future Carmelites were to rely on begging (hence 'mendicant') for their income. Their houses could now be built in towns, following the traditional claustral plan which had been developed in the early years of Christianity by St Benedict. The ideal plan was to have the cloister on the south side of the church where it was warmest, but there were exceptions. There were various reasons that the cloister was sometimes situated to the north of the church, probably the commonest being access to a source of water, essential for drinking, washing and draining away effluent. Urban houses may also have needed to plan their precincts according to the space allocated to them.

It seems that the four English pre-revision Carmelite houses continued to consider themselves to be the true Carmelites, situated in rural locations suited to an eremitical way of life and conforming to the 'form of life' devised by St Albert in the early thirteenth century. But at least two of them changed with the times, with both Hulne and Aylesford adopting the post-revision claustral plan as they developed. The absence of physical evidence means that little can be said of the buildings of Lossenham, but documents confirm assemble and hear the friars preaching. Its presence at Hulne suggests that the church was part of a post-revision complex with a formalised plan. The total length of the church was 37 m and the width 6 m, with no distinction in width between nave and quire. Although the south wall stands to almost its full height in places and can be dated by two thirteenth-century windows, one in the quire and one in the nave (Figure 6.7 and 6.8) the north walls of both quire and nave survive only as foundations. The east wall was largely reconstructed in the eighteenth century (St John Hope 1890: 113; Pevsner 1970: 196).

Figure 6.7 (left) Hulne Friary, the thirteenth-century window in the nave:
Figure 6.8 (right) window in the quire.
Source: based on St John Hope (1890, between pp 114 and 115), with kind permission of the Royal Archaeological Institute..

The vestry, chapter house and reredorter in the east range of the cloister have thirteenth-century windows, suggesting that at least that part of the cloister was constructed at the same time as, or shortly after, the church. Discussing Aylesford, Rigold suggested that the first community of friars there would have needed no more than an east range for their accommodation and activities, and it might have been the same at Hulne (1965: 11).

The south and west ranges of the cloister exist only as undatable foundations and fragmentary standing walls such as the north wall of the refectory ('frater' on Figure 6.6) which St John Hope concluded was an 'Elizabethan' rebuild, that is, part of the post-Dissolution secular occupation (1890: 119–21). Many other buildings date from the late fifteenth century onwards, but there is evidence of early work in the infirmary hall and its adjoining chapel. They had been converted into a single family house by the time St John Hope was writing, but fortunately some lancet windows in both the hall and chapel are still preserved and indicate a thirteenth-century date for their construction (St John Hope 1890: 124). Thus, it seems likely that the earliest Carmelite friary in England was not as it appears in Figure 6.6 but consisted only of a long rectangular church, part of an east range, and an infirmary well away to the south (to avoid the spread of infection?). It is also likely that even this fragment of a claustral layout was built after the 1247 revision.

Aylesford, Kent

Aylesford Friary was founded in 1242 on land granted by the lord of the manor, Richard de Grey, 2nd Baron Codnor, a crusader who travelled back from the Holy Land with the hermits in 1241–2 (Egan, 1992b: 2, 4–11). All the refugees may have been accommodated on de Grey's land in Kent until a group set out for Hulne under the protection of de Vescy, and then those who intended to found their own hermitage in Aylesford remained 'technically as de Grey's guests' until the beginning of 1247, when the bishop of Rochester gave them permission to build a dwelling and a church, both on de Grey's land (Rigold, 1965: 3). Before that they must have worshipped in Aylesford parish church and lived in temporary accommodation on de Grey's estate.

Figure 6.9 The fourteenth-century bridge over the River Medway at Aylesford. Source: © Stephen Craven from geograph.org.uk - 1741212.jpg

In January 1247 the same bishop encouraged members of his flock to contribute to the building of a church for the Carmelites by granting an indulgence to those who did so, and there were more donations from Richard de Grey. It is rather surprising that the house was in any fit state to host the General Chapter in early September 1247, but it did do, even before the church was completed. The Chapter may have opened with a celebratory

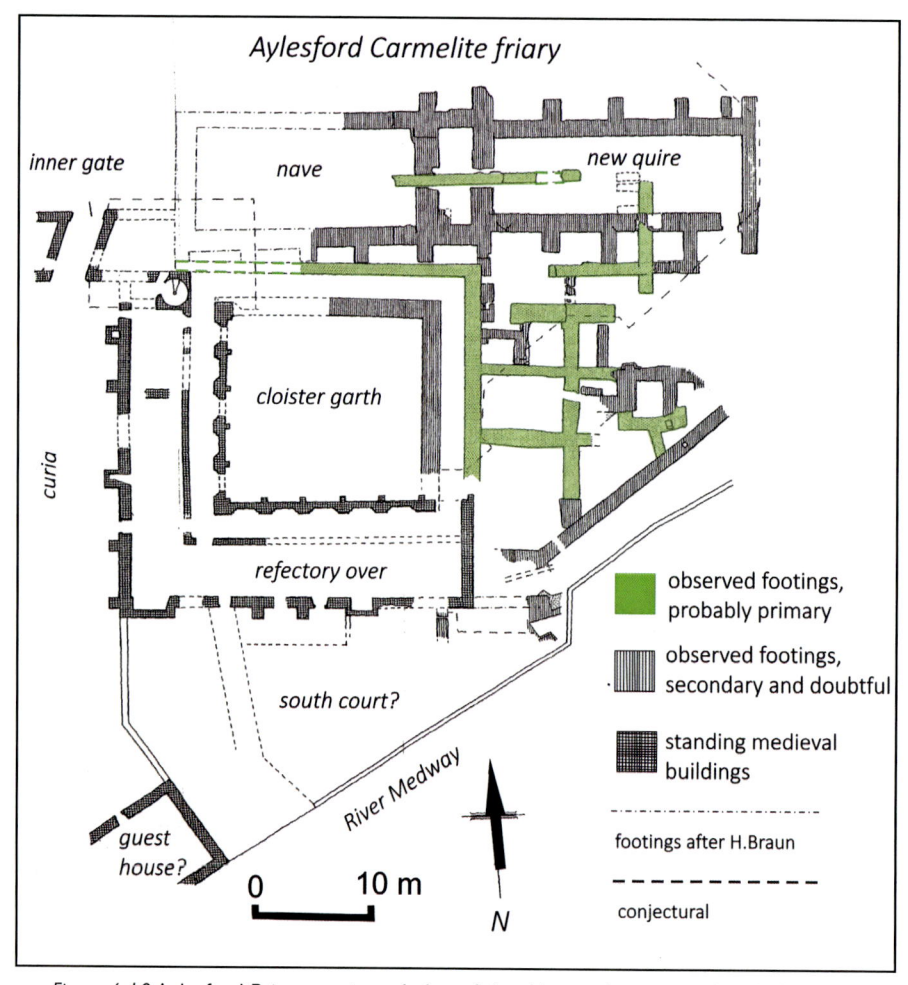

Figure 6.10 Aylesford Priory, projected plan of the thirteenth-century church (outlined in green) based on 'observed footings, probably primary' (after Rigold 1965, fig. 1). Reproduced by kind permission of Kent Archaeological Society.

meal, as Henry III gave 2 marks (£1.6.8d) 'for their pittance [provisions] on the day when they are to celebrate their chapter' (*CLR 1245–51*: 163). That General Chapter was highly significant as it was then that the 'form of life' of 1212 was superseded by the revision of the Rule, changing the eremitical community envisioned by St Albert into the Mendicant Order of Carmelites and heralding the beginning of urban friaries.

The church and cloister were on the right bank of the River Medway, near an early river crossing on the road from London still marked by a medieval bridge (Figure 6.9). Aylesford Priory (as it is now called) has the unique distinction of still being a house of Carmelite friars, the head house of the Carmelite Order in Britain and a centre of pilgrimage. However it did not

Figure 6.11 Aylesford Priory, the modern church with the medieval quire replaced by the shrine of St Simon Stock (centre back) and the fourteenth-century nave an open space for open-air services. Photo: © H. Clarke.

have a continuous history as a friary, for the medieval house was dissolved in 1538 and after that it passed through many hands, until 1949 when it was acquired by the Carmelites and became a friary once again.

Some of the medieval buildings survived the centuries of secular occupation and were modified to serve modern needs even before the Carmelites returned. The footings of the claustral layout were recovered when the friary was being made habitable in the 1950s, and the plan was drawn out and published by Rigold in 1965 (Figure 6.10). There have been a few minor archaeological interventions in recent years, mainly watching briefs (for example, one that confirmed the existence of the medieval moat around part of the precinct (Nenk et al. 1995: 223), but otherwise nothing has been found that has added much to publications by Braun in 1950 and Rigold in 1965.

Since 1949 there has been much building work on the site of the medieval church, with an open-air 'nave' laid out over the medieval nave and a shrine to St Simon Stock erected in what would have been the quire (Figure 6.11). Although nothing remains of the medieval church, footings uncovered in 1959 enabled Rigold (1965: 8–10) to work out the plan of two superimposed churches (Figure 6.10 earlier buildings in green). The earlier church (built 1247) was a simple rectilinear structure, *c.* 7 m wide and up to 30 m long. It conformed to the design and the dimensions of thirteenth-century Carmelite church plans such as that of the mother house on Mount Carmel (23.35 m x 6.35 m by the mid-thirteenth century; see Figure 6.3), and the much longer church at Aylesford's contemporary, Hulne (37 m x 6 m; see Figure 6.6).

Footings of what seems to have been the east range of a cloister indicate that it was built at the same time as the first church. Rigold suggests that an east range would have been sufficient to accommodate all the needs of the first community of friars, containing 'dormitory and reredorter upstairs and nothing very important in the undercroft [ground floor]' (1965: 11). The church and east range at Aylesford show similarities to those at Hulne, and their building history must be comparable. We can be confident that Aylesford was not started until 1247 and pretty certain that Hulne would have got under way at much the same time. Hulne's cloister was completed on conventional lines, although its church was never changed.

Figure 6.12 Aylesford Priory, the outer court or 'curia', showing part of the stone-built guest house (right) and much restored western range. Photo: © H. Clarke.

Figure 6.13 Aylesford Priory, the outer gatehouse dating from the fifteenth century. Photo: H. © Clarke.

Aylesford's cloister was probably fully built by the early fourteenth century, when it needed to accommodate the 20 friars who lived there in 1326 (VCH Kent II: 202). By 1348 building had started on a replacement which had the conventional plan of a fourteenth-century church, with the nave slightly wider than the quire, from which it was separated by a 'walking place' with a tower and steeple above. Although construction seems to have started in a rush, the church was not completed until 1417.

The south and west ranges of the cloister were probably built in the fourteenth century, concurrently with the church. They defined an 18.2m square cloister garth (garden). Modernization in the eighteenth and nineteenth centuries and a fire which gutted the interiors in the 1930s have left few original features, but further evidence for the medieval friary can been seen in the outer courtyard (or 'curia'), the south range of which still contains the guest house against the river Medway and access to the quay (Figure 6.12). Visitors would have arrived by boat, as would the ragstone used in the buildings and most of the commodities needed for the day-to-day running of the house. The precinct boundary consisted of a moat (now filled in) flanked by a late fifteenth-century outer gatehouse (Figure 6.13).

Lossenham (or Losenham), Kent

Unfortunately Lossenham cannot help in tracing the development of early Carmelite buildings. Not even its location is known in detail, although it is accepted that it stood in the parish of Newenden, on the left bank of the River Rother (Figure 6.14).

The only physical clues are intriguing rather than helpful. Some walls were visible at the end of the eighteenth century (Hasted, 1798, 168–9) and footings were discovered when field drains were being laid in the 1840s (Hussey, 1852: 108), but neither observation was accurately recorded. The approximate location of the friary site is assumed to be in agricultural land to the east of the group of buildings known today as Lossenham Manor, Lossenham Priory Farm and Lossenham Farm. Hasted states that the medieval manor house was 'almost adjoining the friary', (1798: 168) and building rubble and masonry fragments can still be found in the fields and surrounding ditches; for example, a fragment of small column base of Caen stone was recently discovered lying loose under a hedge (Figure 6.15).

Otherwise, documents are the only source for its history. We know that it was founded between 1242 and 1247 by Sir Thomas Aucher, lord of the manor of Lossenham (Egan 1992b: 2, 51), and that it must have grown quickly, as in 1263 there were ten friars, each of whom received 4d from Henry III's gift of 3s 4d (*CLR* 1267–72: p. 122, no. 1063). Building was also getting under way,

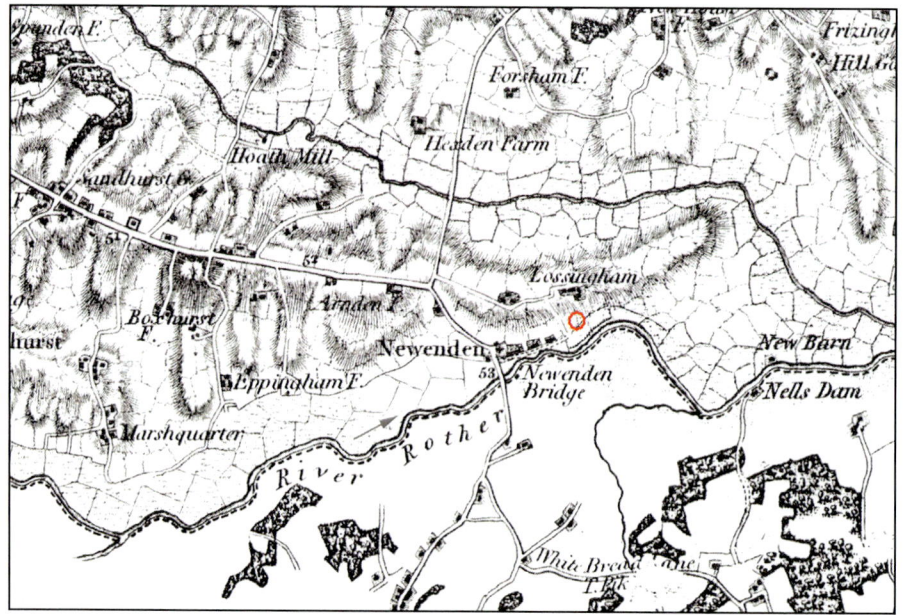

Figure 6.14 Lossenham Friary, map of the area in 1801. Mudge's map, The County of Kent in 1801, original scale 1 inch to 1 mile.
Reproduced by kind permission of Kent Archive and Local History Service.

Figure 6.15 Lossenham Friary, fragment of the base of a small column of Caen stone, probably from a window, found in a ditch in the presumed area of the precinct.
Photo: © G. Clarke.

for in 1271 the friars received six oaks from the royal forest (*CCR* 1268–72: p. 361) and another five were given in 1272 (*CCR* 1268–72: p. 455). Such rapid expansion seems not to have been popular with some local parish clergy, for in 1276 (*CIM* p. 318, no. 1039) James, rector of Warehorne (a village about 16 km to the north-east) was found guilty of encouraging his servant William to burn down the entire friary, which he had done in the previous year (*CPR* 1272–81, p. 173). The damage was estimated at £80, a large enough sum to suggest that a considerable amount of building had been completed by then. Comparison with Aylesford and Hulne would suggest that no more than a simple rectangular church and the east range of a cloister was at its core.

There are no records of the rebuilding over the next decades or of the finances needed for it, but from 1368 onwards a few wills survive, recording bequests of small sums for masses to be said for the souls of the testators, or sometimes just to the house in general. Presumably most of the cost of rebuilding was borne by the Aucher family, descendants of the founder, whose residence stood next to the friary throughout the Middle Ages.

The high point of Lossenham's history must have come in 1517 when the Provincial (not General) Chapter was held there. There were then 39 friaries in the English province, each of which would have sent its prior and his attendants. Probably more than a hundred delegates and their entourages needed accommodation, and it is difficult to imagine how such an apparently insignificant house provided it, even if most attendees brought their own tents. Indeed, even though hosting the Provincial Chapter was a great honour, it must have been the beginning of the end for this sad little Whitefriars. The poverty of the place two decades later is underlined in a letter that Richard Ingworth, bishop of Dover, wrote to Thomas Cromwell in late July 1538 when Ingworth visited the friary to close it down. The letter runs:

> went from thence to Losenham .... There be honest men. The stuff [i.e. the friary's possessions] is priced at £6 10s with [including] the bell and chalice. The house is poor in building and no lead, but tile, and much of it ready to fall. It is to be let, with the orchard, garden and land, at 5 marks [£3.33p] a year (*L&P* no. 1456).

Unusually, the full inventory of 'stuff' on which Ingworth based his letter has survived (Robertson, 1882: see Appendix), and from it we can see that the buildings and their fittings were of little worth, even though the church with its 'stepull' and bell and the 'Hall' bedecked with 'hangyngs' may have displayed a little style. The list includes both objects which had been used in church services and domestic utensils, the paucity of which really brings home the poverty-stricken conditions in which the friars lived. It could be, however, that the poverty reflected in the inventory was illusory. The brethren had had plenty of notice of their impending fate, and could have disposed of whatever there was of value before the Commission arrived for the coup de grace. Ingworth himself complained about 'priors who sell the convent's goods' (*L&P* no. 1457), and that might be what had happened in Lossenham. It is unlikely that the friary was ever a place of great wealth, certainly not as flourishing as many of the Carmelite friaries in towns.

That is not to say that Lossenham had no dealings with the outside world. Although isolated to modern eyes, its site was not inaccessible, and by the end of its existence Lossenham was not the remote place that it presumably was at the time of its foundation. Its precinct extended to the river Rother (Figure

Figure 6.16 Lossenham Friary, with the River Rother as precinct boundary. Photo: © G. Clarke.

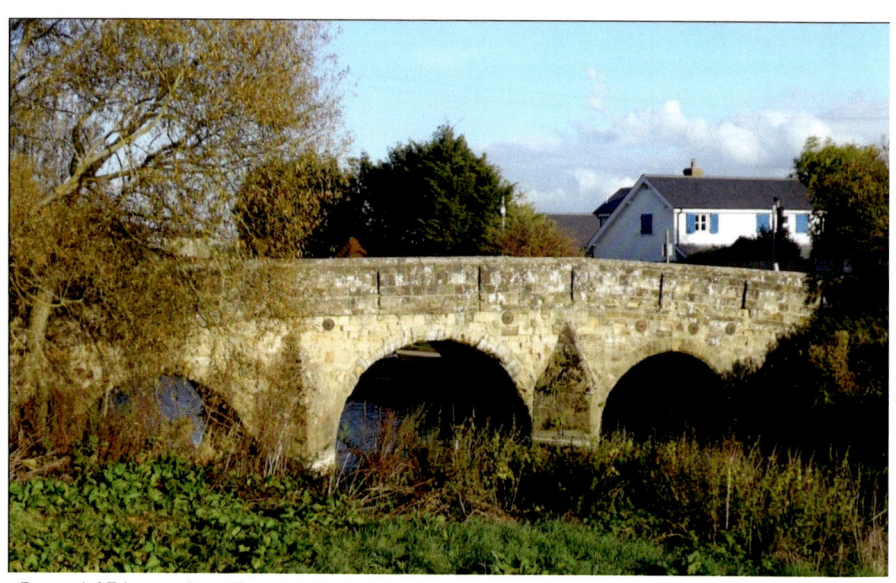

Figure 6.17 Lossenham Friary, the bridge crossing the River Rother on Rye to London road. This bridge was built in 1706 to replace the 1507 structure. Photo: © G. Clarke.

6.16), which throughout much of the Middle Ages was navigable downstream to the English Channel and upstream as far as Robertsbridge. The river bank was studded with villages and small towns, and at Newenden itself a wooden bridge was built across the river in 1507 to replace a ford and facilitate the overland transport of fish between Rye and London (Figure 6.17). Lossenham, then, was near an important crossing of land and water routes which could have contributed towards its livelihood through the years. Although a quiet spot today, Lossenham could be viewed as an ideal centre from which the Carmelites could have travelled to neighbouring villages and small towns to preach and to beg and to keep the friary solvent.

Burnham Norton, Norfolk

Finally, we turn to the fourth of our early Carmelite houses. Some time between 1242 and 1247 it was founded, reputedly at a place called *Bradmer* in Norfolk. Its site is not known, although it is likely to have been on the north Norfolk coast, perhaps just west of present-day Burnham Norton village, near where a 'Bradmere House' stands today.[4] The only evidence for the existence of Bradmer is in an early sixteenth-century history of the Carmelite Order compiled by the friar John Bale (1495–1563), who cites as his authority a lost register of Burnham Norton. There is some doubt about the reliability of Bale's account, especially as he writes that Bradmer was inhabited from 1223, an unacceptably early date according to Egan (1992b: 18). Nevertheless, he appears to accept Bradmer as the fourth house, with some reservations, and that the founders were Ralph Hempnale and Walter Calthorp.

John Bale is also the only source for the move from Bradmer to Burnham Norton in 1253. Again, Egan has reservations (1992b: 19) but is prepared to accept Bale's date because the next reference to Burnham Norton is not until 1298, when the friary had clearly been in existence for some time. This is suggested by a document which records that a Walter de Calthorp granted land ('a rood of meadow') to the friary (*CPR 1292–1301*: p. 354). If 1253 is correct, then Burnham Norton was not founded until six years after the revision, later than the Carmelite houses in London and Cambridge, both established in 1247. The Carmelites were present in York some time before 1253. Thus, we have the strange situation of Bradmer being the fourth house to be founded after the arrival of the Carmelites in England, and Burnham Norton being the fourth foundation after the revision, which shifted the focus of the Order to urban sites.

The Norfolk friary seems to be an exception to the post-revision foundations in towns, but there may be an explanation for this apparent anomaly. If it was, as John Bale claims, a refoundation of Bradmer, the donors of the land on which the new house was sited might have also been Bradmer's founders Ralph Hempnale and Walter Calthorp (Egan, 1992b: 19). They were noblemen with local connections and perhaps with land in the rural county rather than the towns of Lynn or Norwich. Bale also claims (Egan 1992b: 67) that friars from Burnham were sent to Norwich in 1256 (see Chapter 7) to be the first brethren in a new friary there.

Figure 6.18 Burnham Norton friary gatehouse and west front of the church.
Photo: © G. Clarke.

Conclusions

Looking at these four hermitages as a group has revealed some interesting similarities which may not have been pointed out before, and which are summarized here.

Three of the four early houses were situated beside a river, where a bridge or ford carried a main road. A road from London to Maidstone and the Weald passed through Aylesford. Lossenham was on the route of the road from London to Rye. Burnham Norton stood on the south side of Brancaster Old Road and the crossing of the river Burn, a pilgrim route to Walsingham. Hulne is the odd one out. Although its precinct was bordered by the River Aln on its south side there is no evidence for a crossing there: not surprising, perhaps, as it flowed through the de Vescy's private park in which the friary stood. And also, the bridge in Alnwick itself was near enough to serve the friary as well as the town. All three had supposedly been founded as hermitages in isolated sites, but all of them had access to good communications by road and river. As hermits, the friars may not have taken advantage of them, but as mendicants they could have travelled far and wide to fulfil their vocation.

There are no traces of the initial phase of any of the hermitages. As usual when founding a rural religious house, the first building on the site would have been made of the most accessible, but perishable, materials, generally timber. The only traces we might expect to find are through archaeological excavation, and they might have been obliterated by later masonry structures. Additional difficulties in the hunt for the initial phase are that the hermitages were occupied for only five years (1242-7), there seems to have been no accepted layout so it is unlikely that cohesive patterns could be found in scatters of post holes, and the hermits would have had very few possessions to leave behind for modern archaeologists to find. It would be extremely lucky to find anything at all.

Hulne and Aylesford show that the earliest remains found on their sites were built of stone, and followed a plan that was not adopted by the Carmelites until after the revision of 1247. Thus, they cannot have been built until 1247 or later. Comparison of these early buildings shows striking similarities. Each had a rectilinear church with a single range running from the south side of its quire. This appears to be the east range of a cloister which had not yet been built in its entirety. There is documentary evidence for the church at Aylesford, which was begun in early 1247, the year of the revision, and perhaps the General Chapter met there when adopting this revolutionary change. It could be argued, then, that Aylesford's church and east range made up the first building project to adopt the new claustral arrangement — architectural features that Hulne followed soon after in the thirteenth century. An examination of the other two rural houses will show if their plans can be interpreted in the same way.

Now there is nothing to be seen of Lossenham, but it is known that it was built before 1276, when it was destroyed by fire. The colossal amount of £80 had been spent on its construction so it must have been virtually complete by that date (church, cloister, some outbuildings perhaps). It would probably have looked like a small version of Hulne and Aylesford but possibly with only the church in stone. When it was rebuilt it would have followed the same pattern, with the cloister being completed as and when finances allowed. There may have been some agricultural buildings outside, near to the precinct, and perhaps a boathouse on the bank of the Rother. Many of the buildings may still have been of timber, but the fragment of a small Caen stone column (probably from a window) suggests that some of the more important structures were of masonry. The site of Lossenham is a greenfield site, very tempting for an archaeologist. The ground may preserve the ephemeral traces of an early hermitage phase which could be discovered through today's archaeological techniques, one of which (a geophysical survey) was carried out at Burnham Norton during the Imagined Land project.

Burnham Norton differs from the other three in that it was founded as a replacement for Bradmer in 1253. Bradmer will have the same difficulties of discovery as the hermitage phase of Aylesford and Hulne, but its successor Burnham Norton presents no such problem. There are still some masonry structures and visible earthworks, and the geophysical survey revealed many features which still lie below ground and await interpretation.

Notes

1 *Wadi 'Ain as-Siyah* is the Arabic name for the valley in which the Hermitage was situated and is described as such in Pringle. The modern Israeli name for the valley is *Nahal Siach* and is now an outdoor adventure trail. According to Pringle Elijah's spring is about 200 m away from the site and the spring from the hermits drew water is now sometimes called Elisha's spring.

2 As the revision mitigated the eremitical rule (making it easier to live by) it often became known as just as 'the mitigation'.

3 The most trustworthy source for the transfer to England is a comment by Thomas of Eccleston, a Franciscan friar writing 1258–9, who states that 'it was Richard de Grey of Codnor who brought the Carmelites to England when Richard of Cornwall returned from his Crusade to the Holy Land (January 1242)' (Egan 1992a: 87).

4 For further discussion of the possible site of the location of Bradmer see Chapter 3.

Appendix: Inventory of Lossenham: objects used in church (Robertson 1882)

Item	Value
one white vestment	5s
one blue vestment	6s 8d
a vestment and chasuble	3s 4d
two chasubles	12d
chalice (weight 14oz)	49s
three old corporasses	8d
one other altar cushion	8d
processional cross	3s 4d
four candlesticks	6s 8d
one little [sanctuary]bell	20d
two latten [pewter] basins and one ewer	12d
two candlesticks and a sockett	8d
two chests	2s
bell in steeple	10s
one old cope	6s 8d
an old stained canopy and altar cloth with stained frontlet	2s
one holy water stoop	8d
book of Catholycon	4d

Domestic equipment:

old hangings and rags	8d
five old sheets	2s 8d
two old nowty pans, small	12d
one brass pot, small	20d
one broken frying pan	4d
thirteen platters and four dishes	6s 8d
one spit	8d
one old brewing pan	2s 6d
one old coverlet	12d
two iron candlesticks	6d
two ladders	6d
hangyngs in Hall [Refectory?]	4d
one iron ?	2d
two old feather beds with bolster	6s 8d
various old clothes	12d
one cupboard	12d
one old chair	1d

Few of these former Carmelite friary sites have been the subject of detailed archaeological excavation. The most comprehensive investigations to date were undertaken in Norwich during 2000-3, within the area occupied until recently by Jarrold's printing works (Figure 7.1). The archaeological investigations, principally by NPS Archaeology (formerly the Norfolk Archaeological Unit) uncovered an unexpected level of below-ground survival, which has enabled new interpretations of the friary plan to be developed. Furthermore, the many artefacts recovered have allowed some reconstruction of the buildings in terms of their fabric and appearance, while providing crucial evidence for daily life in the friary. The discovery of numerous burials has also provided a tangible link to both the Carmelites who once lived in the friary and the laity who chose to be buried there.

Following the completion of the fieldwork, a post-excavation assessment report was produced in 2004 outlining the methodology to be used for analysis and the eventual publication of the results (Shelley 2004). Oxford Archaeology East was subsequently commissioned to undertake these latter stages of work. Many of the subsequent interpretations of the friary remains (including the symbolic location of the fourteenth-century church) are based on those first developed by Andy Shelley. His major contribution to this project, along with that of his team, cannot be overstated.

This chapter provides a summary of the results of the investigations at Norwich Whitefriars, focusing on the evidence related to the medieval friary. The aim is to provide some additional (urban) context for the programme of investigation planned at the sister house at Burnham Norton. Underpinning the analysis is the documentary research undertaken by Elizabeth Rutledge, the results of which are included below in brief. A monograph detailing the full archaeological sequence uncovered at Jarrold's Whitefriars, which includes the post-Dissolution use of the site and the ultimate encroachment by industrial development during the nineteenth and twentieth centuries, is due to be published imminently (Clarke forthcoming).

An overview of Norfolk's other Carmelite friaries[2]

Burnham Norton's friary was clearly an early Carmelite foundation, when the eremitical influence was still prevalent and more rural locations were preferred. Relatively little is known about the first site at Bradmer, where the house was seemingly established between 1245 and 1247 (more likely the latter date). The friary was relocated to its current site in 1253, and occupied an area of 2.3 hectares (5.68 acres) to the south of the village (O'Sullivan 2013: 74). Upstanding remains include a fine fourteenth-century gatehouse, parts of the precinct wall and the west wall of the friary church, along with numerous earthworks. Details of the Burnham Norton Friary are, of course, covered by other chapters in this volume.

In contrast, very little of the Carmelite friary in South Lynn to the south of King's Lynn (known as Bishop's Lynn until the Reformation) survives above ground. The friary, also known as Whitefriars, occupied an area estimated to have been 3.25 hectares (8 acres) within the town defences, adjacent to the road leading to the south gate and close to the quay on the River Ouse (O'Sullivan 2013: 186). The primary remains comprise the friary's north gateway, a fairly small brick structure with ashlar dressings that is thought to date from the fifteenth century.[3] The interior elevation is relatively plain, while the exterior face is more decorative, with ashlar string courses and a set of three statue niches, although no statues remain. The gateway is now freestanding as the precinct wall has been demolished on either side.

No documented investigations have been undertaken at the site, although adjacent archaeological trial trenching in 2009 uncovered evidence relating to a bridge leading to the gate, along with the western continuation of the precinct wall. Human skeletal remains were found during the 1980s and 1990s to the east of the gateway in Whitefriars Terrace. Their discovery indicates that the friary cemetery was located in the northern part of the precinct. Although the site of the church is not known, it seems that the tower might have remained in use as a dovecote until its collapse in the early seventeenth century (NHER 5481). Historical sources indicate that the initial building programme was under way in the 1270s and 1280s, with the altar dedicated in 1276. The church was struck by lightning in 1363, soon after which the Whitefriars entered into a series of agreements (known as corrodies), presumably to provide additional means of funding the rebuilding work. The nine corrodies were between lay people (mostly the more affluent townsfolk) and the convent, and related to the provision of accommodation within the friary, even including purpose-built apartments. Over the friary's lifetime, the number of friars present fluctuated between 26 (in 1300) and a maximum of 42, the latter recorded in 1326. However, this total had fallen to 11 – including the prior – by the time the house was dissolved on 30th September 1538 (O'Sullivan 2013: 186–7).

Yarmouth's Carmelite friary was located on the north side of the town between the market place and the North Quay. The precinct appears to have covered an area of c. 3.21 hectares (7.93 acres), although the exact boundaries are not known. The only upstanding structure that might be attributable to the friary is a section of wall incorporated into the rear wing of a later building. It contains the remains of two brick arches of probable early sixteenth-century date, the location of which may indicate that the main friary buildings were located within the southern part of the precinct. The site is now built over, although human skeletons probably from the friary cemetery were unearthed during the nineteenth century, and more recently buried wall foundations were revealed during demolition and construction works at the site during the 1960s and 1980s (O'Sullivan 2013: 351; NHER 4306). Few documents survive for this friary, a probable royal foundation; it suffered a disastrous fire in 1509 and was dissolved by December 1538.

The foundation date of the friary at Blakeney (sometimes known as Snitterley) is open to some interpretation, and is discussed elsewhere (O'Sullivan 2013: 49–50). As with Yarmouth, few documents survive to elucidate its history, including its suppression. The precinct was located to the east of the small medieval port town of Blakeney, and occupied an area of 13.5 acres (5.46 hectares). Surviving remains include two pointed arches within the north-east corner of Friary Farmhouse and a medieval flint wall with a later gateway located to the north of the farmhouse (O'Sullivan 2013: 49–50; NHER 6158).

Based on current evidence it is clear that despite their different settings, relatively little is known about the plan or development of these friary complexes, making the investigations at Norwich all the more significant.

Norwich Whitefriars

The Carmelite friary at Norwich was established on typically marginal, flood-prone land on the north bank of the River Wensum, adjacent to Whitefriars Bridge in the north-eastern part of the city (Figure 7.1). Here, ancient river gravels (First Terrace) are overlain by deposits of peat and alluvium, above which are extensive make-up deposits which were probably imported from at least the twelfth century onwards. Ecclesiastical construction during the thirteenth century necessitated ground-raising on a massive scale in these riverside areas. At Whitefriars, make-up deposits up to 4 m thick were recorded close to the River Wensum.

Norwich was one of the foremost towns in Norman England. It acquired a royal castle (c. 1067), a new market with associated church (St Peter Mancroft) and a cathedral by the end of the eleventh century, all south of the river. Although there appears to have been little development to the north of the river immediately after the Conquest, there was considerable expansion of settlement during the following centuries. This notably included the north-eastern part of the city, and was seemingly associated with the bishop of Norwich. Both St Paul's Hospital and Church (Cox 1906: 447–8) and St James's Church were founded by the bishop in the twelfth century on land cut out of his manor of Thorpe. This area was accessed by a bridge over the River Wensum (St Martin's, later Whitefriars) which was in existence by at least c. 1106 (Ayers and Murphy 1983: 57).

The area that became the precinct of the Norwich Carmelite friars lay within a part of the city that was colonised by industries such as tanning and dyeing, although it also attracted some middle-status residences. Both the street frontages were developed here, with at least five messuages (dwelling houses) along Cowgate between the church of St James and the river, and another five to the north between the church and the city wall, along what is now Barrack Street (Rutledge forthcoming). One of the Cowgate messuages was the initial plot granted by Philip of Cowgate to the Carmelites. By the end of the fourteenth century the friary precinct extended from the river up to Barrack Street (excluding St James's Church) and from Whitefriars (formerly Cowgate) east to the city wall, encompassing an area of 2.2 hectares (Figures 7.2 and 7.3 overleaf). This area is somewhat smaller than the other Norfolk Carmelite precincts, perhaps reflecting the fact that available land was at more of a premium in Norwich than elsewhere in the county.

Investigations at Norwich Whitefriars

Archaeological investigations were undertaken as part of the mitigation works necessary in advance of the redevelopment of part of Jarrold's print works, since demolished. In 2003 an excavation area (700 m2) within the footprint of a proposed new office block (Figure 7.2), alongside various associated works, revealed wall foundations, drains, tiled floors and burials related to the friary. Numerous finds were also recovered, ranging from small personal items such as (belt) strap ends and a needle case to large fragments of architectural stone related to the fabric of the friary buildings. Most of the Whitefriars' site had been built over during the late post-medieval and modern periods, causing some significant but often localised damage to the below-ground remains. However, two significant elements of the friary survived as standing elements within this part of the precinct: the 'Anchorite's arch' and a medieval undercroft. The arch stands in the southern part of the site, close to the river, while the undercroft (fourteenth-century with a fifteenth-century vault) is located close to the road, and was excavated and recorded in 1978 prior to its use as a print museum (NHER site 36).

Although there had been a small number of investigations within the precinct (supplemented by chance finds during various building works), these had generally been limited in size and located in more peripheral areas. Consequently, much of the presumed layout of the friary was based on the interpretation of cartographic and historical evidence applied to traditional models of monastic development. These interpretations have since been augmented and to some extent challenged by the results of the programme of desk-based assessment, historic building recording, watching brief, evaluation, excavation and the subsequent analysis.

BURNHAM NORTON FRIARY

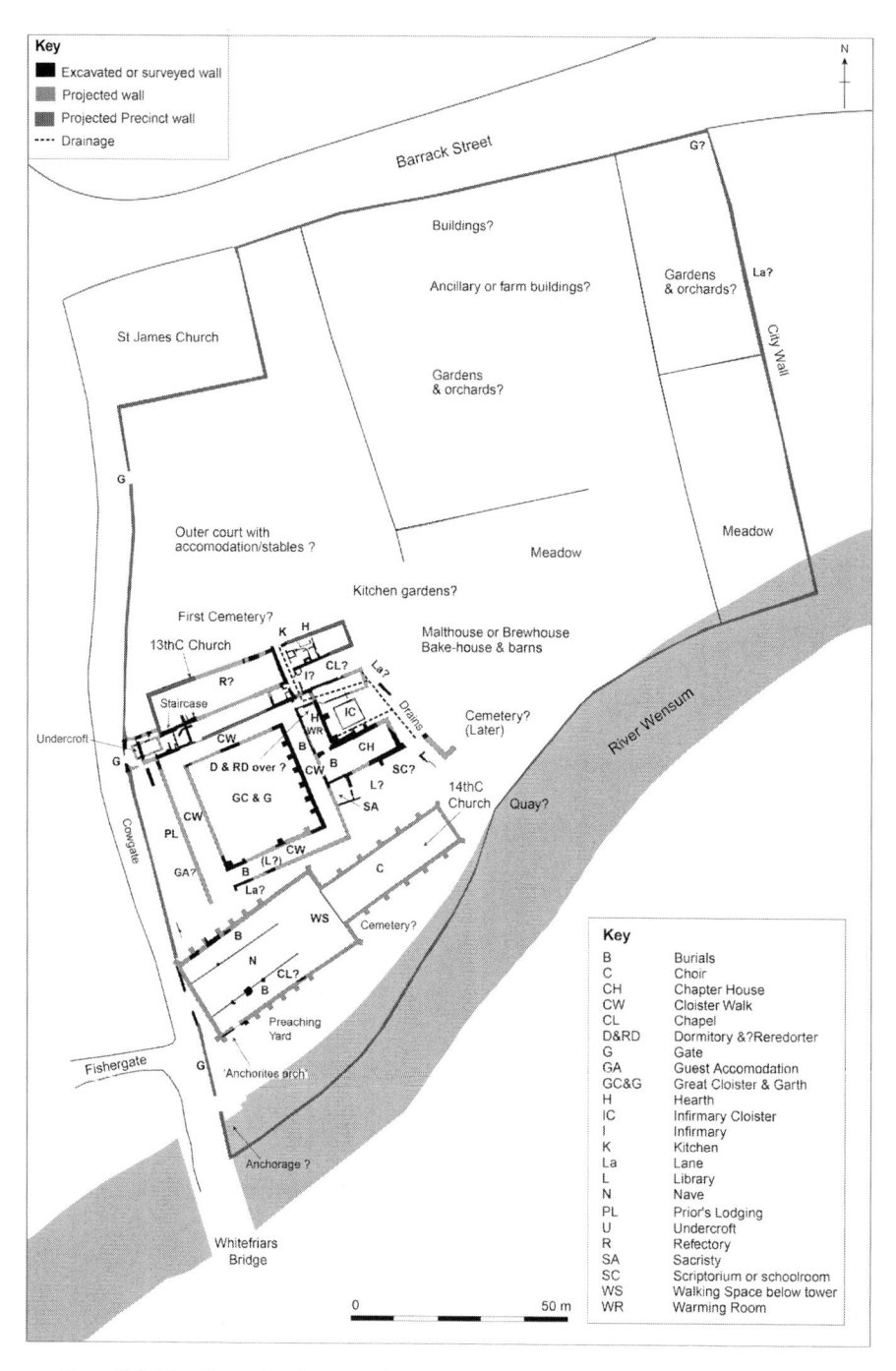

Figure 7.2 The Carmelite friary and its precinct, based on documentary research and excavated evidence. © OA East.

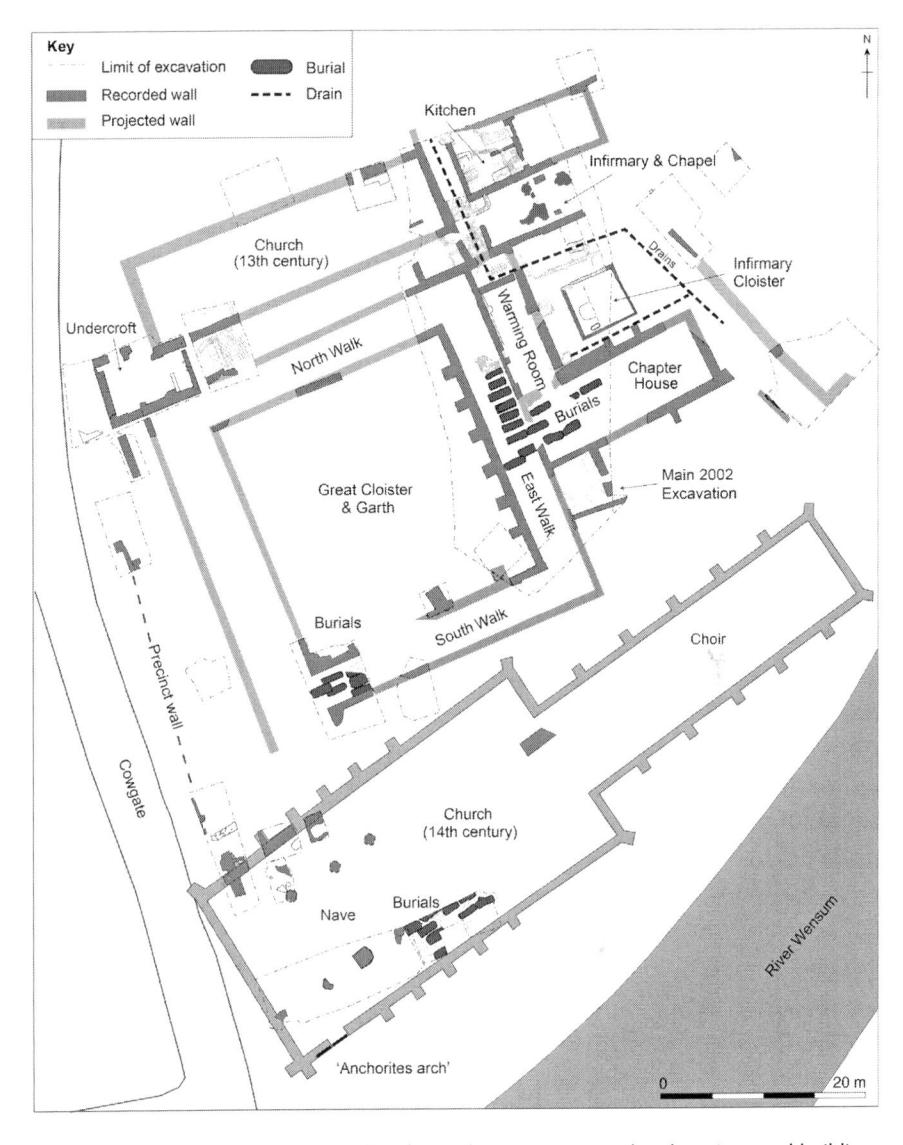

Figure 7.3 Detail plan of Norwich Whitefriars showing excavated and conjectured building remains with interpretations. © OA East

The first church (middle to late thirteenth century)

Although the excavations provided the most extensive evidence yet for the layout of the friary, very little of this can confidently be assigned to the earliest period of establishment and occupation. It is probable that the friars initially occupied and extended the existing buildings along the Cowgate frontage, many of which would originally have been of timber construction.

However, it would have been paramount to begin building the church as soon as possible, and this would have been of far more substantial construction. During excavations within the undercroft in 1978, a large masonry wall foundation, believed to have been related to the first church, was found (Atkin and Evans 2002: 194-7). Further evidence of this wall, which incorporated angle buttresses and chamfered oolitic limestone plinths and a doorway, was revealed extending to the east during the more recent excavations (Figure 7.3). Other masonry foundations were also exposed which appear to have formed the eastern end and parts of the northern and western walls, although no clearly contemporary internal features were identified.

This early church was aligned north-east to south-west within the central and broadest part of the initial plot granted to the Carmelites. It appears to have been of basic rectangular plan, and measured approximately 32m (104ft) north-east to south-west, and 9m (28ft) north to south externally. It is likely that the associated burial ground lay to the north, although no definitive evidence of this has so far come to light. Two (unexcavated) graves apparently containing disarticulated human remains were identified in a yard area that was later occupied by the infirmary cloister, and these may represent disturbed burials from an early cemetery.

Friary expansion (*c.* 1322 to 1382)

A major building campaign commenced from 1322 as the Carmelites gradually acquired adjacent plots of land to the east and north-east of their initial holding. This enabled them to expand their precinct and begin construction of the cloister, new friary church and other key buildings. In 1326 there were 50 friars documented at Whitefriars, showing that it was thriving community, although this number would have fluctuated. The building campaign also necessitated the closure of two lanes, one of which led down to the river, and the realignment of Cowgate (Whitefriars) further west. The sequence of land acquisition and associated bequests is documented elsewhere (Rutledge forthcoming, Copsey 2006), but essentially culminated in the new choir being completed in 1344, followed by consecration of the churchyard in the following year. However, the church (nave) was not fully completed and dedicated until many years later in 1382. This delay may in part have been a consequence of the Black Death in 1348/9, which had an enormous impact on Norwich, with many citizens succumbing to the plague. Despite (or in reaction to) this setback, further bequests to the friary followed in 1351 and enabled a new stone gate and dormitory to be built.

Prior to the investigations at Whitefriars, existing interpretations of the friary layout (Campbell 1975: map 6; Woodfield 2005: fig. 4; Penn 2001; Hutcheson 2000: fig. 1 and others) generally placed the church to the north of the cloister and to the south of St James's parish church. This would be in keeping with the position of the first, thirteenth-century church, but not with the larger church built in the subsequent century. The plan of the precinct (Figures 7.2 and 7.3) revealed by the investigations shows the new church positioned at a slightly awkward angle to the south of the cloister, close to the bend in the river.

The fourteenth-century church and 'Anchorite's arch'

The early to mid-fourteenth century 'witnessed a great phase of rebuilding of the mendicant churches, which transformed the landscape of late medieval Norwich' (Harper-Bill and Rawcliffe 2004: 105). Against this backdrop, it would have been imperative for the Carmelites to compete with the other mendicant orders who had also established their houses within the city walls. To this end the Whitefriars set about constructing an impressive new choir with a nave that was large enough to accommodate the laity both for preaching and for burial, at least for those who could afford the latter. This impetus would also explain the positioning of the church to the south of the cloister. Such a location not only provided the widest building plot, but also included space for a preaching yard with easy access from Cowgate. Furthermore, this positioning of the church with its central tower would have ensured maximum visual impact for those coming from the city south of the river and over Whitefriars bridge.

Based on the measurements of the English chronicler William Worcester (1415-82), Rutledge (forthcoming, based on Harvey 1969: 234-5) has estimated the total length of the church to have been about 225 ft 9 in (c. 68.85 m), with the nave measuring 63 ft on the south side. This is slightly shorter than the churches built at the Norwich Greyfriars and Blackfriars (overall lengths 250 ft and 254 ft respectively) but significantly larger than the earlier church to the north. The full length of the fourteenth-century church was not revealed by the excavations, with only small parts of the nave being exposed. Any remains of the choir were probably largely destroyed by the construction of St James's Mill in the nineteenth century (see Figure 7.15 at the end of this chapter). However, the measurable external dimension of the surviving foundations indicates a nave of c. 19.6 m (c. 64 ft 9 in) wide, which broadly corresponds with William Worcester's measurements.

In addition to the main external walls (with substantial buttresses), a number of pier or column bases were found, forming parts of the north and south aisles within the nave. The walking space beneath the tower would have separated the choir from the public nave, and linked with the cloister to the north. There were several phases of tiled floors which had been patched and repaired following the insertion of numerous burials, none of which were excavated. The main cemetery was presumably located to the south and east of the church, although this area was low-lying and might still have been prone to flooding from the adjacent river.

Establishment of the location of the fourteenth-century church is of further significance as it sheds light on the interpretation of the upstanding 'Anchorite's arch'. Rather than being part of the Anchorite's house (which was probably removed when the river bank was cut back and a new bridge constructed in the 1920s), the arch is clearly the remains of a doorway (Figure 7.4). Its position in relation to the excavated remains shows that this door was the main 'public' entrance into the nave from Cowgate to the west and from the preaching yard to the south. This association was first proposed by Andy Shelley (pers. comm.), underpinned by a detailed map regression exercise taking into account other fossilised wall fragments in nearby buildings (since disappeared). The NHER entry (site 26156) describes it as a 'mid-fourteenth-century stone arch within the remains of a flint and brick wall with three orders of mouldings with attached shaft'. The fabric of the archway appears to be similar to the excavated friary walls recorded elsewhere on the site, and its date is broadly in keeping with the documented period of construction and expansion at Whitefriars.

Figure 7.4 The 'Anchorite's arch' with new office building behind, from south.
© OA East

The cloister and related buildings

The great cloister lay to the immediate east of the Cowgate frontage, with a central garth (probably a garden) and the church to the south (see above). Overall the size and plan of the cloister probably compared favourably to other friaries in the city; at just under 107 ft/32.6 m (Rutledge 2007: 54) the east walk of Norwich Greyfriars measured only slightly longer than the 105 ft/32 m recorded at Whitefriars. The cloister walks were on average between c. 3.4 m and c. 3.8 m (12 ft 4 in) wide (Figures 7.3 and 7.5), comparable with the cloisters at many other friaries including London Whitefriars, Norwich Blackfriars and Coventry Whitefriars.

Figure 7.5 Overhead 'working shot' of the great cloister under excavation, from south-east.
© B. Ayers/NPSA

BURNHAM NORTON FRIARY

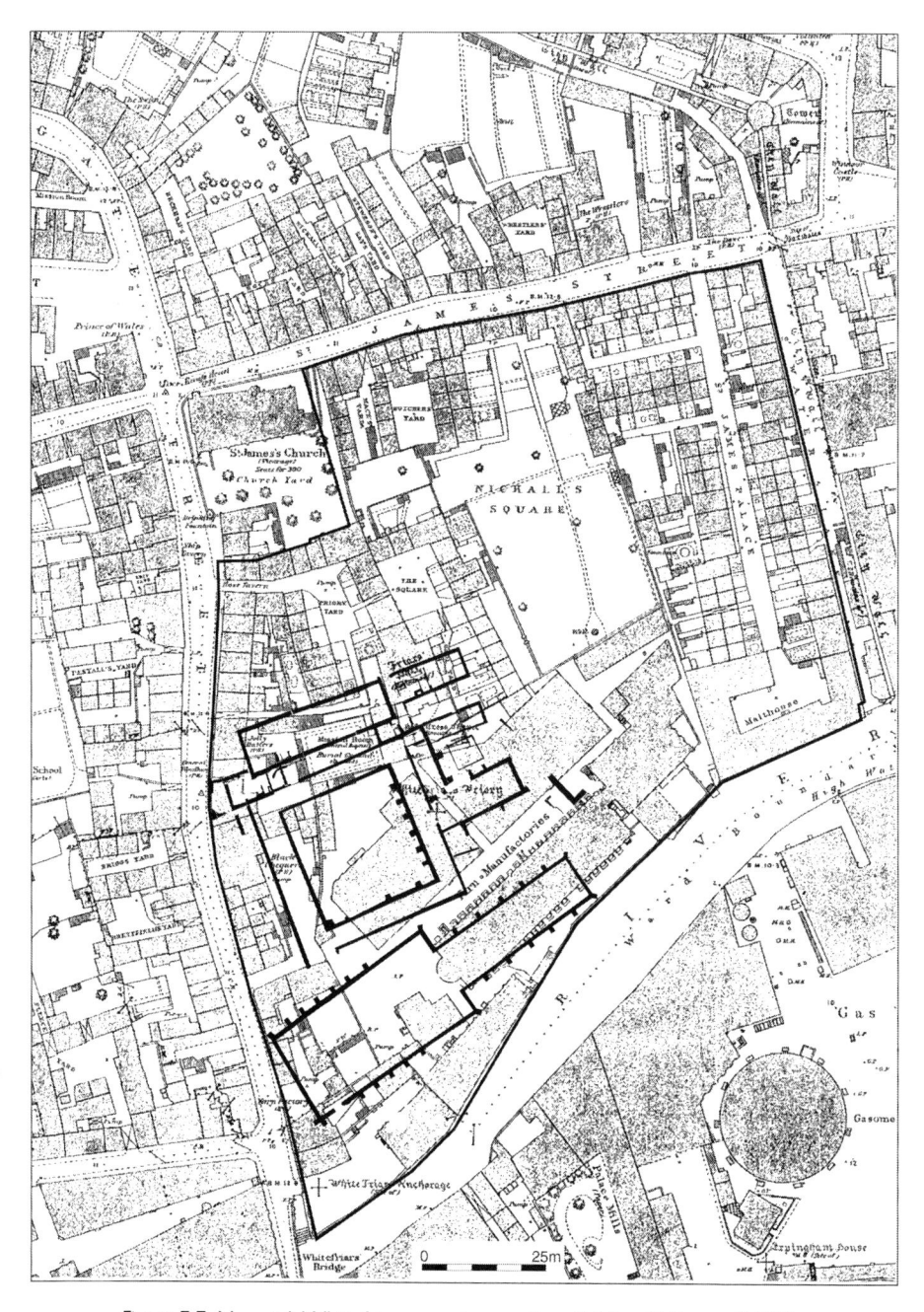

Figure 7.7 Norwich Whitefriars overlain on First Edition O S map (1885).
© OA East

on a different alignment from the other buildings. Buildings were certainly located along the frontage in the area between the thirteenth-century church and the boundary to St James's Church, as flint walls have occasionally been recorded here during various archaeological investigations (NHER site 318; Atkin and Evans 2002: 197–8; NHER site 234; Emery and Ayers 1999: 278). These might have been tenements or even shops which were rented out to provide additional income for the friary. A malthouse is documented at the site, while other buildings might have included a brewhouse, cheesehouse, bakehouse, laundry, dovehouse and stables.

Large areas of the precinct would have been green, open spaces (Figure 7.2). Gardens, orchards, possibly vineyards, small fields, paddocks and meadow probably extended across much of the eastern half of the precinct towards the city wall and down to the river. Vegetable and herb gardens would also have been created, presumably close to the kitchens. Although most of these areas have not been excavated, probable horticultural features dating to the fifteenth century have been identified in the north-east corner of the precinct close to Pockthope Gate, and are likely to be remains of the friary gardens (NHER site 430; Hutcheson 2000). Ponds, which would have been a resource for fish and waterfowl as well providing water for small livestock and cultivated crops, are also mentioned in Dissolution documents. A small stream or cockey that might have been culverted by the fifteenth century is also documented. There are at least two references suggesting the presence of a jetty or quay on the waterfront (Sandred and Lindström 1989: 11; Kirkpatrick 1845: 153), essential for the importing of building stone and other construction materials.

Very little documentary or physical evidence for the precinct wall at Whitefriars has been uncovered. It is not certain when it was constructed, although there are references in a deed to an entrance gate opposite Fishergate (Rutledge forthcoming). Fragments of wall foundations found adjacent to Cowgate/Whitefriars are likely to have been remnants of the early precinct wall before the friary was extended in the fourteenth century. Part of the north-east section of the precinct wall is depicted on a drawing of Pockthorpe Gate by John Ninham, published in 1861. There are also likely to have been internal boundary walls separating the burial grounds and garden areas from the main conventual buildings. Some of these may be represented by a number of apparently buttressed walls depicted on the first edition Ordnance Survey map.

The later years of the friary until the Dissolution (until *c.* 1538)

A number of changes to the Whitefriars buildings were initiated, which probably date to the fifteenth century; documentary evidence places some of these works at the very end of the century. However, both the architectural stone and window glass recovered from the site date to the previous phase of expansion and construction, with little being demonstrably later than around 1400. This suggests that the later modifications were not on such a grand scale as previously, and reused materials wherever possible. An example of this is where gravestones and lintels were used as thresholds or flooring in the new passageways and doorways. The fifteenth century also witnessed an increased use of brick, replacing the expensive freestone of the preceding centuries. Further evidence for changes in this period are represented by the extant undercroft adjacent to Cowgate (Figure 7.8). In the fifteenth century, the undercroft was significantly remodelled, with the partial demolition of the south wall and insertion of freestone-faced semi-octagonal piers. Also probably related to this phase was the construction of a new staircase in the south-west corner of the former thirteenth-century church, and the insertion of a closed drain into the floor. These, along with the possible creation of new entranceways, suggests a change in function for this building or at least for the adjacent and overlying chambers (Atkin 2002: 195–6).

Figure 7.8 The extant undercroft in 1978 showing fifteenth-century vaulting.
© Norwich Survey (Atkins and Evans, 2002)

One of the major additions in this period was the creation of a second, smaller cloister to the east of the main cloister. This is interpreted as an infirmary cloister, with the infirmary located on the northern side. Adjacent to it were a probable kitchen and possible chapel. The latter interpretation is based on the presence of a large dump of window glass found in the eastern half of the building, although this might not have originated within this building. Another significant development was related to improvements in drainage and sanitation, with the creation of several brick-lined drains, garderobes and sumps/soakaways.

A spacious new library was constructed following a bequest in 1450. In 1520 this was described in the writings of John Bale (1495–1563) – who was educated at the friary – as the 'most beautiful in the Order' (Copsey 2006: 30). In this period there were also a number of bequests which indicate that upkeep of the friary was an ongoing concern; by the end of the fifteenth century it had fallen into a dilapidated state (Copsey 2006: 20).

Construction and appearance of the friary

Similar construction techniques were evident at Whitefriars to those recorded elsewhere in the city, notably at Greyfriars, typified by significant ground-raising and the creation of an extensive chalk raft or building platform. Cut through this were steep-sided trenches infilled with bands of compacted deposits, above which most of the major walls were constructed. The fabric of the walls comprised flint, brick and mortar, with limestone or brick mouldings and dressings. Several of the more substantial walls were supported by buttresses and underpinned by relieving arches where they were associated with major buildings such as the church, or carried an upper storey, as would have been present over the east (and possibly south) range.

In addition to the below-ground remains such as walls, floors, doorways, fireplaces and other structural elements, an impression of the appearance of the friary can also be gained from the surviving upstanding elements. These include the undercroft and the 'Anchorite's arch', both described above. Another structure that is widely thought to have originated from Norwich Whitefriars is the highly decorative Arminghall Arch, although the strong possibility remains that it once stood at one of the other Norwich friaries (see Rutledge forthcoming). According to Lindley (1987), the arch was relocated after the Dissolution and used for the south porch of Arminghall Old Hall, a late Elizabethan house built by the Mingay family. It has since been conserved and reconstructed in the Magistrates' Court on the opposite side of the river. The arch (Figure 7.9) is elaborately carved with vine-leaf decoration, among which are dragons and other beasts, with the bearded head of a man at the apex of the pointed arch and figure niches containing seated kings on either side (Lindley 1987: 22). On stylistic grounds the arch is thought to date to between c. 1320 to 1340, with the likelihood of it being a work of the 1330s (Lindley 1987: 27). This fits well with the beginning of the Whitefriars building campaign and construction of the new church, or at least the choir. It is possible that the arch was commissioned as part of the church, and that it served as the entrance to the choir from the walking space. Another possibility is that it came from the chapter house, given that substantial robber trenches were found where the doorway would have been located. However, if indeed it was part of the Carmelite friary, it would perhaps have been most appropriate as an ornate public entrance into the monastery, forming the front face of a porch or gateway (Lindley 1987: 24).

Figure 7.9 The Arminghall Arch. © NPSA

This evidence is supplemented by the significant assemblages of architectural stonework, painted window glass, lead window cames, ceramic building materials, and to a lesser extent structural ironwork and other fixtures and fittings. The ceramic floor tiles recovered from Whitefriars include a number of glazed examples, of which some were brown or uncoloured, but most were green (including some dark and some bright green) or yellow. Plain tiles such as these were used to form chequerboard floors, as was found in the church and cloister walks (Anderson forthcoming). Walls that were not whitewashed were occasionally finished with carefully knapped flintwork to create a decorative flush face; ashlar string courses were recorded and limestone plinths were commonly used, particularly in association with buttresses of the more important buildings (Figure 7.10). Freestone generally appears to have been employed in decorative elements such as windows (both plain and ornate), arcades, lintels, jambs and various mouldings, as well as funerary monuments. Brick was also used decoratively as well as structurally (in relieving arches and quoins), being present in vaulting and as a lining to apertures and doorways.

Figure 7.10 Detail of cloister buttresses.
© NPSA

The painted window glass (1,444 fragments in total) is largely of fourteenth-century date, with much dating to the period of expansion in 1380–1400. The assemblage shows strong affiliations with the long-established Norwich school, and it is almost certain that a local glazier was employed for this work. Of particular note are several heraldic fragments comprising square pieces with lions passant gardant on yellow glass, which strongly suggest that they were from the arms of England before *c.* 1405 (Figure 7.11). It is possible that these came from the same window as a scallop border, and the combination might indicate that this window was donated by John of Gaunt, duke of Lancaster, perhaps for the church or another important building (King forthcoming). These fragments came from the largest and most significant group of window glass (1,115 pieces) from the site, recovered from a post-Dissolution dump in what has been interpreted as the infirmary chapel. However, it is possible that the glass (and associated window tracery) was taken from elsewhere in the complex and processed in this room (King forthcoming).

Figure 7.11 Painted window glass: a lion.
© OA East

Daily life at Norwich Whitefriars

Much of the friars' lives would have been taken up with religious services, study, writing, teaching and preaching to the wider community. Presumably some of their time was allocated to tending the gardens, orchards and other areas within the precinct, although some of these duties, along with cooking and other domestic activities, might have been undertaken by servants. The excavations at Norwich Whitefriars have brought to light further evidence for some of the activities undertaken in this community, as well as providing information on diet through study of the animal bone and other remains from the site.

Despite the fragmented nature of the faunal assemblage, it is possible to infer that the Whitefriars, at least towards the latter end of their tenure, had a fairly good diet, with access to a variety of meat. This included sheep (mutton), and to a lesser extent cattle (beef) and pig (pork), alongside rabbit and roe deer (venison). It is likely that the friars, although originally dependant on begging, were partly self-sufficient, supplementing their diet with home-grown vegetables, fruit, herbs (and medicines) alongside other produce from within their own gardens. Fish and waterfowl might have been provided from their ponds. They might have owned a dovecote to provide eggs and occasional meat, and even ground their own flour, baked their own bread, brewed beer and made their own cheese.

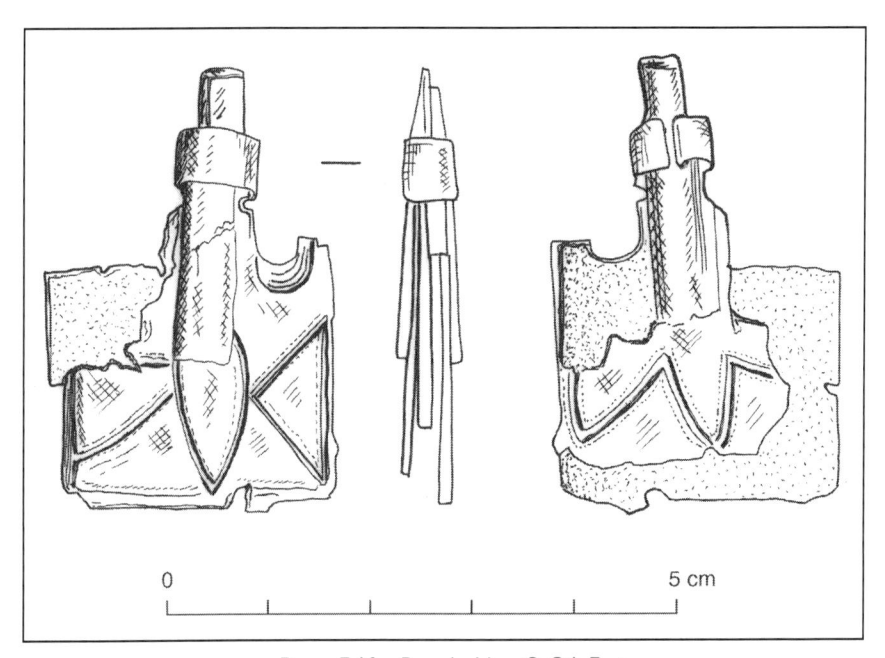

Figure 7.12a Page holder. © OA East

Further evidence for life in the friary is provided by the assemblages of artefacts, with many objects relating to dress accessories, literacy and weighing. Of note are a group of simple rectangular strap-ends that must have been worn as part of the habits of the friars. A high number of book-fittings was recovered, alongside a very fragile page-holder (Figure 7.12a) which could be taken as evidence for a considerable library (as described in later documents at Whitefriars). A similar motif, a saltire (St Andrew's cross) of incised zigzag design, appears on many of the strap-ends, the page-holder and possibly some of the book-fittings that had been reused as strap-ends (Figure 7.12b). This motif does not occur among the large assemblage of strap-ends from London, and no parallels have been found from other monastic sites, suggesting that this was a distinctive feature of Norwich Whitefriars' metalwork. These objects were probably produced specifically for the friars, either by a smith in the city or by a bronze-smith among their community (Crummy forthcoming).

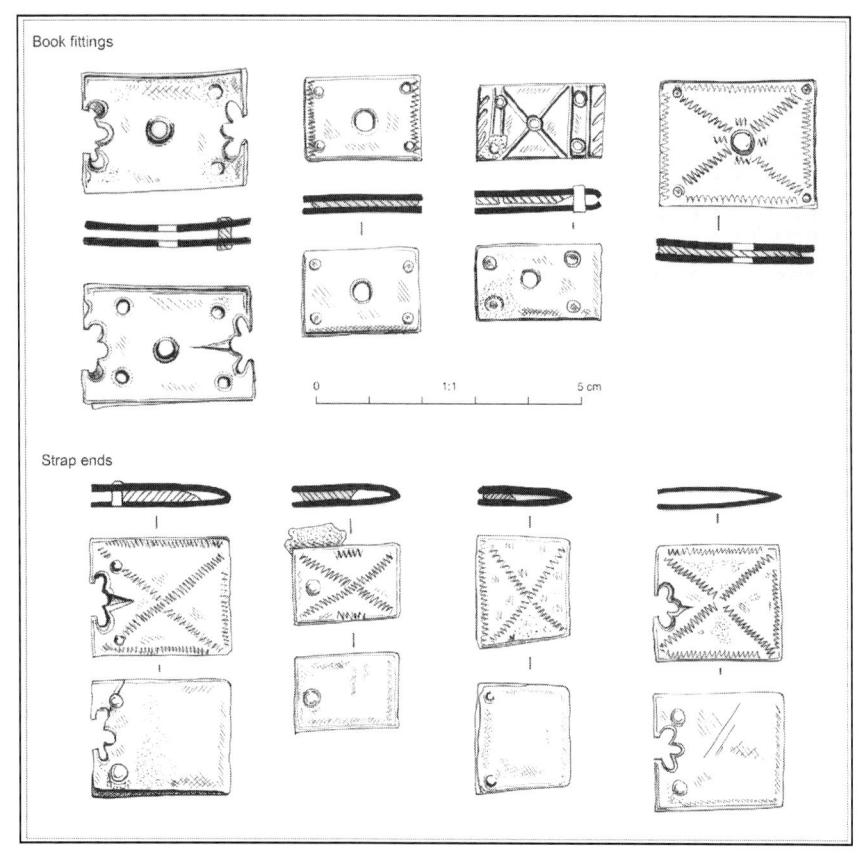

Figure 7.12b Strap ends and book fittings with saltire design. © OA East

The presence of a copper-alloy coin weight points to contact with traders, while many of the simple lead weights might relate to the medicines prepared for the sick in the infirmary or the preparation of communal food. Evidence for sewing is provided by four thimbles and a gilt copper-alloy needle case (Figure 7.13), the latter found close to the left arm of an adolescent buried in the east cloister walk. Mending garments and other sewing skills would have been a necessary accomplishment for at least some members of the community. Dental analysis of the monastic skeletal remains identified lesions on the teeth indicative of activities such as threading needles, which might support this. Other metal finds include a single rolled lead fishing-weight, several knives and two hone stones which could relate to food provision and preparation. A possible surgeon's or craft tool is represented by a saw blade.

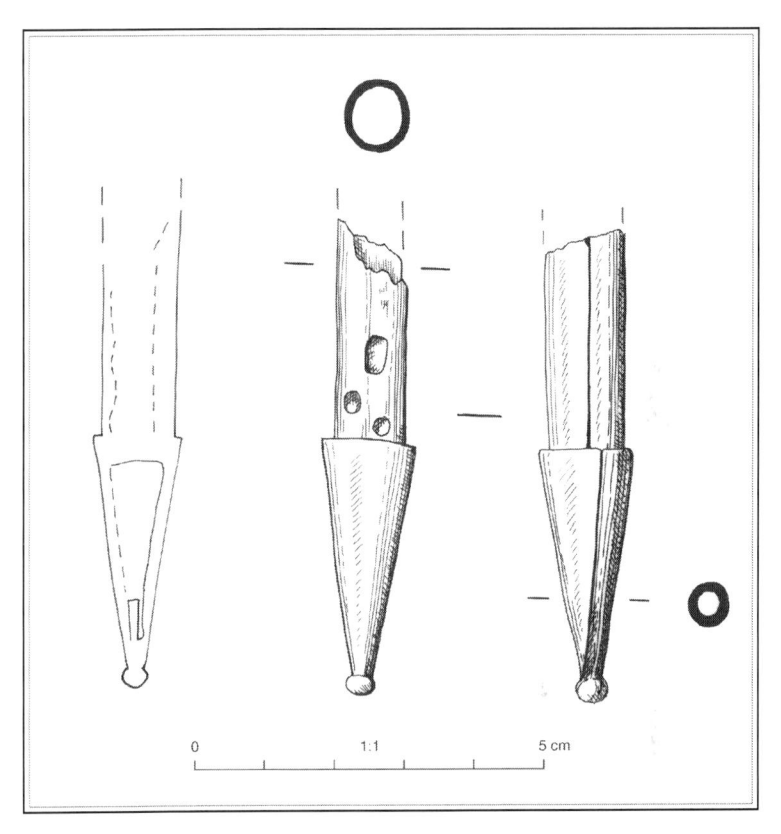

Figure 7.13 A gilded needlecase.
© OA East

Most of the late medieval pottery vessels, particularly German stonewares, were related to drinking, although one more unusual form was a chamber pot. Cooking and dining were also well represented in the assemblage. A mixture of kitchen/cooking pots and decorative tablewares was found, the former including skillets, pipkins and dripping dishes, the latter jugs, cups and a chafing dish with anthropomorphic decoration. Among the finds are two lamps (one stone and one ceramic), probably associated with the greater need for light after dark in a monastic establishment. A roughly made ceramic dripping dish in an uncommon form might have been ordered for a specific purpose related to monastic needs. The small late-medieval vessel glass assemblage includes several fragments of flasks and tubing, which in late monastic contexts is often associated with distillation to produce medicines or inks. Butchery, hornworking and leatherworking were also evidently carried out in different areas of the precinct (NHER site 430; Hutcheson 2000).

Monastic burial

Urban friaries and their new churches impacted on the older monastic foundations and the parish churches of the secular clergy by diverting away potential alms, burial payments and bequests. This was certainly the case with the Carmelite friary, as it lay within at least two parishes and close to another, all belonging to the (Benedictine) Cathedral Priory, which subsequently took measures to maintain its parochial income (Rutledge forthcoming). Like the other Norwich friaries, the Carmelites received bequests from almost half of all Norwich testators (clerical and lay) between 1370 and 1532. The friary seems to have been less popular, however, as a place of lay burial, with only 20 bequests over the same period for burial in the church or cemetery, as opposed to 28 for the Austin Friars, 39 for the Franciscans and 45 for the Dominicans. It is not possible to be certain whether the 23 individuals excavated from within the friary buildings at Norwich Whitefriars represent members of the monastic community or lay people, or a combination of the two. The latter is perhaps the most likely, as although the remains are predominantly of males (18), there are also two females and three non-adults (possibly oblates). This mixed population can be seen to be a reflection of the greater integration of urban friaries with local communities. Information from contemporary documents (wills) indicate that burials at Norwich Whitefriars included 39 friars alongside various individuals from a relatively wide range of social backgrounds such as knights, merchants, a fishmonger, a fuller, a notary and a clerk. A number of wives and widows also requested burial within the friary.

Various burial groups in distinct phases were examined during the excavations, including graves located within the church (which were not excavated), cloister walks and chapter house (Figures 7.3 and 7.14). All articulated skeletons were placed in the usual Christian manner, with little variation other than in arrangement of arms and hands. Alignments followed that of the surrounding walls and friary buildings, being slightly north of east and south of west; those within the church followed the even more extreme north-east/south-west axis necessitated by the location of this building.

Although no direct evidence of coffins was found, the rectangular shape of many of the graves might indicate they were cut to receive coffins. The use of coffins for burial at the friary is attested to by the discovery of at least two oak coffins with skeletons during construction works in 1958. Although their precise locations are not known, one of the skeletons was conjectured to be the remains of Lady Eleanor Talbot (Ashdown-Hill 2000: 14–18), who died in 1468 and is known to have been buried in the friary church.

Chapter houses were popular places for burial in the larger monasteries, and the burials are often found in tightly packed rows (Coppack 1990: 72), perhaps reflecting the integral importance of this building in the lives of the religious community. Cloisters were often seen as the 'spiritual core' of monasteries. The walks or alleys formed an integral part of the processional life of the community, connecting the church and monastic ranges. Burial within these areas was often structured according to gender and age, especially within friaries (Gilchrist and Sloane 2005: 57–9).

Figure 7.14 Example of one of the monastic graves. © NPSA

Overall, the health of this excavated group of burials corresponded with the late medieval average. However, higher prevalence rates for some conditions were noted at Whitefriars than was normal for the period. The presence of a well-healed radius fracture suggests that some types of injury were treated successfully, probably in the infirmary. Degenerative joint disease, inflammation of the shins, sinusitis and evidence for childhood stress were common, while fractures and congenital anomalies were also noted. An unusually high frequency of cavities, gum disease and dental abscesses was observed for the period, indicative of poor oral hygiene (Caffell and Holst forthcoming).

Conclusion

Dissolution of the four Norwich friaries in 1538 had an enormous impact. Large areas of the city had been dominated by monastic precincts and ecclesiastic institutions, and it was home to numerous hospitals, chantries, anchorages and a school. Their removal would have affected the inhabitants visually, but perhaps more profoundly it affected them economically, socially and spiritually. Norwich was already in decline in the sixteenth century, and the Dissolution probably accelerated this recession, at least initially (Ayers, 1991: 4–5).

The friars in particular had been a very active and visible presence in the city and surrounding region for nearly 300 years, yet within a few years following the Dissolution three of their large churches had disappeared and many of their remaining buildings had been ransacked or plundered. The site of the Carmelite friary was granted away in 1542 and the former precinct was gradually encroached upon (Figure 7.15), echoing its more industrial past before the Whitefriars colonised this area of the city.

Notes

1 See www.heritage.norfolk.gov.uk
2 This section draws on O'Sullivan (2013).
3 It is listed as II* (1212056).

NORWICH WHITEFRIARS

Figure 7.15 View north from the Cathedral spire showing the urban infill of the former friary site, with Whitefriars bridge on the left and St James' Mill on the right.
© G. Plunkett with permission

Acknowledgements

As with any archaeological project of this nature, a large number of people and organisations have been involved at various stages, both directly and indirectly, to ensure its successful completion. The excavation and post-excavation assessment were funded by R G Carter Ltd, with the post-excavation analysis and publication stages funded by Jarrold & Sons Ltd. The main excavations that form the basis of this chapter, and the forthcoming monograph, were directed under tight time constraints by Andy Shelley, former senior project manager at NPSA (formerly the NAU). His interpretations formed the backbone of the analysis and publication.

The NAU field and post-excavation team deserve particular mention (full acknowledgements are included in the forthcoming monograph). Brian Ayers kindly supplied copies of his own slides taken during the excavations, and is thanked for his continued interest in the project throughout the post-excavation and publication stages. Photographs of Norwich taken by the late George Plunkett were kindly supplied by his son Jonathan. Elizabeth Popescu managed the post-excavation programme for OA East, providing many useful insights into the archaeology of Norwich.

Thanks are also extended to the various specialists whose reports are summarised in this paper, notably Sue Anderson (pottery and ceramic building material), Dr Anwel Caffell and Malin Holst (human skeletal remains), Nina Crummy (metal finds), David King (window glass), Chris Faine (animal bone), Alice Lyons (vessel glass), Mark Samuels (architectural stone), Ruth Shaffrey (stone objects) and Elizabeth Rutledge (documentary research).

8

Benefactors great and small: late medieval wills relating to Burnham Norton Friary

John Alban

Introduction

The principal purpose of the orders of friars was preaching and prayer. However, like all religious houses, the Carmelite priory at Burnham Norton needed sources of income to sustain itself as an institution. The priory's own medieval archives did not outlast the Reformation and the Dissolution of the monasteries. In the absence of a surviving *corpus* of administrative and financial records emanating from the house itself, probate records existing elsewhere are crucial for throwing light upon some key elements of its funding. The monastic orders lived in largely self-sufficient communities boosted by revenues from often extensive estates and rental portfolios, which could include rural manors and urban tenements. However, friaries were highly dependent on charitable donations or other gifts and alms, and on bequests made by benefactors in their wills. Although Burnham Norton Friary did derive some of its income from its small estates,[1] it was mainly reliant upon the charitable donations which came from all levels of society in Norfolk, and which particularly emphasised and cemented the house's relationship with the local community. This dependence on grants, bequests and alms from external sources lasted from the earliest days of the friary until the time of its dissolution in 1538.

This chapter examines the numerous bequests made in favour of the friary between the thirteenth and the sixteenth centuries, by a variety of benefactors from all walks of life – from the founders of the house down to the 'ordinary' people who lived in the Burnhams and elsewhere in Norfolk. The wills of testators who over a long period of time made pious bequests to the friary survive in fair quantities in the archives of the various probate jurisdictions which pertained to Norfolk. In particular, the probate records of the Norwich Consistory (Bishop's) Court and of the Archdeaconry of Norfolk, held in the Norfolk Record Office (NRO), provide a wealth of information, which helps in part to offset the unfortunate lack of documentary evidence from the friary itself.

The establishment of a Carmelite friary within the North Norfolk parish of Burnham Norton traditionally dates to 1241 (Cox 1906: 425-6). However, some doubt has been cast on this early date, since Burnham Norton was only the fourth Carmelite house to be established in England, after the priories at Hulne (Northumberland) and Aylesford (Kent), both in 1242, and Lossenham (Kent), founded between 1242 and 1247. The date of foundation, at the priory's first site in a place called Bradmer in the parish of Burnham Norton, must therefore have been later than the dates on which the others were established. It is now considered to have occurred within the latter timeframe, being the last house to be founded before the rule of the order was revised in 1247 and before the friary was re-established at its current site in 1253 (Egan 1969: 143, 159; Copsey 2017: 3; Knowles and Hadcock 1971: 233).

The founders of Burnham Norton Friary

Associated with the traditional date of 1241 are the names of Sir Ralph de Hemenale (or Hempnale) and Sir William de Calthorpe, who are considered to be the original founders of the house.[2] Moreover, while the exact date of the priory's establishment is uncertain, we can at least be sure of the names of its founders, although precise information about them is also vague. The distinguished Carmelite historian Professor Keith Egan, for example, remarked that 'No William de Calthorpe can be shown to have a connection with this friary' (1969: 160). This is perhaps not a surprising statement, since while both surnames were those of well-known and prominent knightly families in medieval Norfolk (Rye 1913: 91, 327), personal details of the two founders remain sketchy.[3] However, this William de Calthorpe may possibly be identified with the William de Calthorpe who was the nephew and heir of Walter de Suffield, bishop of Norwich,[4] from whom he inherited manors in Calthorpe, the place from which the family took their name. Some time during the reign of Henry III (1216-72), through his marriage with *Cecilia*, the sister and heiress of *William de Burnham*, he acquired the manor of Burnham Thorpe, part of which extended into Burnham Westgate.[5]

Modern commentators have identified the other founder, Ralph de Hemenhale, as being the lord of a portion of Polstead Hall manor, which lay jointly within Burnham Norton and Burnham Westgate (e.g. Francis 2003: 9). It is more than probable that the de Hemenhales did hold part of that manor during Henry III's reign, although there is scant surviving documentary evidence that they were lords there at that time.

However, they were certainly in possession of parts of it by the reign of Edward I (1272–1307), since in 1285–6:

> 'the sheriff of *Norfolk* had a precept to make a just division of the *Polsted* estate, between *Ralph de Hemenhale,* and *Emme* his wife and *John de Gymingham*, in *Burnham Norton*' ...

and also to ensure delivery to Ralph and Emma of their rights in that part of Polstead Hall manor lying in Burnham Westgate (Blomefield 1805–10, vol. 7: 16, 34). While precise archival evidence of his holding land in the Burnhams in the 1240s is lacking, Ralph de Hemenhale's involvement with the foundation of the friary strongly suggests that he already had a close connexion with that area by that decade, and probably held some estates there. However, from the latter part of the thirteenth century onwards, there is a fair amount of surviving documentary information about both families, which reveals their continuing presence as important manorial lords in that part of Norfolk throughout the later Middle Ages.

Figure 8.1 Coat of arms of de Hemenhale, c. 1300, in Threxton church.
Photo: © J R Alban.

Figure 8.2 Coat of arms of de Calthorpe, c. 1418, in Ashwellthorpe church.
Photo: © J R Alban.

Figures 8.1 and 8.2 illustrate the coats of arms of the two founding families of Burnham Norton friary.

The Norfolk antiquary Francis Blomefield records that the de Hemenhales took their name from the eponymous village (now Hempnall), some 13 miles south of Norwich.[6] From at least the early thirteenth century they were the lords of Sir Ralf's or Curple's Manor at Hempnall, which they held of the Fitzwalter barony of Bainard's Castle (Blomefield 1805–10, vol. 5: 185–6). The de Hemenhales clearly regarded their position as vassals of such important lords as the Fitzwalters as being of some significance, thus the feudal dependency between the two families was reflected in their respective coats of arms.[7] At various times during the Middle Ages, the family possessed manors in many different parts of Norfolk, including ones in the hundreds of Clacklose, Diss, Eynford, Freebridge, Loddon, Shropham and Wayland. Of particular relevance to their involvement with Burnham Norton Friary was the cluster of estates in the North Norfolk hundred of Brothercross in which they held whole or partial interests. These included Walsingham Priory manor in North Creake, Reynham's or Lexham's manor in Burnham Westgate, and Polstead Hall manor, which lay in Burnham Westgate and Burnham Norton. From at least the 1330s, they were also recorded as holding the advowson of Burnham Ulph (Blomefield 1805–10, vol.1: 1–39; 438; vol. 2: 365; vol. 5: 185–6; vol. 7: 16, 36,70, 322; vol. 8: 187; vol. 9: 90; vol. 10: 164).

The de Calthorpe family also held extensive estates in Norfolk, concentrated mainly in the north and west of the county, in the hundreds of Brothercross, Clacklose, Freebridge, Happing, Holt, North Greenhoe, Smithdon, South Erpingham and Tunstead; they also had manorial interests in the southern hundreds of Diss and Loddon. As already mentioned, they took their name from Calthorpe,[8] in South Erpingham hundred, where they were established by the twelfth century (Blomefield 1805–10, vol. 6: 514–21). As noted above, through his marriage with Cecilia de Burnham William de Calthorpe acquired manors in Burnham Thorpe, which were held of the de Warenne earls of Surrey.[9] Elsewhere in the hundred of Brothercross, the de Calthorpes also had extensive manorial holdings in Burnham Overy, Burnham Westgate, and in North and South Creake, again most of them held of the de Warennes as capital lords (Blomefield 1805–10, vol. 7: 21–2, 71–2, 80).

Throughout the later Middle Ages, members of both families frequently appeared as parties in or as witnesses to deeds, as well as playing their parts in local administration. The de Calthorpes also served as knights of the shire in Parliament for Norfolk on three separate occasions, between 1306 and 1491, and as sheriffs of Norfolk five times between 1442 and 1500 (Le Strange 1890: 16–18, 40, 47). However, none of the de Hemenhales appears to have held either office. Moreover, during the fourteenth and early fifteenth centuries, several members of both families followed the martial calling of their class and served in English armies in France.

The benefactions of the founders

Details of the original grant and any associated costs that de Calthorpe and de Hemenhale incurred in establishing the friary are unknown, but they would have regarded their gesture as a significant one, not least for the benefit of their souls, and of those of their ancestors. Such benefactions were strongly motivated by the search for salvation in the next world. Founding a religious house could also be viewed as a demonstrable public act, which would consolidate their status in local society, as well as enhancing their lineage: such patronage often created a family tradition of continuing links with the foundation. Establishing the friary would certainly have involved endowments of some portions of land for accommodating the Carmelites, first at Bradmer and then at the later site in Burnham Norton. Such grants were often effected by a charter, thus it is feasible that the two founders issued the friars with an instrument of foundation, granting land, rights and privileges: indeed, Blomefield speculated on the probability that 'they had a patent granted them' (1805–10 vol. 7: 19.) Originals of such documents rarely survive from this period: at best, the original text of a lost foundation charter might have been entered later into a cartulary. If a re-grant or confirmation of it were made by a subsequent lord or the monarch, it might have been incorporated into the type of charter known as an *inspeximus* (Thompson 1994; Davis 1958). Unfortunately, neither an original nor a copy of such a charter appears to have survived for Burnham Norton Friary.

What is known is that over succeeding centuries, members of the founders' families continued to maintain links with the friary, possibly regarding themselves as its patrons, and making the occasional additional grant to support it. For example, at some unrecorded date during the thirteenth century, a Sir William de Calthorpe – perhaps the same man who was named as one of the founders – made a bequest of 20s. to the friary (Bryant 1914: 21). In the 1290s Walter de Calthorpe, possibly the son of Sir William de Calthorpe and his wife Cecelia de Burnham, was involved in making a gift of additional land to the friars. However, this grant was not a straightforward one, because it involved the conveying of land to an ecclesiastical body and therefore came under the scope of the Statutes of Mortmain of 1279 and 1290, which placed restrictions on the passing of property to the church – a practice which would have ultimately resulted in the loss of revenues to the crown. After the enactment of these statutes, whenever a feudal tenant wished to make such a gift, an application to do so had to be made to the king, who would then normally cause to be instituted a commission *ad quod damnum* ('to what damage?'). These commissions would examine the matter and determine whether such a grant or licence would be prejudicial to the interests of the crown or others. If the applicant's case were accepted, the crown would issue a licence to alienate in mortmain.[10] Thus, in May 1297, following an application by Walter de Calthorpe and William Reynald 'to grant land in Burnham to the prior and Carmelite friars there, retaining land in Burnham' an inquisition was duly ordered (TNA, C143/26/12). On 16 June 1297 the crown issued to Walter de Calthorpe a 'licence for the alienation in mortmain to the prior and Carmelite friars of Brunham of a rood of meadow there for the enlargement of their place' (*CPR 1292-1301*: 354).

Licences for alienations in mortmain, not surprisingly, became a recurring consideration in those instances where gifts of land were made to the friary. In 1353 Edward III granted such a licence jointly to Ralph de Hemenhale, a member of the family of the other founder, and Richard Ferman of Burnham Sutton, in respect of 3 acres of land in Burnham Norton, conveyed to the friars, 'for the enlargement of their manse' (*CPR 1350-4*: 506).

The de Hemenhales appear, understandably, to have maintained a continuing connexion with the friary. For instance, in his testament of 24 September 1391, Sir Robert de Hemenhale made provision for himself to be buried in *choro fratrum de monte Carmeli apud Brunham* ('in the choir of the friars of Mount Carmel at Burnham'), although, in the event, his wishes may have been overridden and he may, instead, have been interred in St John the Evangelist's chapel in Westminster Abbey.[11] In addition, he left to the friars his greater black gown (*nigrum gones meum maiorem*) and 1 mark (13s. 4d.) in money, while a further sum of 40s. was to be set aside for distribution to paupers on the day of his burial and for the expenses of his funeral itself. It is perhaps significant that de Hemenhale's bequests to the friary head the long list of provisions which he made in his testament and his last will,[12] and his wish to be buried there may well have reflected his desire to demonstrate a spiritual affiliation with the order through the continuing physical presence of his body within the church (see Röhrkasten, 2004: 467). It may therefore also be that the de Hemenhales saw themselves as patrons of the friary at Burnham Norton and thus considered it as their family place of burial, in the same way as the Howard dukes of Norfolk, as a key element of their own commemorative strategy, regarded Thetford Priory as theirs (Stöber 2007: 171-82; Claiden-Yardley 2014: 63-4, 115-16, 186-7, 217-18, 277-9; Weever 1767: 551-60). Indeed, Egan notes that the Sir Ralph de Hemenhale who died in 1328 may have been the friary's patron in the previous year (1969: 160). In contrast, there is no surviving evidence that any of the de Calthorpes were interred in Burnham Norton Friary. However, members of that family are known to have been buried in the Whitefriars in Norwich, in Burnham Thorpe Church (of which they were the patrons), and in North Creake Abbey (Blomefield 1805-10, vol. 6: 517; vol. 7: 14, 77).[13]

Other benefactors 'great and small'

The de Hemenhales and de Calthorpes were not the only members of the higher orders of society to make provision for the friary, although Burnham Norton appears not to have commanded the same levels of benefaction from the nobility and gentry as did some other larger and more notable houses.[14] T Hugh Bryant, in his study of the churches in the hundred of Brothercross, claimed that Walter de Suffield, bishop of Norwich between 1224 and 1257, was a benefactor of the house in 1256. This repeats a statement made – seemingly without substantiation – by Dugdale, which has been echoed by several later commentators, although there is possible doubt about it (Bryant 1914: 21; Copsey 2017: 4; Francis 2003: 10; Dugdale 1846, vol. 6, pt. 3: 1573). As noted above, de Suffield was himself a member of the de Calthorpe family and thus had links with the Burnham area, so it appears logical that he acted in such a capacity and left a legacy to Burnham Norton Friary. However in his testament, dated 19 June 1256, he made bequests to the Dominicans and Franciscans, but made no mention of the Carmelites of Burnham Norton – or indeed of any Carmelite house – prompting us to wonder whether Bryant misinterpreted the terms of the testament, or merely followed Dugdale: there appears to be no other known surviving instrument of de Suffield's by which such a grant was made (Bryant 1914: 21).[15]

Burnham Norton Friary did, on occasion, also benefit from general bequests from the nobility. For instance, it profited from the munificence of Isabel de Beauchamp, the dowager countess of Suffolk, who in her will (made on 26 September 1416 and proven a month later on 28 October) left 5 marks a year to each of the four orders of friars in Suffolk and Norfolk, to sing for her soul and to provide specified alms (Jacob and Johnson 1938: 95, cited in Copsey 2017: 6).[16] On another occasion the friary also benefited, albeit indirectly, from papal largesse. While it was itself not a direct grant of moneys, a papal indulgence issued in 1392 by Pope Boniface IX was intended to generate continuing funds to the friary by granting relaxations of penance to any pilgrims who visited the chapel situated over the friary's gatehouse and gave alms for its conservation (Bliss and Twemlow 1902: 433).

In the Middle Ages, gifts to religious houses were made for many reasons, but most particularly donors were strongly motivated by the search for salvation for themselves and their family in the next world. Such benefactors were drawn not just from the ranks of the nobility or gentry, but from all strata of society, and included ordinary people as well as those from the local elite. Thus, over the three centuries from its foundation to its dissolution, the Carmelite house at Burnham Norton also benefited particularly from numerous smaller donations of money and goods from inhabitants of north Norfolk, and especially from the area around the Burnhams. Many of these were simple bequests involving small sums, which could be as low as 20d. For example, John Gybbys of Brancaster in his will of 19 January 1499 bequeathed such an amount 'to the friars of Burnham Norton' (Harper-Bill, 2000: 57, cited by Copsey 2017: 7);[17] Thomas Laws, the vicar of Burnham Overy, made a small bequest of 40d. on 27 April 1429, *Conuentui fratrum Carmelitarum ordinis Beate Marie de Brunham* ('to the convent of the brothers of the order of Carmelites of the Blessed Mary of Brunham');[18] and 5s. was left 'to the Carmelites of Burnham' by Andrew Horscroft of South Raynham, in his will of 10 May 1499, 'for celebrating half a Gregorian trental for his soul and those of his benefactors' (Harper-Bill 2000: 69, cited by Copsey 2017: 7).[19]

In 1517 John Fenne bequeathed an even smaller sum of 8d. 'to the Friers gild', which was otherwise known as the gild of St Mary of Bedlam, in the Carmelites' chapel at Burnham Norton.[20] This small gild was a frequent recipient of bequests, with for example Nicholas Palmere, a chaplain of Great Snoring, leaving it 6s. 8d. in 1387.[21] Alice Balton of Burnham Sutton left *Confraternitati seu Gildee sancte marie virginis tente a capella beate marie super portas domus fratrum Carmelitarum in Burnham unum quartum ordii* ('to the confraternity or gild of St Mary the Virgin held by the chapel of the Blessed Mary, above the doors of the house of the brothers of the Carmelite order in Burnham, one quarter of barley'). Alice also left to the friary itself a quarter of maslin (a mixture of rye and wheat) and two and a half quarters of barley, as well as making a long string of other pious bequests to churches and gilds in Burnham Sutton, Burnham Westgate and elsewhere.[22]

The friary frequently received bequests of fractions of a mark, which was worth 13s. 4d. For instance, on 18 August 1476 John Wade, senior, of Burnham Ulph left a quarter of a mark, 3s. 4d., to the house of Carmelite friars in Burnham.[23] In his testament of 21 November 1486 Robert Waryn of Burnham Norton bequeathed half a mark, 6s. 8d., 'to the Carmelite friars of Burnham Norton to pray for his soul'.[24] Similarly William Shropham of Burnham Norton, by his testament of 30 April 1495, left 6s. 8d. to the friars of Burnham Norton and also bequeathed a comparable sum to the Franciscan friars of Walsingham. By his last will, made on the same date, he added that 'Also þen I Wylle þat þe Freres of Burnham haue xx s.'[25] In 1501, Henry Seman of Burnham Norton left 6s. 8d. 'to the convent of Carmelite friars of the said township [Burnham Norton] to pray for my soul and for all the benefactors', plus a further 6s. 8d. 'to the chapel of the aforesaid friary'.[26]

The 6s. 8d. bequeathed in 1514 by Nicholas Goldale of Burnham Norton, to the friary there, was only one of several legacies to local mendicant houses across Norfolk:

Also I bequethe to the Wyght Fryres of Burnham vjs viijd. Also I bequeth to the grey Fryres of Walsingham, vjs viijd. Also I bequethe to the Wyght Fryres of Lenne [Lynn] a quarter of barly. Also I bequethe to the Augustene Fryres of Lenne a quarter of barly. Also I bequethe to the blak Fryres of Lenne a quarter of barly. Also I bequethe to the Grey Fryres of Lenne a quarter of barly.[27]

As well as his provisions for local friaries, Goldale also made a large number of other pious bequests to churches in the area of the Burnhams. He wished to be 'buried in the Churche of saint Margaret of Burnham Norton afforeseid be fore the bellhowe dore'; bequeathing 10s. to the church for tithes forgotten; 20s. for its reparations, with a further 20s. for the gild halls. He also left the sizeable sum of 18 marks:

to an honest prieste to sing in the Churche of saint Margaretes be the space of ij yeres together ... for my soule and the soules of my Wiffes of Helyn and Helyn and for the soules of my father and moder of James and Isabell Johanna Porter and William Hagon.

The gilds of St Margaret and St Nicholas in Burnham Norton were each left 6s. 8d., while he bequeathed a quarter of barley each to the gild of St Saviour in Burnham Westgate and the gild of the Resurrection in Burnham Ulph. From the sale of his messuage in Dersingham, his executors were to give 6s. 8d. to the high altar of the church there, with an additional 20s. for its reparations.

Goldale was a member of a family in Burnham Norton about whom relatively little is recorded, but who from their occasional appearances in the records seem to have had a certain local prominence.[28] The bequests in his will suggest that he himself was a man of some substance. Another family member, Jaffery (Geoffrey) Goldale, by his testament and last will of 28 September 1532 bequeathed 'to the Freers of burnham ij combe of Barly',[29] but he too also made a series of bequests to the church at Burnham Norton.[30] Like Nicholas, he indicated that he wished to be buried in the churchyard there, 'before the Belhowse dore', leaving 3s. 4d. to the high altar for tithes unpaid, 6s. 8d. for the church's reparation, while to each of the two gilds of St Margaret and St Nicholas there he left two coombs of barley.

Bequests by the same testator to multiple ecclesiastical bodies – such as those made by Nicholas and Geoffrey Goldale – were not unusual: over a period of several hundred years, Burnham Norton Friary was often included as a beneficiary in instruments of this kind. For instance, by his testament of 23 February 1374 John de Berneye made bequests of 2 marks to the Franciscan friars of Norwich and of 20s. to each of the other orders of friars in the city, while he left 1 mark to each of the mendicant orders in Great Yarmouth and Lynn. He also bequeathed 1 mark each to the Carmelite house in Burnham Norton and to the small Carmelite friary at Snitterly, or Blakeney, situated 15 miles to the east. In return, he required that all the benefiting houses should pray for his soul and for those of his parents.[31]

A legacy of 1 mark was also left to the friars of Burnham Norton in the will of Elsabeth Norton, the widow of Richard Norton, drawn up on 5 January 1499 (see the Appendix to this chapter).[32] Elsabeth made a number of other pious bequests, including the significant sum of 10 marks for purchasing an ornament or book for St Margaret's Church, Burnham Norton, where she wished to be buried. She also made smaller grants of 6s. 8d. towards the repair of each of the churches of Burnham Westgate, Burnham Ulph and Burnham Sutton, as well as 10d. to the gild of Saint Saviour for masses.[33] A significant bequest had also been made a few years earlier, when Cecilia Walpole, widow of Burnham Westgate, in her last will and testament of 1 January 1492/3 left 40s. to the friary for the repair of the cloisters there (*ad reparacionem Clauster' ibidem*).[34]

While many of the testators who left bequests to the friary came from the immediate area of the Burnhams, others came from farther afield. The chaplain Nicholas Palmere of Great Snoring, who it was noted above, left 6s. 8d. to the gild of St Mary in the friary in 1387, also bequeathed 6s. 8d. to Robert de Merston, prior of the Carmelite order at Burnham, and a similar sum to every one of five other named friars of the house.[35] In addition, he left 3s. 4d. to each of the other friars not named and 2s. to each of the novices there. He also made several other bequests, variously to the Franciscans at Walsingham and to the parish churches at Great Snoring and South Creake. Most significantly, he wished for his body to be buried in the friary at Burnham Norton.[36] In 1465 John Bettes of East Barsham, by his last will of 15 December, left 3s. 4d. to the friary at Burnham Norton and a similar sum to the Austin friars of Lynn Bishop (*de Lenne Episcopi*), as well as 40d. to other friaries in the same town.[37]

On 13 December 1457 Nicholas Esthawe, a wealthy inhabitant of Bishop's Thornham, 6 miles to the west of Burnham Norton, left 26s. 8d. (or 2 marks) to the friars of Burnham, one of a large number of pious and charitable bequests contained in his testament.[38] To the parish church of Thornham, where he wished to be buried in the porch, he left 40s. for tithes forgotten and 10 marks for the upkeep of the fabric. As well as his bequest to the friary of Burnham Norton, he seems to have had a general affinity for the mendicant orders, leaving 20s. to the Franciscan convent at Walsingham, 26s. 8d. to the Austin Friars of Lynn, and 6s. 8d. to every other house of friars in the county of Norfolk. He showed concern too for the secular church: as contributions towards the maintenance of their fabric, he left 20s. to Brancaster church, 13s. 4d. each to the churches of Titchwell and Holme, 26s. 8d. to Hunstanton church, and 10s. each to the churches of St Peter and St Andrew in Ringstead, plus 6s. 8d. to every other church in the North-West Norfolk hundred of Smithdon. He also left 10s. to every township in the same hundred, according to their size, while his other charitable bequests included 26s. 8d. to the gild of the Holy Trinity of Lynn, and 6s. 8d. to the gild of the Holy Trinity of the Soken there (*de Soken ibidem*).[39] He had a particular consideration for his home town of Thornham, leaving 3s. 4d. to every gild there, together with 13s. 4d. towards the upkeep of the gild hall at Thornham, as well as a generous grant of 12d. to every household (domicilio) in the town on the day of his death (Farnhill 2001: 205).[40]

If Nicholas Esthawe had sympathetic leanings towards the mendicant orders, William Fowler of Burnham Norton appears to have had an even closer affinity with the house of Carmelites there. He made his testament on 16 January 1446/7, and this was followed by a last will (*ultima voluntas*) dated 1 February 1446/7.[41] In his testament he expressed his wish to be buried within the friary at Burnham Norton and also nominated Nicholas Merlow, the prior of the house, as one of his three executors, the other two being his wife Margaret and William Grome. In addition, he left 6d. to the altar of St Margaret's Church in Burnham Norton, and 6d. towards the reparation of the church, together with a further 6d. for a light for the Blessed Virgin Mary there. By his last will, he gave instructions that his houses, then in the hands of his feoffees, one of whom was the same William Grome, should be sold and that the profits from the sales should be distributed, with 20s. to be given to the friary at Burnham Norton. He also wished that one mass for his soul should be said annually in St Margaret's Church, Burnham Norton by a friar from the convent. Fowler died shortly after making these provisions, as both the testament and the *ultima voluntas* were proved on 16 February 1446/7 (Foss 1986, vol. ii, part 1: 255–6, cited in Copsey 2017: 6–7).

Surviving probate records shed light on the piety of other local families, including the Gigges family of Burnham Overy, several members of which made bequests to the friary. By his last will and testament of 11 March 1466/7, Thomas Gigges of Burnham St Clements (Burnham Overy) left legacies in money to the church of St Clement where he wished to be buried. Also, he left funds to the poor house in the parish of St Clement and St Andrew, Burnham; the church of St Margaret, Burnham Norton and the church of Stanhoe; but only 2s. to the Carmelite priory of Burnham.[42] His namesake and descendant Thomas Gegges, in his testament of 1 December 1505, also wished to be buried in St Clement's Church, to which he left several legacies, namely 6s. 8d. for the 'hey awter', 6s. 8d. for the reparations to the church and 20d. each for 'oure ladye lyte ther' and 'the gylde of Seynt John ther'. He also made bequests to several other churches, including those in the parishes of Burnham Norton and Burnham Sutton, Wood Norton and Guist. To the friary at Burnham Norton he left 6s. 8d.:

> that is to say, to the prior 12d., and to every friar being a priest 4d., and to every novice 2d., and to their pittance 12d., they to keep a solemn *dirige* and a mass for my soul and all my friends' souls at my burying.

He further bequeathed 12d. 'to the 'gylde of oure lady ther', anticipating the bequest of 8d. which John Fenne granted 'to the Friers gild' in August 1517.[43]

Some five years later, by her will and testament of 20 September 1510, Thomas Gegges's widow Olyve, who like her husband desired burial in the Lady Chapel of Burnham Overy Church, left 20s. to the 'hey altare' there, 20s. for church reparations and 3 coombs of barley, which were to support the 'comyn lighte of the same churche'. A further 5 coombs of barley were given to 'the gild of Sancte Clement', while she also left 6 coombs of barley to 'the whight friers of Burnham'.[44]

From the magnitude of the pious bequests in their wills, the Giggeses, the Goldales and the Esthawes of Thornham appear to have been families of some local substance, although of a social status somewhat lower than the de Calthorpes and the de Hemenhales. W J Blake's observation on the difficulties of identification of medieval Norfolk families posed by scanty surviving documentary information has been noted above (see note 3). However, something is known about the Gigges family, who from the early fifteenth century appeared as manorial lords in North Norfolk, having risen from yeoman stock to become one of the wealthiest families in Wighton, their prosperity largely derived from sheep farming. On 28 August 1423 John Gygges of Wighton made a grant to Thomas Gygges of Burnham St Clement of the manor of Vewters, with its appurtenances in the various Burnhams – Overy, Thorpe, Sutton, Ulph, St Edmund, Westgate, Norton and Deepdale – as well as in Holkham, North Creake, Wighton and Warham.[45] Although there seems initially to have been a dispute over the title to this estate, by the middle of the 1440s Thomas was sufficiently established there to be described as a 'gentilman', a title also enjoyed by his descendant Thomas Gegges, the testator in the will of 1 December 1505.[46] The Gigges family was clearly further down the social order than the successors of the two founders of the friary, but nevertheless by the fifteenth century they had risen to hold manorial interests in the Burnhams and elsewhere. This placed them among the lower gentry in Norfolk, giving them a certain local standing and influence, and also making them friary benefactors of middling rank.

Conclusion

During its three centuries of existence, the Carmelite friary of Burnham Norton regularly benefited from bequests made by benefactors great and small, who from the evidence of the surviving wills and testaments came mainly from within the area of the Burnhams or slightly beyond. Some bequests were expressly and solely made to the advantage of the friary; in other cases, legacies left to the friary might form part of a wider series of pious bequests offered to a broad range of ecclesiastical and charitable bodies in Norfolk. It was possible for a testator to make provisions primarily for the maintenance of his or her parish church and to wish for burial there, but at the same time ensure that some gift was made to the friars of Burnham Norton. Clearly the friary featured prominently in the lives of local people, so much so that several chose to be buried there.

The friary was a beneficiary in wills and testaments almost up to its dissolution, although as happened in the case of some other religious houses, there was a tailing-off of donations in the early 1530s, as a probable result of political uncertainties surrounding Henry VIII's policies towards the Church.[47] The last known bequests to Burnham Norton Friary were made by Geoffrey Goldale's testament of 28 September 1532, while Dugdale noted that Henry Fermor was also a benefactor in the same year.[48] One commentator has suggested, 'after this date, few donations were given to any religious houses because it was thought politically unwise' (Francis 2003: 12).

Medieval friaries did not depend on revenue from estates, but survived mainly on charitable donations, thus the mendicant orders preferred to settle in towns and cities, where the bulk of the population – and potential income – was to be found and also where the greatest spiritual needs possibly were. Being in a more remote, rural location meant that the opportunities for attracting income were lower for the Carmelites at Burnham Norton than for a friary located in one of Norfolk's urban centres, at Norwich, Lynn, Great Yarmouth or Thetford. Nevertheless, Burnham Norton Friary's survival until its dissolution in the sixteenth century is testimony to the fact that it was a sustainable entity. Of course, because of the disappearance of the friary's own archives, we have no precise information about many of its sources of income, such as the alms which the brothers must have regularly received. Persons travelling the ancient routeway from Walsingham, via Peterstone and Burnham Overy, through Burnham Norton and on to Brancaster might often have broken their journey at the friary and given alms. Those seeking to benefit from the papal indulgence of 1392, by making a specific journey to visit the friary's chapel, certainly gave alms. Members of the local community in the Burnhams and beyond may have occasionally made charitable donations to the house, other than in their wills. In the absence of firm evidence, we can only speculate on all this. However, surviving probate records, in several archive repositories, have permitted us a reasonably detailed insight into the long series of charitable bequests that Burnham Norton Friary received from the earliest days of its existence, and which continued for almost 300 years.

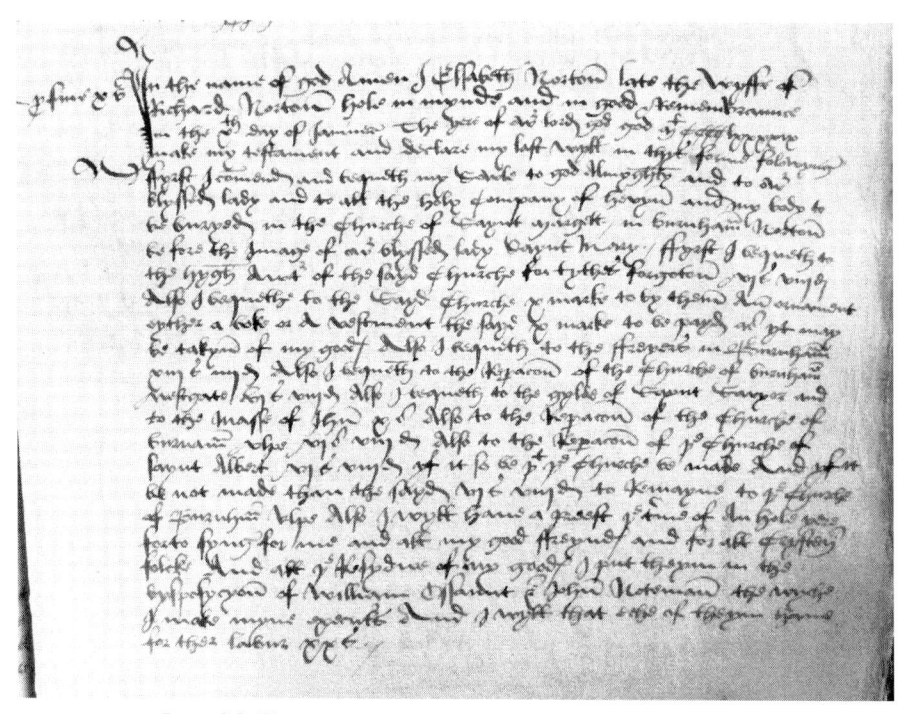

Figure 8.3 The testament and last will of Elsabeth Norton, 1499.
Norfolk Record Office, NCC Will Register Sayve, fo. 32.

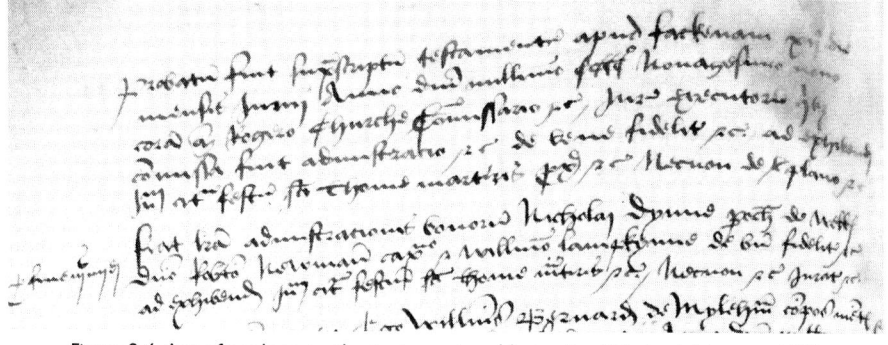

Figure 8.4 Act of probate to the testament and last will of Elsabeth Norton, 1499.
Norfolk Record Office, NCC Will Register Sayve, fo. 32v.

Appendix: Transcript and translation of the testament and last will of Elsabeth Norton, 1499[49]

Transcript[50]

[fo. 32] In the name of god Amen. I Elsabeth Norton late the Wyffe of Richard Norton hole in mynde and in good Remembraunce on the vth day of Januier the yere of owr lord god god [sic] m^lCCCClxxxxix make my testament and declare my last Wylle in thyt forme folowyng.[51]

Fyrst I commend and bequeth my Sowle to god Almyghty and to owr blyssed lady and to alle the holy Company of hevyn and my body to be buryed in the Churche of Saynt margett in burnham Norton be fore the Image of owr blyssed lady Saynt Mary. Fyrst I bequeth to the hyghe awter of the sayd Churche for tythes forgoten vj s viij d. Also I bequeth to the Sayd Churche x marke to by them An ornament eyther a boke or a vestment the sayd x marke to be payd as yt may be takyn of my goodes. *Also I bequeth to the Freyers in Burnham xiij s iiij d.*[52] Also I bequeth to the Reparacion of the Churche of burnham Westgate vj s viij d. Also I bequeth to the gyld of Saynt Savyor[53] and to the Masse of Jhu' x d. Also to the Reparacion of the Churche of burnham vlpe vj s viij d. Also to the Reparacion of the Churche of saynt Albert[54] vj s viij d yf it so be þat þe Churche be made And yf it be not made than the sayd vj s viij d to Remayne to þe Churche of Burnham Vlpe. Also I Wylle haue a preest þis terme of An hole yere forto syng for me and alle my good Freyndes and for alle Crysten folcke. And alle the Resydwe of my goodes I put theym in the dysposycyoun of William Ossament and John Noteman the whyche I make myne executors. And I wylle that eche of theym haue for ther labor xx s.

[fo. 32^v] *Probatum fuit suprascriptum testamentum apud Fackenam xij° die mensis Junij Anno domini millesimo CCCC Nonagesimo nono coram etc. Rogero Churche Commissario etc. Jurati executores quibus commissa sunt administracio etc. de bene fideliter etc. ad exhibendum Inventarium ante festum Sancti Thome martiris proxime etc. Necnon de plano [et vero compoto] etc.*

Translation

[fo. 32] In the name of God, Amen. I, Elsabeth Norton, late the wife of Richard Norton, whole in mind and of good memory, on the fifth day of January [in] the year of our Lord God 1499, make my testament and declare my last will in this form following.

First, I commend and bequeath my soul to God Almighty and to our blessed Lady, and to all the holy company of Heaven, and my body to be buried in the church of Saint Margaret in Burnham Norton, before the image of our blessed

Lady, Saint Mary. First, I bequeath to the high altar of the said church, for tithes forgotten, 6s. 8d. Also I bequeath to the said church 10 marks to buy them an ornament, either a book or a vestment, the said 10 marks to be paid as it may be taken from my goods. Also I bequeath to the friars in Burnham, 13s. 4d. Also I bequeath to the reparation of the church of Burnham Westgate, 6s. 8d. Also I bequeath to the gild of Saint Saviour and to the Mass of Jesus, 10d. Also to the reparation of the church of Burnham Ulph, 6s. 8d. Also to the reparation of the church of Saint Albert, 6s 8d, if it so be that the church be made. And if it be not made, then the said 6s 8d [is] to remain to the church of Burnham Ulph. Also I wish to have a priest [for] this term of a whole year, to sing [masses] for me and all my good friends and for all Christian folk. And all the residue of my goods, I put them at the disposition of William Ossament and John Noteman, whom I make my executors. And I wish that each of them [shall] have 20s. for their labour.

[Translation of the (Latin) Act of Probate:]

[fo. 32ᵛ] The above written testament was proven before us, Roger Churche, Commissary, etc., at Fakenham, the twelfth day of the month of June 1499. The executors to whom administration was committed were sworn etc. to display well and faithfully etc. the inventory before the feast of St Thomas the martyr next [i.e., Thomas Becket, 29 December], etc. And also [to render] a plain [and true account], etc.

Notes

1 The *Valor Ecclesiasticus* of 1535 recorded the friary as drawing income from:

> 40 acres of land in Burnham Norton, 26s. 8d.
>
> 14 acres of land in Burnham Westgate, 9s. 4d.
>
> 14 acres of land in Burnham Sutton, 9s. 4d.
>
> Total income: £2. 5s. 4d.

(Caley and Hunter 1810–34: iii, 371, cited in Copsey (2017: 9). Dugdale gives the same gross value, but says that 'the clear value, after reprises, was £1. 10s. 8½d' (1846, vol. 6, pt. 3: 1573). The friars may have also gained some income by controlling the ford on the River Burn, near the Brothercross at Burnham Overy (Francis, 2003 [2018]: 10).

2 '*Radulphus Hempnale et Guilhelmus Calethorpe, viri nobiles et aurati equites, conventus Brunhamie fuere fundatores primi, anno domini, 1241*' ('Ralph Hempnale and William Calethorpe, noblemen and knights, were the first founders of the convent of Burnham, in the year of the Lord 1241' (Egan 1969: 160; Copsey 2017: 3); and see also Blomefield (1805–10, vol. 7: 19); Dugdale (1846 vol. 6, pt. 3: 1573).

3 Roger Virgoe remarked that 'very little is known about the private lives of even the most notable figures of late medieval Norfolk' (1969: 406). See also Blake (1951), especially p. 247, for his observation that 'it is very difficult to place the families below the rank of knights, our information is so scanty', thus there are many instances where names are the only

things that we know for certain about some medieval Norfolk gentry.

4   Blomefield (1805–10 vol. 3: 486): '*Walter de Suffield*, so called from *Suffield* in *Norfolk*, the place of his first preferment, his sirname being *Calthorp*, a name assumed by his ancestours from *Calthorp* in *Norfolk*, the ancient place of their residence, which manor this bishop bought, with that of *Erpingham* ... and settled them on *William de Calthorp*, his nephew and heir, and on the heirs of *William*; so that by this and other gifts, he raised his family very considerably'. See also Harper-Bill (2004).

5   In 1271 Henry III granted a William de Kalethorpe a weekly Saturday market at his manor at Burnham and a yearly three-day fair there, to be held on the vigil, the feast and the morrow of St Peter ad Vincula (31 July–2 August) (CCR 1257–1300: 174).

6   Grid ref. TM 2396 9451.

7   The de Hemenhales bore the Fitzwalter arms of or, a fess between two chevronels gules, differenced with the addition of three escallops argent on the fess.

8   Grid ref. TG 1856 3183.

9   In the same way as the de Hemenhale arms were based on those of their feudal superiors, the de Calthorpe arms reflected that family's own feudal connexion with their de Warenne overlords, differencing the de Warenne arms of chequy, or and azure with the addition of a fess ermine.

10 *Mortmain* literally means 'dead hand', signifying that if an estate were owned by a religious corporation which never died, there would in consequence be no liability for feudal incidents, levies which were usually payable to the crown upon the inheritance of a successor to an estate. In such circumstances a religious body would hold the estate in perpetuity, and since it had no successors no taxes were paid, leading to a permanent loss of revenue to the monarch.

11 It is not absolutely certain that de Hemenhale's final resting-place was in Westminster Abbey. His supposed burial there is unattested by a tomb or brass, or by any of the various tomb-lists held in Westminster Abbey Muniment Room, the British Library, the College of Arms or All Souls College, Oxford. However, several scholarly commentators (e.g. Cockayne 1910–98, Vol. 3, p. 345; Saul 2001, p. 26, n. 93; Curran 2016: 72) have suggested that this was the case. They ultimately based their statements on a tradition stemming from *Holinshed's Chronicles of England, Scotland and Ireland* (Vol. 4, p. 790), where it was claimed that 'the fift and last husband of ... Ione de la Poole, was sir Iohn Harpenden knight, buried at Westminster, besides hir first Husband [Sir Robert de] Hemandale'. However, Barbara Harvey more cautiously observed that 'the tradition, *if correct* [author's italics], establishes Hemenhale's place of burial as the chapel of St John the Evangelist in Westminster Abbey' (1977: 370).

12 His testament in Latin, together with his last will in French, are in TNA, PROB 11/1/32.

13 Blomefield remarks of Creake Abbey (1805–10 vol. 7: 77), that 'It appears by the will of Sir *William Calthorp of Burnham Thorp*, dated *May* 31, in the 10th of *Henry* VII. that many of his ancestors were here buried, in a chapel' and mistakenly cites as his authority as '*Regist. Poppy Norw.*' of 1501. However, Calthorpe's testament of 1494 is actually in NRO, NCC will register Wolman, fos 206–7, with probate granted on 27 November 1494. Calthorpe laid down that 'my pore body be buryed in þe Whyte Freyres at Norwych where þe place of my sepulture is made'. The church at Burnham Thorpe houses the magnificent military brass of another Sir William de Calthorpe (d. 1420), Blomefield noting that 'Sir William's will is dated December 19, 1420, and proved on the 29th of the said month, wherein he appoints

Sibil his wife and Will. Paston, Esq. executors, and was buried in Burnham Thorpe chancel' (Blomefield 1805-10, vol. 6: 516-17; NRO, NCC will register Hirning, fo. 75).

14 Although Dugdale says that 'It was a foundation of some importance' (1846, vol. 6, pt. 3: 1573).

15 De Suffield's Latin testament, which is held in the NRO, NCR, 24B/2, and also analysed in English in Blomefield (1805-10 vol. 3: 487-92), uses the terms 'friars preachers' and 'friars minor' (*fratrum predicatorum et minorum*), rather than Dominicans and Franciscans, which may have caused Bryant or Dugdale some confusion. Of course, Dugdale might have had sight of a document which no longer survives.

16 She was the widow of William de Ufford, second earl of Suffolk, KG (1338-82).

17 Probate was granted on 4 June 1499.

18 NRO, NCC will register Surflete, fo. 38^v (note that this register has an alternative foliation number in pencil at the bottom of each recto folio, this folio being fo. 66^v, according to this revised sequence). Probate granted 7 May 1429.

19 Probate granted 25 May 1499.

20 NRO, NCC will register Robinson, fos 44^v-45. Last will made 21 August 1517, probate granted 20 March 1520/1. See also Farnhill (2001: 179).

21 NRO, NCC will register Harsyk, fo.81^v. His testament was made on 17 February 1386/7 and probate granted after 25 March 1387, but a torn section in the folio means that details of the day and month are missing.

22 NRO, ANF will register Liber 4 (Grey) fo. 336. Will and testament made 15 October 1476, probate granted 2 December 1476.

23 NRO, ANF will register Liber 4 (Grey) fo. 305^v.

24 NRO, NCC will register Norman, fo. 22. Probate granted 7 January 1486/7.

25 NRO, NCC will register Wolman, fos 213^v-214. Probate granted 14 May 1495.

26 NRO, NCC will register Popy, fos 92-92^v. Testament made 14 December 1501, probate granted 4 January 1501/2.

27 NRO, NCC will register Coppinger, fos 60^v-62. Goldale's testament, in English, was made on 4 September 1514 and probate was granted during an undated episcopal visitation.

28 For example, in 1450, John and Katherine Goldale donated to St Margaret's Church, Burnham Norton its magnificent hexagonal wineglass pulpit, decorated with images of the four Latin Doctors of the Church, as well as those of the two donors (Bryant 1914: 26). Throughout the fifteenth and sixteenth centuries, members of the family made occasional appearances in deeds, e.g., TNA, WARD 2/52A/178/66; WARD 2/53/178/242; WARD 2/53/179/70.

29 *Oxford English Dictionary (OED)*: '3. coomb | comb, n. A dry measure of capacity, equal to four bushels, or half a quarter'. It was in use in Norfolk as a dry measure from the Middle Ages until the late eighteenth century.

30 NRO, NCC will register Mingaye, fos 16^v-18. Probate was granted on 15 November 1532.

31 NRO, NCC will register Heydon, fo. 42. Probate was granted on 8 June 1374. The small Carmelite friary at Blakeney was founded 1304-16 (Knowles and Hadcock 1971: 233; Cox 1906: 425).

32 NRO, NCC Will Register Sayve, fos 32-32^v. The Appendix contains the full text, with translation, of Elsabeth's testament and last will.

33 In St Mary's Church, Burnham Westgate, where Blomefield records that 'In this church were the guilds of St. Salvator, and that of St. Margaret' (1805-10, vol. 7: 38). See also Farnhill (2001: 179).

34 NRO, NCC will register Wolman, fo. 85. She requested to be buried in St Mary's Church, Burnham Westgate, to which she bequeathed 3s. 4d. to the high altar and 6s. 8d. for reparations, while she also left a similar sum of 6s. 8d. to Plumstead Church. She died shortly after making her will, probate being granted on 5 February 1492/3.

35 Great Snoring is 11 miles south-east of Burnham Norton.

36 NRO, NCC will register Harsyk, fo.81^v. The friars named were John Wauncy, Adam de Desenham, Thomas de Bucham, Thomas de Harpelee and Thomas de Baunsted.

37 East Barsham is 12 miles south-east of Burnham Norton. NRO, NCC will register Cobald, fo. 79^v. Probate was granted on 8 March 1465/6.

38 A probate copy of Esthawe's testament, for which the probate was granted on 13 January 1457/8, is at TNA, E40/13389, with a published description under A.13389, in Maxwell Lyte (1906: 503-4). There are also two paper copies of Esthawe's *ultima voluntas*, or last will (under the name Nicholas Esthagh), which bears the same date as the testament, in NRO, HARE 5975, 227X3 and HARE 5976, 227X3. The latter also contains an act of probate dated 13 January 1457/8 and a memorandum that the testament was annexed.

39 That is, South Lynn, or *le Soken de Suthlenne*. See Hillen (1907: 167, fn *). I am grateful to Susan Maddock, honorary research fellow, School of History, University of East Anglia, for pointing out this reference and also for indicating occurrences of the term in primary sources in the King's Lynn Borough Archives, such as in the Hall Book in 1465 (KL/C 7/4, p. 219). The gild of the Holy Trinity in the *Soken* was associated with All Saints' Church there (Farnhill, 2001: 202).

40 There were four of them: Holy Trinity, St John the Baptist, St Mary and St Thomas the Martyr.

41 While the terms 'will' and 'testament' are now generally interchangeable in modern usage, originally there were differences between them: testaments dealt with personal estate or property, which could be bequeathed, while wills were concerned with real estate, which was devised. However, devise of real estate by will was not acknowledged under common law until the enactment of the Statute of Wills in 1540, thus before that date, a will (sometimes termed a 'last will' or *ultima voluntas*) might often be drafted after the making of a more formal testament, to which it could function as an appendix. Indeed, by the fifteenth century, probate courts increasingly came to treat last wills made in this way as codicils to the testament. The medieval distinction between wills and testaments thus became blurred over time, and the term 'will and testament' subsequently came into common use in testamentary documents (see Camp 1974: x; Sheehan 1963: 193-5).

42 The church of St Andrew's, Burnham Market was consolidated with St Clement's in Burnham Overy in 1421. NRO, ANF will register Liber 4 (Grey) fo. 185. Probate was granted on 17 May 1467. A probate copy of the will is held at TNA, E40/5971, with a published description as A.5971 in Maxwell Lyte (1900: 247).

43 TNA, E40/12778, with a published description as A.12778 in Maxwell Lyte (1906: 381-2). See note 19.

44 NRO, NCC will register Johnson, fo. 24. Probate copy at TNA, E40/12352, with a published description as A.12352 in Maxwell Lyte (1906: 293–4).

45 The testator in the will and testament of 11 March 1466/7. Walter Rye tentatively suggested that this Thomas Gigges was the same as Sir Thomas Gigges of Rollesby whose daughter Eleanor married Roger Townshend of Raynham in about 1444 (1913: 246). TNA, WARD 2/52A/178/70.

46 In December 1442 Thomas conveyed the same estates to feoffees to uses (TNA, WARD 2/52A/178/76). He possibly felt obliged to do so to in order to protect the property from the threat of legal challenge, as there may have been some dispute as to title. A clue may lie in the fact that on 7 August 1423, by letters of attorney given at Sculthorpe, John Drewe, clerk, appointed Thomas Jygges as his attorney, 'to take seisin of the manor of Veautres with all messuages, lands, tenements, etc., in Burnham St Clement, Burnham Thorp, Burnham Sutton, Burnham St Andrew, Burnham Ulph, Burnham Westgate, Burnham Norton, Burnham Deepdale, Holkham, Wighton, and Warham, which lately belonged to Simon Veutre' (TNA, E 42/340; WARD 2/51/177/39). Whatever the situation, it appears to have been resolved in January 1446, when Sir Richard Veutre quitclaimed Thomas Jiggys, gentleman, of land in the manor called 'Veutres', lying in the townships previously mentioned and which had formerly belonged to Simon Veutre, but excepted lands which were seised or held by Margaret, widow of William Lexham, of Burnham Westgate, Roger Coltham, of Burnham Thorpe, and William Grome, of Burnham Norton (TNA, WARD 2/51/177/50).

The younger Thomas was himself thus described in a deed of 1505, by which Robert Gygges of Wyghton enfeoffed him, Olive his wife, Roger Touneshend, esquire, Thomas Blakeney, esquire, and Christopher Gygges of Wyghton, 'gentilman', of three pieces of land in the fields of Burnham Overy (TNA, E 40/11071). For background information on the Gigges family, see Trend 2017: 118–68, with generational details and a family pedigree, 1383–1506, at 198–203.

47 Although not in the case of some London friaries (Holder 2011: 21).

48 NRO, NCC will register Mingaye, fos 16^v–18; Dugdale (1846 vol. 6, pt. 3: 1573).

49 NRO, NCC Will Register Sayve, fos 32–32^v.

50 This transcript preserves the original spelling and punctuation of the manuscript, although full stops have been used in place of the short, oblique feint slashes by which the scribe indicated the end of a sentence or section. The original use of capital letters has also been retained. Where the intended full forms of words are known for certain, abbreviations have been extended.

51 The date in the will is given as 5 January 1499, thus we would assume that the correct New Style date is 5 January 1500. However the date of probate, which of course is later than the date on which the will was made, is given as 12 June 1499. On the basis that the date of probate was recorded by the commissary and therefore had official status, it has thus been assumed that the will was executed in 1499, especially since all the acts of probate in this register are dated 1499.

52 Author's emphasis.

53 The gild of St Saviour in St Mary's Church, Burnham Westgate (Farnhill 2001: 179).

54 The parish church of Burnham Sutton, dedicated to St Ethelbert or St Albert, which has been ruinous since before 1845.

9

The Carmelite journey 1247 – 1538: with a focus on Burnham Norton

Brendan Chester-Kadwell

Overview and historical background

The Carmelites arrived in Western Europe in the middle years of the thirteenth century. They were Christian hermits from Mount Carmel who later became known as the Whitefriars from the colour of the mantle, part of their habit. By the early years of the fourteenth century they, along with the other Orders of friars, had become an effective element in the pastoral work of the Western Church. As one of the early foundations, the friary at Burnham Norton contributed to the Carmelite 'mission' until their activities in England were suppressed in 1538 — a period of about three hundred years.[1]

Inevitably, the role that the Carmelites assumed, both in England and the rest of Western Europe, was conditioned by the challenges and opportunities present in the Western Church over this extended period. The thirteenth century had opened with what could best be described as a crisis for the Western Church, where confidence in its ability to effectively fulfil its pastoral role had faltered. The nature of this crisis and its implications for the life of the Church is essential for understanding the context within which the mendicant way of life developed. The issues that caused the leaders of the late twelfth and early thirteenth-century Church to fear for its future and the actions they took to address them will be examined more closely in the following paragraphs.

The late twelfth-century crisis in the Western Church

There were four areas of concern that together were perceived critical to the survival of Christendom — 'Christendom' being the term given to the earthly manifestation of the Latin Church. These were: the existential threat posed by the military advances of Islam (and later, the Tartars); the worry that four civilisations were in various ways superior to Christendom — Ancient Rome, Byzantium, Islam, and Judaism; failures within the organisation of the Western church — especially laxity within the monastic orders, the quality of the secular clergy, and the wealth and worldliness of many churchmen; and finally, concerns over the morality of the laity and guilt over the failure of Christians to do better in spreading the gospel and converting non-believers (Duffy 1997: 112-14; Knowles 1950: 78-9; Tanner 2016: 57-8).

It is easy to forget that in the Middle Ages, prior to the emergence of European imperialism from the late sixteenth century, Christianity was not yet a global religion (Tanner 2016: 57). The recapture of Jerusalem by Saladin in 1187 had sent shockwaves through Western society. Subsequently, the surviving Latin (Christian) states in the Holy Land remained under immense pressure after the failure of the Third Crusade to recapture the holy city (1189-92). Christianity had largely been pushed out of North Africa and was struggling for dominance in the Iberian Peninsula. The capture and sack of Budapest in 1241 by the Tartars only exacerbated the fear that Christendom might be overcome completely. The cultural achievements of Islam and Byzantium, the greater success of members of the Jewish faith over Christians in many fields, and the failure of the medieval West to achieve the cultural heights of ancient Rome, all fed into this neurosis.[2]

Within Christendom itself, the moral laxity and worldliness of many churchmen brought the Church hierarchy into disrepute with devout Christians. This in turn helped undermine lay morality and the often ill-prepared parochial (parish) clergy were not well equipped to provide the pastoral care and levels of catechesis (teaching of the rudiments of the faith) required. By the second half of the twelfth century, future leaders of the Church were already recognising that something needed to be done to reform Christendom. Thus, when Lothar of Segni (later to become pope Innocent III (1198-1216)) was studying at the University of Paris in the late 1180s, the theological emphasis was on practical themes such as the celebration of the liturgy, lay morality and the reform of the Christian life (Duffy 1997: 112). Innocent III became a great reforming pope who put his energies into the practical business of pastoral and spiritual renewal, culminating in the Fourth Lateran Council (1215) —although, it took a further eighty years for the reforms of the council to be effectively implemented.

The brilliance of Innocent III was his ability to harness the often spontaneous and free ranging religious energy of the times for the broader needs of a reforming Church. For example, he saw in Francis of Assisi a charismatic force and was able to find a positive ministry for it — at a time when Christendom was being threatened from within by the heresy of the Cathars (Albigensians) and others.[3] Innocent III enabled the formation of the mendicant orders at a time when it wasn't obvious what this would actually mean, although he didn't himself live to see the fruit of their work.

Origins and influence of the mendicant orders

To understand the path that the Carmelites took in the second half of the thirteenth century, it is necessary to look at how their commitment to a lifestyle evolved from 'hermit' to 'mendicant'. The mendicant 'charism' — evangelising poverty — arose nearly fifty years before the arrival of the Carmelites in England, out of the need for church renewal and was developed first through the Franciscan and Dominican Orders. The pattern of ministry that they established became the model for the Carmelites as well.[4] The emergence of the Franciscan (the Friars Minor) and Dominican friars (the Order of Preachers) in the early years of the thirteenth century was to revolutionise apostolic ministry in the Western Church as the two orders of friars swept across Europe out of Italy and Southern France respectively.[5] It is difficult to fully comprehend the impact of these two movements upon their contemporary Church without an extensive analysis. However, a flavour can be gained by looking at just one or two of the novel aspects of both orders.

In the case of the followers of St Francis, their way of life was directly inspired by Francis's own personal vision of striving to imitate the way that Christ led his own life as closely as possible. Unlike the established monastic orders --or the less formal eremitical associations that had become so popular by the opening years of the thirteenth century -- this was not to be achieved by the withdrawal from the world and circumscribed by a formal Rule that legislated for every action of the daily routine:[6]

> While he [St Francis] made a full and explicit allowance for a contemplative and solitary element in the body of his followers, Francis was always clear in his declaration that it was their vocation as a body *to preach to all men, faithful and heathen alike*, both by the *example of a life of service lived among men*, and by direct, formal, widespread *evangelisation...* They formed from the first one great body, not an aggregate of communities; they were not bound as individuals to perpetual stability in a particular home, nor even to continual residence in any home; in the eyes of St Francis, the friar, like his Master, had no home, and must be *prepared to spend much of his life on the road or as a pilgrim lodger...* (Knowles 1950: 120) [author italics]

This Franciscan ideal was to become the norm for all the orders of friars, although each had their own particular way of expressing it.

The Order of Preachers emerged under the guiding hand of the Spanish priest, Dominic Guzman (St Dominic), during the same period as the Friars Minor, but from very different origins. Dominic himself was an Augustinian or black canon who, circa 1205-7, undertook to convert the Albigensian heretics of Languedoc, gathering around himself a group of fellow preachers, the basis for his future institute. In 1216, in a response to a request from Pope Innocent III Dominic chose the Rule of St Augustine of Hippo for his Preachers.[7] In 1220, at the first general chapter for the order held at Bologna, the Order of Preachers adopted the poverty of a mendicant order (Knowles 1950: 146-9). St Dominic developed a clear forward-looking set of objectives for the Preachers. Their Augustinian origin was reflected in the way that all the Dominicans were ordained priests (unlike the Minors who were, at least at the outset, lay brothers). This in turn influenced how the Minors (and indeed eventually all of the other mendicant orders) developed their ministries. By the end of the thirteenth century members of these orders were increasingly ordained to the priesthood, and promotion to positions of authority within the orders eventually depended on achieving this status (Andrews 2015: 20).

The significance for the pastoral life of the thirteenth-century Church of the coming of the orders of friars was in their independence from the regular diocesan structures. This was a completely new concept, which although taken for granted in the later church was truly revolutionary in its day. By the nature of its organisation, the diocesan structure was static and conservative and the more fluid organisation and independence of the friars were both a challenge and an irritation for the secular clergy. Until then the pastoral care of the faithful was almost exclusively the responsibility of the diocesan bishop and his assistant clergy (principally the order of presbyters, or priests).

The diocese was a territorial unit sub-divided into parishes each also with established territorial boundaries. The parish priests were responsible for the 'cure of souls' of all those living within the boundaries of their parish.[8] This was a responsibility that they guarded jealously and which caused considerable friction from time to time between the secular clergy and the friars throughout most of the thirteenth century. Generally speaking, on the other hand, the friars were mobile, ultimately responsible to the Pope, but with authority to work in an individual diocese with the bishop's permission. However, in practice, the mendicants were virtually autonomous and eventually established a parallel pastoral system that worked alongside the normal parish system. However, it took some time to achieve this (Knowles 1950: 186).

The contentious issues, between the mendicants and the secular, parish clergy, principally concerned the administration of the key elements of pastoral care and who could perform them. These included the ritual fulfilment (celebration) of the sacraments, as well as other functions such as burials and most importantly the right to preach.[9] Some commentators have emphasised the financial implications of the rivalry between parochial clergy and the friars (for example, the competition for income). However, the arguments raised by both sides at the time seem to suggest that what was at least as much at stake was the exercise of authority and the maintenance of influence. The principal areas of contention were centred on preaching, the hearing of confessions (sacrament of penance), and the status of the mendicant orders at the Universities. The history of the dispute between the mendicants and the secular clergy was complex and changed in its nature over the period in question. In the early decades of the thirteenth century many secular clerics had neither the skill nor desire to preach or administer the sacrament of penance to the degree required by the Lateran Council. Reforming bishops often welcomed the opportunity to use the friars to fulfil the obligations laid upon them to evangelise the laity. It was not until the middle decades of the century, when a better-prepared body of secular clergy was available that a stronger resentment against the friars emerged. This resentment was strongest in the towns where the friars were present in numbers and appeared to be in direct competition for the loyalty of the laity: it was fuelled by the fear of a loss of authority and income by the diocesan parish clergy (Copsey 2004: 5; Knowles 1950: 182-6).

The controversy around the issue of how pastoral care was provided by the secular clergy and the mendicants lasted until the end of the thirteenth century. It was eventually resolved by the issuing of *Super Cathedram* in 1300.[10] The contents of *Super Cathedram* was summarised by Knowles as follows:

> The mendicants were free to preach in their own churches and in public; they were forbidden to appear in parish pulpits without invitation. For confessions, the provincials were to choose a number of their subjects in each diocese proportionate to the population; these were to be presented to the bishop for licence; he might reject individuals, but was not free to reduce the agreed numbers; should he refuse to grant any licenses the requisite faculties were supplied from the plenitude of the Apostolic power. The friars were at liberty to bury all who might wish, but a fourth part of all dues and legacies were to go to the parish clergy. (Knowles 1950: 186).

This accord may partially account for the way that the mendicants in general — and perhaps the Carmelites in particular — developed their ministry during the course of the fourteenth century.

A brief introduction to the journey of the Carmelites

It was under the challenging circumstances of the thirteenth-century Church that the Carmelites needed to establish their place as an authentic part of western Christendom, and to find a sustainable way of life. This propelled them away from an eremitical, contemplative Christian lifestyle to one of involvement in the world, active in evangelising, becoming what is known as mendicant, living by receiving alms.

The second great challenge for the Order was maintaining their connection with the lay community through the turbulence of the fourteenth century. This was a task that they had in common with the other mendicant orders as well as the secular clergy. The most difficult trial was that presented by the great plague which affected the whole of Western Europe and later became known as the Black Death. The psychological effect of the Black Death on the general population was to focus their spiritual lives more acutely on the eventuality of their own death and their concern for a heavenly reward after death. This impacted strongly on the ministry of mendicant orders generally and the friars at Burnham Norton would have responded to this need. [11]

During the course of the fourteenth and fifteenth centuries, despite the difficulties, there was a period of expansion and consolidation by the mendicants in which the Carmelites shared. This established a positive, mutually beneficial relationship between the laity and those responsible for their pastoral care that was based on respect and reflected the interests of both parties.

However, towards the end of the fifteenth century and into the sixteenth, the Renaissance, with its roots in the revival of knowledge in the culture of classical Greece and Rome, brought about a new way of thinking that became known as humanism. Humanistic writings challenged many of the established practices of the Church that had been developed in the later Middle Ages, encouraged the reform of religious institutions and set the seeds of both the Catholic and Protestant reformations. In England, the impetus for reform together with the particular political circumstances of the time, led to the Protestant Reformation in the English Realm and the abolition of the religious orders there.

Burnham Norton Priory was closed in 1538 following the Act of Suppression of religious houses (1536).[12] The last years of the Carmelite mission in Burnham Norton would have been dominated by disputes and uncertainty, which would also have challenged the religious beliefs and practices of the laity. This is the background against which the relationship between the Carmelites and the lay communities developed, and eventually ended.

The Order of Carmelites and their rise in Western Europe 1247 to 1326

The process by which the Carmelites became an active part of the Western Church was complex. They were a new religious order to Western Europe in the 1240s, but with a longer history in the Middle East (see Chapter 6).[13] Under pressure from the Islamic re-conquest of the Crusader states, groups of Carmelite brothers migrated west in the late 1230s, some of whom arrived in England about 1242. As hermits on Mount Carmel their charism was to bear witness through the contemplative life — one directed outwards towards God, but also inwards to themselves. Once the Order had emigrated to the West the emphasis changed quite quickly to one of pastoral engagement with the wider community at its core. This change in focus is understandable considering that the Order's arrival coincided with an unsettled period in the history of the Church. The Carmelites came to recognise that their charism was changing to meet the needs of the contemporary Church — which was learning to accommodate itself to radical change in how pastoral care for the laity was delivered.[14] The process by which the change to the Carmelite charism happened is obscure, but the Mitigation to the Carmelite Rule that was adopted in 1247 laid the foundation for their emerging ministry. About eighty years later in 1326 Pope John XXII (1316-34) included the Carmelite Order in the provisions of *Super Cathedram*, which marked the full integration of the Order into the pastoral mission of the Latin Church.

Initially, upon arrival in the West, the Carmelites received support from Pope Innocent IV (1243-54) through a series of letters encouraging the bishops to welcome them as brethren seeking refuge from the Holy Land. In 1247 Innocent IV gave approval to a change to their Rule allowing them to establish houses where they could and not just in 'desert areas'. Slight as this 'mitigation' now seems, it allowed the Carmelites to move into the vicinity of towns and was the first formal step of their journey to a more communal lifestyle committed to poverty and the evangelisation of the laity (see also Chapter 6). This was a period of challenging re-adjustment for an Order founded on a response to a charism of contemplation, now being led towards a response to a charism of evangelical poverty. The Franciscans, who had faced a similar dilemma in their early years as an order, had established the path that the Carmelites were now committed to following. However, the Carmelites had not at that time received a final confirmation of their permanent establishment as an Order.

It was at the Second Council of Lyons, called by Pope Gregory X (1271-76) in 1274, that the continued existence of the Carmelite Order was being called into question. Many of the bishops were worried by the continued proliferation of new religious congregations: partly because it was more difficult to manage a large number of diverse religious communities but also because of the fear of heresies, and the desire to ensure that religious communities were following a sensible, prudent and effective Rule. The establishment of new orders had technically been forbidden by Canon 13 at Lateran IV in 1215, but largely ignored (Copsey 2004: 6-7; Tanner 2016: 59). The bishops' determination at Lyon II to enforce Canon 13 proved very troubling for the Carmelites who struggled to prove that their Rule had been established before the key date of 1215. However, whilst a number of orders of mendicants (for example, the Friars of the Sack) were directed to adopt one of the approved mendicant rules, Lyon II placed the Carmelites (and also the Augustinians) on probation pending further consideration. In the event Pope Boniface VIII (1294-1303) lifted this threat to the Carmelites' independence in 1298 (Andrews 2015: 21).

When Boniface VIII defined the role of the other mendicant orders with regard to the secular clergy in *Super Cathedram* in 1300, the Carmelites were not included. In 1317, under a different pope, John XXII, the Carmelite Order was granted exemption status (meaning they were responsible directly to the Pope and not local Bishops). In 1326 Pope John added the Carmelites to the *Super Cathedram* of 1300. This completed their promotion to mendicant status and the Carmelites could thereafter claim parity with the Dominicans and the Franciscans, in at least the legal sense. However, official recognition of the Order by the ecclesiastical authorities was only one element in the process of acceptance. A working relationship with the secular clergy, which the Papal Bull *Super Cathedram* defined was also essential, but as important was recognition and promotion by the laity.[15]

Inclusion in *Super Cathedram* marked the final stage of the acceptance of the Carmelites as a permanent mendicant order, but there were many staging posts along the line. Critical to the Carmelites' success was their willingness to adapt to the pastoral needs of the Church during the later decades of the thirteenth century, thereby demonstrating the Order's ability to fulfil the mission required of it. As the thirteenth century proceeded, the pastoral role of the mendicant orders crystallised around their expertise as preachers and confessors. The Carmelites also needed to develop the requisite skills and their success was marked by a number of Papal bulls. In 1253 Pope Innocent IV confirmed the Order's right to preach and hear confessions (*Devotionis Augmentum*), followed in 1261 by a bull of Alexander IV (*Speciali Gratia*) allowing the laity to frequent Carmelite churches — both essential for the development of the Carmelite pastoral endeavour.[16] The hearing of confessions, with its central role in spiritual direction, was considered to be a priestly function and preaching was normally reserved to the higher clergy. It is not surprising, therefore, that the Carmelites increasingly became clericalised with many more ordinations to the priesthood. At the same time the role of the lay brothers diminished and they were formally excluded from positions of authority soon after the Council of Lyons. By 1281 lay members were excluded from the higher functions of the Order and had lost the right to vote at local, provincial and general chapters (Andrews 2015: 20).

The establishment of the Carmelites in Burnham Norton

The apparently steady advance of the Order in its progress to become mendicant must have involved many difficult decisions. In Burnham Norton the re-establishment of the friary on its new site in 1253 raises a number of interesting possibilities. Although it was not unusual for early foundations to be re-established on more favourable sites later, this usually applied to post-mitigation urban foundations. Burnham is the only one of the early, pre-mitigation friaries to have been treated in such a way, based on the suggested date of its original foundation (Egan 1992: 18-19).

The move seems to have involved leaving an isolated marshland site for a new one central to the Burnham settlements.[17] It has been amply demonstrated in the first three chapters of this book that the Burnhams were active in trade at this period, well endowed with churches (almost on an urban scale, Chapter 2), and well connected with other North Norfolk ports and destinations such as Walsingham (Chapter 1). The decision to move to the later site suggests that the intention was not just one of choosing an alternative (perhaps more convenient) rural site, but to a busier (more 'urban') location better suited to the mendicant life style. The foundation of the Carmelite friary in Norwich, three years later in 1256, supposedly by brethren from Burnham, might also reasonable be considered part of a strategic plan of expansion by the Order into Norfolk (Egan 1992: 66).[18]

The desire to expand and found new houses, however, relied on the support and generosity of the laity. Therefore, the Carmelites needed to be both responsive to their needs and effective at meeting these needs, as well as fulfilling the expectations of the church authorities. Whilst the thirteenth century laid down the foundations of their new role, it was developed subsequently in a relationship with the laity, of both high and low 'estate', in the fourteenth and fifteenth centuries.[19]

The advent of change to the pastoral practices of late medieval religion

There were important developments in the pastoral practices of the medieval Church during the thirteenth, fourteenth and fifteenth centuries. Some of these developments were under the direction of the bishops, such as the seminal Decree Twenty-one adopted at Lateran IV; some were in response to momentous events such as the Black Death and the impact of climate changes, while others occurred in response to the rise of literacy, and the increasing self-awareness and independence of the individual worshipper. These factors will be explored in more detail in this section. It will enable a better understanding of how the practical work of the Carmelites at Burnham Norton, and elsewhere, enhanced the lives of the communities in which they served. In this section, the church community is described as the 'people of God' or 'the Christian people': this embraces all those baptised into the Catholic faith and who retain equality as members of the Church regardless of their function within the structures of the Church.[20]

In order to understand the work of the mendicant orders, and the Carmelites in particular, in late medieval England, it is necessary to describe the differential status of pastor and laity. It is easy to imagine that in theological terms the gulf between the lay and the clerical state was a wide one. In fact the difference between the two was one of function rather than precedence. That is, the ordained minister was marked out by the sacrament of Ordination as befitted his role (or function) in the life of the Church, but there was an equality of membership of the Church between laity and pastor through the sacraments of Baptism and Confirmation, which was shared by both. While it is true that the lifestyle of the laity was different in many respects from that of the religious and secular clergy, they shared a common spiritual life as Christians. Both were products of the same community and all shared a common system of belief. It was the function of the pastor that separated him from the lay member, but the laity also had a role to play in the operation of the church community without which the work of the pastor would become inoperable. Pastoral care may have been organised by the bishops and their clerical helpers, but it needed the willing participation of the laity to succeed; it was a partnership between those who provided pastoral care and those who benefited from it. During the course of the thirteenth century the role of the laity had begun to become more central to how local church communities were organised and pastoral care received. As the contribution of the laity developed further during the fourteenth and fifteenth centuries the practices that developed became normalised into the life of the Church.[21]

Decree Twenty-one of the fourth Lateran Council (1215)

The pressure for change in how the laity were catechised and concerns about the ability of the clergy to cope with the demands that such a change required, were reflected in the teaching of the Fourth Lateran Council.[22] The Council Fathers passed a number of decrees that either directly or indirectly affected the pastoral care of the laity (Tanner 2016: 59). The principal one was Decree Twenty-one that stipulated that anyone over the 'age of reason' must go to confession once a year and receive communion at Easter, as follows:

> All the faithful of both sexes shall after they have reached the age of discretion faithfully confess all their sins at least once a year to their own (parish) priest and perform to the best of their ability the penance imposed, receiving reverently at least at Easter the sacrament of the Eucharist, unless perchance at the advice of their own priest they may for a good reason abstain for a time from its reception; otherwise they shall be cut off from the Church (excommunicated) during life and deprived of Christian burial in death. Wherefore, let this salutary decree be published frequently in the churches that no one may find in the plea of ignorance a shadow of excuse. But if anyone for a good reason should wish to confess his sins to another priest, let him first seek and obtain permission from his own (parish) priest, since otherwise he (the other priest) cannot loose or bind him.

Whilst this seems slight in the telling, the Decree goes on to lay out the pastoral approach to be adopted:

> Let the priest be discreet and cautious that he may pour wine and oil into the wounds of the one injured after the manner of a skilful physician, carefully inquiring into the circumstances of the sinner and the sin, from the nature of which he may understand what kind of advice to give and what remedy to apply, making use of different experiments to heal the sick one. (Decree 21, IV Lateran Council 1215 in Schroeder 1937).

The pastoral implications for implementation were great and led to considerable effort on the part of the English bishops to ensure that Decree Twenty-one, and others designed to improve the quality and education of the clergy, were successful.

The expectation was that a parish priest would give each individual penitent a thorough examination of their conduct according to the person's circumstances, testing their knowledge of the Faith and calculating an appropriate penitential solution to aid improvement. The additional workload for the parish priests was considerable, especially as the education of many was inferior to the demands of the task. It is not surprising, therefore, that many of the English bishops turned to the Friars Preachers and Friars Minor to help with confessions in the decades following Lateran IV. For example, Robert Grosseteste, bishop of Lincoln (1235-53), Alexander Stavensby of Lichfield (1224-38), Roger Niger of London (1229-41) and William of York, bishop of Salisbury (1247-56), amongst others, were all recruiting the friars to preach and assist in the hearing of confessions in their diocese (Knowles 1950: 180-81).[23]

The demands on the laity were also great, for they had to be instructed in the right form of making their confession and they would be expected to learn their catechism and specific prayers, principally the *Pater Noster* but also where possible the Creed as well. The absolution of sins involved the person in the performance of a penance, the severity of which varied according the nature of the sin and the personal circumstances of the individual. Deciding the nature of the penance was complicated and required the kind of specialist training that the friars had received. The confessional became an important occasion for catechesis as well as the mechanism for absolving the repentant sinner from the guilt of those sins committed after baptism (Rahner and Vorgrimler 1983: 370).[24] Textbooks were written to aid the less well-prepared or experienced confessor to make the best decision when administering the Sacrament of Penance and to aid him in the process of catechising the laity (Duffy 1992: 54-7).

Encouraging the laity to take part in the Sacrament of Penance more frequently, with its linkage to the process of catechesis, also complemented the significance of the Mass in the lives of the Faithful: the celebration of the Eucharist retained its centrality in medieval Christian worship.[25] However, the vigour of the policy of more frequent confession and the emphasis on perfection may have deterred ordinary lay folk from receiving frequent communion out of a sense of unworthiness — even though the policy was intended to encourage more frequent communion. As the active participation by the laity in the actions of the Eucharist declined in response to changes in liturgical form and the continued use of Latin as the liturgical language, its place was largely taken by the practice of private devotions during Mass prior to the reception of communion (Metzger 1997: 130-6).[26]

To some extent the development of private devotions during Mass by the laity demonstrated a commitment to their own spiritual development, as well as reflecting the growth in literacy during the course of the fourteenth and fifteenth centuries. In England, a late thirteenth-century Mass book in the vernacular (actually a modified translation of a twelfth-century work originally written in French) was available for those who could read — generally known as the Lay Folks Mass Book.²⁷ This book was frequently updated until the early years of the sixteenth century. It was subsequently joined by other English prayer books related to the Mass that became more widely available following the invention of printing. Over the same period literacy became more common in terms of the general population and devotional texts and pictures were widely circulated (Duffy 1992: 213, 221; Tanner 1984: 110-11). In this way, worshippers could follow the Order of the Mass in much the same way that lay people did up to modern times during the Catholic Mass in Latin (Duffy 1992: 117-123). This continued to be the practice until the introduction of the vernacular following the Second Vatican Council in the 1960s.

Figure 9.1 The seven sacraments font at St Mary's Church, Great Witchingham, Norfolk. The image for baptism is shown on the central panel of the font in this illustration.

The Black Death (accentuated by the social and economic effects of fourteenth-century climate change) was a seminal moment in late medieval experience that significantly shifted contemporary perceptions of the proper attitude of the believer towards God. After this time the emphasis was more strongly on the penitential, an appreciation of the 'Passion of Christ' as an 'act of redemption', and the significance of humankind's 'receptiveness to saving grace'. Although Catholic doctrine had not changed, the agony of Christ's 'passion' and the guilt of sinful Man were themes that appeared more frequently in preaching and catechetics. In Catholic iconography the symbols of the passion and representations of the Last Judgement become more generalised and were strongly reflected in contemporary church art, devotional practices, and in the promulgation of the scholastic theologian's teaching on purgatory.[28] However, the iconography of the period (where it survives) needs to be considered alongside the central liturgical action of the Mass and the sacraments (see Figure 9.1).[29]

Burnham Norton friary and the pastoral life of the local community

Determining the exact nature of the relationship of the Burnham Norton friary with the laity and secular clergy of the Burnhams, during the 300-year period when the friars were there, is largely a matter of conjecture. However, a range of activities can be discerned, some based on documentary evidence — such as wills. Other involvements that are less tangible can be sensibly proposed, given that the life of the contemporary Catholic Church in many ways has not shifted from its essential base of sacraments, prayer and ministry. In a wider liturgical sense, lay participation took place through processions and other pious acts in common surrounding various seasonal celebrations. This would include the great feasts of the Church like Easter (particularly Palm Sunday), Christmas, and Corpus Christi. However, there would also be lesser feasts (often with a mainly local significance,) such as the dedication of a parish church or, as may have been the case of the friary at Burnham Norton, a locally significant feast in honour of St Mary.

One particular form of lay participation was attendance at events when the friars preached. These it seems were very popular, lively and up-to-date, if the evidence of a letter from the prior of the Cathedral Priory written in 1360 is to be believed; even though requests for sermons in wills are generally lacking in Norfolk Wills (Tanner 1984: 11). The friars at Burnham Norton had extended their preaching nave in the fourteenth century, which suggests they were attracting a larger congregation to hear their preaching.

Norman Tanner's study of the late medieval church in Norwich provides a basis for understanding how this relationship might have developed in the Burnhams (Tanner 1984: 11). The friary at Burnham Norton benefited from bequests in the wills of local people and by benefactors in other Norfolk places. John Alban has identified a total of twenty-three extant wills between 1374 and 1532 referring to Burnham Norton friary, of which twenty relate to the fifteenth and early sixteenth century (Chapter 8).[30] This is a very small number compared with the sample of over 900 used by Tanner in his study and the Burnham wills cannot be seen as a statistically meaningful sample (Tanner 225). However, as might be expected, the Burnham sample does generally reflect the same pre-occupations of the Norwich testators and a commonality of practices. By their nature, wills deal widely with the testators' concerns for their spiritual wellbeing — especially in relation to the matter of intercession by the living for the soul of the deceased, but also in other ways. First, money is frequently bequeathed for prayers for the benefit of the soul of the testator, including Masses and sometimes Divine Offices.[31] In Burnham these bequests tend not to be particularly lavish compared to those in Norwich, but this is not surprising. There is no direct mention of chantries and the sums would have been too small for a chantry to be founded. However, it is possible that some were intended to be joined to existing chantries. In fact there is no surviving evidence for the founding of chantries at the friary. However, the role of the Gild of St Mary of Burnham may have carried out the function of organising many of the activities associated with perpetual chantries including prayers for the souls of deceased members and benefactors (Duffy 143).

The Gild of St Mary was one of a number of local gilds in Burnham parishes, although it was the only one that is known to be directly associated with the friary. Interestingly, it was located in the chapel over the entrance way into the friary, in the chamber above the surviving entrance immediately in front of the west end of the friary church. Like other gilds it was likely to have been under lay control and this might well be why it was not within the church itself but on the boundary of the precinct. It was clearly focused on attracting pilgrims as is attested by a grant from pope Boniface IX in 1392 that granted an indulgence to anyone visiting the chapel over the gatehouse and giving alms at specified times.[32] It is likely that the friary benefited from the offerings given to the Gild of St Mary by saying masses, preaching and offering other services.[33]

Besides the burials of members of the Carmelite Order, others also sought to be buried at the friary church at Burnham Norton. Those seeking interment were more generous in their bequests, but these larger sums were probably intended to cover the cost of burial, as was often the case in Norwich (Tanner 99). Most of those from outside the order were lay people, although there was at least one member of the secular clergy as well (probably an under representation as the number of wills available to be examined was rather small). In an area with so many parish churches it would be helpful to have a clearer indication of the nature of the relationship between secular clergy. The vicar of Burnham Overy, Thomas Lowe (or Laws) in 1429 left 40d. to the friars (although he may have been an Austin Canon rather than a member of the secular clergy). Although not conclusive, this indicates that relationships could be reasonably good at least.

The Burnham parishes were small and within easy walking distance of each other. Land holdings were also interspersed over a number of parishes, so that manorial estates tended to be fragmented geographically over the Burnhams (Chapters 2 and 3). This may partly account for why in so many of the wills the testator left bequests to a number of the parish churches and gilds in several parishes. This might reflect the likelihood that a person's place of residence could be in one parish, but the land they owned, or the work they did, occurred in one or more other parishes. Testators might identify with a number of church communities under these circumstances. The habit grew up (especially after *Super Cathedram*) for individuals to seek a confessor other than their parish priest and this offered the option to confide in someone outside their own parish of residence. The existence of Burnham Norton Friary, Peterstone Priory at Burnham Overy and North Creake Abbey, provided alternative opportunities for pastoral care in the immediate locality. This would have provided a greater choice of spiritual adviser, preachers, and places of burial. This presented a greater freedom for lay people at a time when the laity was becoming more active in the life of the parishes and more practised at managing their own spiritual devotions.

It must not be forgotten of course that the resident Burnham lay community was only a part of a much wider 'congregation' for the friars. The Burnhams were a vibrant, economically significant part of Norfolk, welcoming itinerant pilgrims en route to and from the Walsingham shrine to Our Lady and the sailors who regularly came and went with ships and cargo in all the important ports and creeks along the north Norfolk coast.

The existence of the friary for 300 years, the significant walled site and the building of a not insubstantial church and gatehouse attest to the long-lasting success of the Burnham Norton Carmelite friars. Many of the men who joined them had the names of local Norfolk men, as is attested in the list of friars in Fr Copsey's Annex.

A reprise: the end of the Carmelite Mission in England

The reforms that were set in motion by the Fourth Lateran Council had become entrenched in the life of the local church by the end of the fifteenth century and must have seemed immutable. However, new forces were at work and new ideas, inspired by the Renaissance, were being explored. The *humanae litterae* promoted by Renaissance scholars were based on the civilised and civilising literature of classical Greece and Rome, through which they saw a new potential in human beings (MacCulloch 2017:4). Humanist thought drew inspiration from Greek scripture and the writings of the Church Fathers rather than the scholastic theologians of the medieval Universities. In the writings of a theologian like Erasmus of Rotterdam (1466-1536) humanism became a powerful motivator for reform of perceived abuses in the Church. Erasmus strongly influenced Sir Thomas More (1478-1535) with whom he also collaborated. Thomas More, perhaps the most influential of the English Humanists, was a controversial figure in his own day and has become so again with the renewed interest in the English Reformation. (It is an irony that Erasmus, the thinker who inspired More the ardent Catholic, should also have inspired Martin Luther the Protestant reformer.)

The Humanist targets were not new and included practices that many believed had become steeped in superstition, were associated with abuses such as those around the sale of indulgences, as well as the power-broking and worldly ambitions of the senior clergy (Duffy 2017: 22-4). Erasmus's dislike of many of the aspects of pilgrimage, for example, would clearly have an impact on the way of life of a community, like that at Burnham Norton, that had become to whatever extent dependent upon the flow of pilgrims. However, this does not support a long-held view that late medieval Catholicism was a corrupt religion and a spent force waiting to be overturned (MacCulloch 2017: 3; Duffy 1992: 4-5). The aim of Catholic reformers like Erasmus and More was to change the Church from within; for them church unity and loyalty to the papacy were essential elements of the Universal Church (Duffy 2017: 21).

Clearly, the medieval Church's mission (and by association that of the mendicant orders) would have been challenged to adapt to a renewed understanding of the Christian practice and ethics, even without the actuality of the Protestant Reformation. Catholic humanism was a transforming (and reforming) philosophy that it might be argued would have changed the way that the Carmelites (as also other mendicant orders) promoted their ministry to the English — even without the trauma of Tudor dynastic politics.

In the event, the work of Carmelites in England was brought to a sudden end when the Order was effectively expelled from the country with the dissolution of their houses in 1538-9. The Carmelite friary at Burnham Norton was dissolved at an unspecified date towards the end of 1538. However, men started to drift away from the house before the dissolution was enacted — for example, Robert Ryder, prior, sought a benefice in 1536, two years after all the orders of friars came under direct royal control and Richard Makeyn was granted permission to become a secular priest some months before the friary was dissolved (see Copsey's Chronology in the Annex).

The mendicants were a phenomenon of the late medieval Catholic Church, with their origins in the thirteenth century. The Fourth Lateran Council of 1215 set the agenda for reform (and in particular pastoral reform) for the remainder of the medieval period and the mendicant orders were central to that endeavour. The Carmelites (comparative late-comers) saw their own future as an Order within that context. However, it would be a mistake to see their development as simply a response based on survival. Their success depended on earning support from the laity and in managing to inspire men to become one of them. The rapid expansion of the Order in the second part of the thirteenth century bears witness to that success. Dedication, enthusiasm and a degree of charismatic ardour must also have been present.

In the context of the Carmelite priory at Burnham Norton there are few specific examples of the relationship between the friars and the local community in the surviving documentary record. However, much can reasonably be conjectured, and the development of the friary site itself bears testament to the success of this House in the fourteenth century. It demonstrates the support the friary received from local benefactors as well as the more itinerant population. The Burnham Norton friars worked hard and successfully, sustaining themselves and their local community through three challenging centuries on the North Norfolk coast. Clearly a set of shared beliefs as well as a shared way of life underpinned the world of the Burnhams, where a dynamic local Carmelite House was an intrinsic part of the fabric of society, at least until 1538. The physical remains of this life can still be seen in a deserted field in the Burnhams, over four and a half centuries later.

Notes

1. Since the schism of the eleventh century, the Christian Church had been split into the Eastern Orthodox Churches and the Western Latin (or Catholic) Church – from the Latin catholicus meaning Universal. However, the 'mission' of all the Churches was believed to be the duty to preach the gospel of Jesus Christ as described in the New testament of the Bible in all places, at all times, to all peoples. The practical result of fulfilling this mission expressed itself in pastoral ministry, and this was the life adopted by the Carmelites. The use of the term 'pastoral' was based on a New Testament metaphor of the shepherd and the flock and whilst primarily focused on the care of the spiritual needs of people it also embraced their physical needs as well.

2. The threat of a comprehensive invasion of Europe from the east was only lifted following the defeat of the Ottoman fleet at Lepanto in 1571 by the fleet of the Holy Alliance formed by Pope Pius V (1566-72).

3. The word heresy comes from the Greek αι϶ρεσισ which means a choice. It signifies an error in matters of faith. It did not indicate a rejection of Christianity itself, but was seen as a stumbling block to true belief. In practice, heresy was only condemned by the Church when it was expressed publicly and was seen as leading others astray. (Rahner & Vorgrimler 1983: 206-8)

4. 'Evangelising poverty' embraces the idea that the message of the Gospel could be spread effectively by those living a life of voluntary poverty and who had dedicated themselves to the task of taking Christ's message to all (evangelising). Those Orders, dedicated to this way of life lived by begging alms and became known as mendicant from the Latin, mendicus, a beggar.

    Charism comes from the Greek χαρισμα, a 'gratuitous gift'. In New Testament theology it refers to the operations of the Spirit of God on the individual believer. The purpose of the charism is to make the Church visible and credible as the 'holy People of God'. The originality of the movement for evangelical poverty in the Middle Ages was regarded by the Church as a new impulse of God's Spirit to confront the Church in a novel way. For a more detail definition of charism see Rahner & Vorgrimler 1983: 64-5.

5. The followers of St Francis became known as the friars minor, or 'little brothers' which reflected their humility and poverty. The group of men recruited by Dominic Guzman were known as the Order of Preachers from their principal interest in that activity.

6. St Francis originally envisioned a company of brothers who would commit primarily to a way of life rather than a formal rule. However, so as to receive the formal recognition he needed to see his ideal prosper, Francis had to accept a formal rule, even if this were different from the typical monastic Rule that had gone before.

7. This was in keeping with the ordinances of the Fourth Lateran Council (1215), which had decreed that a new order should choose an existing rule rather than create a new one (Canon 13).

8. The Latin *cura animarum* may be properly translated as the 'care of souls', which better expresses its Latin original meaning.

9. Since its inception, the Church has used certain formal practices to demonstrate the concept of the 'working of God's grace' in the lives of its members. These were the foundations of the life of the Church, although it was not until the eleventh century that these different performances were given the common name of 'sacraments'. By the late

Middle Ages the seven sacraments of baptism, confirmation (regarded as completing baptism and preparing the person for their future role as Christians), the Eucharist (or Holy Communion – sharing in the community of Christ's disciples by participating in a 'thanksgiving' meal, receiving Christ's 'body and blood' under the appearance of bread and wine), penance (confession), matrimony, orders (the consecration of an individual to a particular office in the Church), and the anointing of the sick were recognised as the central elements of the sacramental life of the Church.

10 The papal bull *Super Cathedram,* first promulgated in 1300, was the accord that reconciled the mission of the Franciscan and Dominican friars (and eventually the Carmelites and other mendicant orders) with the diocesan bishops.

11 The plague first occurred in England 1348/49 with a return in the 1360s, but there were later more localised outbreaks over an extended period into the fifteenth century. The initial occurrence of plague devastated the population and the clergy were more adversely affected than the lay population because of their pastoral role (Knowles 1961: 8-13). The friars at Burnham would inevitably have been drawn into this dangerous ministry although we do not know the rate of death amongst them. In the bishops' registers there is a sharp rise in the number of clergy, especially religious, who received permission to hear confessions in each diocese. The mendicant friars (and Carmelites) feature prominently in these lists and the rapid change-over of confessors would suggest that many of the priests ministering to the sick also caught the plague and died. Frequent changes in the handwriting in the bishops' registers suggests that the scribes were also victims of the plague (the author's thanks to Fr Copsey for pointing this out).

Estimates concerning the number of people who actually died of the plague, either in terms of its first outbreak or in those recurrent events of plague thereafter, is complicated because other factors also influenced the fall in population. Scholars have been divided over the years about the effect of losses directly attributable to the plague, which range from about 20% to 60% of the population. Therefore, settling on a figure of at least 30% is probably reasonable – especially bearing in mind that the plague was a recurring factor over an extended period of time. The broader argument is about late medieval demographics, an especially complex area of study that demonstrates that population variations cannot be tied to one single cause. A clear introduction to the subject can be found on pages 30-44 in Postan M M, 1975. *The Medieval Economy and Society,* Harmsworth: Penguin Books.

12 This, however, is a gross simplification. All the orders of friars had been brought directly under royal control in 1534 and did not figure in the Act of 1536. On the 6th February 1538, Richard Ingworth, bishop of Dover was appointed visitor for all the friaries that were then systematically closed by his authority during the course of 1538/9 (Knowles 1971: 177, 360).

13 The Carmelites had been founded as an eremitical order on Mount Carmel in Palestine receiving their first Rule in the early thirteenth century, probably sometime before 1214 (scholars have differed in their opinion on the exact date, ranging from 1207 to 1212). See Chapter 6.

14 The challenge for the Carmelites was a paradigm of the challenge for the whole Church, in as much as the survival of both depended on a more effective engagement with the lay community.

15 Although the state of the laity has often been seen as an inferior one, in terms of ecclesiastical authority their acceptance is essential. See Rahner and Vorgrimler 1983: 35.

16 For a full list of papal bulls in this time period concerning the Carmelites see the Index

Chronologicus: In primam partem bullarii Carmelitani Rome 1715.

17 The first foundation was at a place called Bradmer, supposedly located in Burnham Norton but not positively identified, although it is thought to have been on the coast (see Chapter 3). In the later years of the thirteenth century the Norfolk coast was subject to a rise in sea level and several very damaging tidal surges. This may have been a contributory factor in the decision to moving further inland, but as the new friary was also adjacent to the boundary with land prone to inundation, this is unlikely to have been the sole reason for the move (see Chapter 1).

18 Lynn, founded circa 1260 (Egan 1992: 2) might also be seen as part of this original initiative. Norwich became the lead priory for Norfolk and the head of the Eastern Distinction (one of four subdivisions of the English province). However, Burnham retained some importance, being the burial place of two provincial priors in the thirteenth century, and between 1346 and 1486 hosted the general chapter seven times (Copsey, the Annex to this volume). General chapters were ideally held every three years and they met in Burnham at approximately twenty-year intervals (Andrews 2006: 22).

19 'The mendicant orders had to "quest" or travel around the surrounding villages looking for alms to support the community. Each Carmelite house would have its own defined area, so as not to clash with any nearby Carmelite communities. However, the quest was not simply a financial collection, the brothers doing the quest would often be entertained in local houses and, doubtless they were pressed to share what information they had about local events, news, etc. In a sense the brothers acted as a 'local newspaper'.' (Fr Copsey, personal comment, 28/08/19.)

20 In this respect, this follows Fr Tanner's study of the church in medieval Norwich which 'is principally concerned with what Christianity meant to and how it was practiced by the mass of citizens rather than with the network of buildings and ecclesiastical authorities which made up the outer face of the local church' (Tanner 1984: i).

21 Much of the research that has attempted to explain the nature and extent of lay participation in the organisation of the local church has occurred relatively recently and typically published over the last thirty-five to forty years. Themes that emerged from religious adherence and sentiments as explored, for example, in Eamon Duffy's seminal work *The Stripping of the Altars: Traditional religion in England 1400-1580* (1992) or, more locally to Norfolk, Norman Tanner's *The Church in Late Medieval Norwich 1370-1532* (1984) is also instructive.

22 Catechesis from the Greek κατηχησισ meaning oral transmission. Catechetics was the process of explaining the basics of Christian belief to the laity. It also involved encouraging lay people to reinforce their understanding by remembering certain prayers, such as the pater noster (Our Father) and the creeds – statements of the basic tenants of the Church, especially the Nicene Creed formulated in 325 AD.

23 Walter de Suffield, bishop of Norwich 1244-57, was also one of the thirteenth-century university trained bishops noted for his piety, diligence, and pastoral care of the poor. For example, in 1249, bishop Suffield founded the Hospital of St Giles principally for the relief of the poor and in his will of 1256 he left over £375 for poor relief (Rawcliffe and Wilson eds, 2004: 74 and 314). Suffield was venerated as a saint after his death, although he was never cannonised (Tanner 2004: 148). Although he is not recorded as having specifically invited the mendicants into his diocese, the Carmelites were settled in Norfolk during his episcopacy and he is reputed to have been supportive of them (see Chapter 8).

24 In order to facilitate lay engagement in the process of confession and catechesis that

emerged from Lateran IV, the laity needed to have confidence that what they said in the confessional would not be used detrimentally to their interests. The second element of Decree Twenty-one was designed to ensure that the confidentiality of the confessional would be preserved. It reads as follows:

> ... let him [the confessor] exercise the greatest precaution that he does not in any degree by word, sign, or any other manner make known the sinner, but should he need more prudent counsel, let him seek it cautiously without any mention of the person. He who dares to reveal a sin confided to him in the tribunal of penance, we decree that he be not only deposed from the sacerdotal office but also relegated to a monastery of strict observance to do penance for the remainder of his life. (IV Lateran Council 1215 in Schroeder 1937: 236-296)

25 In the Mass the faithful came together as a community to hear the Good News and to celebrate in thanksgiving the redemptive act of the Death and Resurrection of Christ. For this reason, the central act of the Mass – receiving Holy Communion – is also often referred to as the 'Eucharist' (from the Greek ευχαριστειν meaning 'to give thanks'). See also note 9, above.

26 The story of how the liturgical celebration evolved from Christian antiquity to the thirteenth century is complex and varied. An overview is available in Joseph Jungman's *The mass of the Roman Rite: Its Origins and development* Vol. 1, 223-45. 1992. The thirteenth-century reforms developed the liturgy in particular ways that eventually altered the design of churches as well. For example, in the parish church the position of the principal altar at the east end of the nave, which was the norm in the eleventh and twelve centuries began to migrate eastwards under the influence of the liturgical developments and eventually into the chancel, back up against the east wall. This, of course, changed the design of the buildings, which reinforced the separation of the congregation from the priestly function in the sanctuary. Certainly by the end of the thirteenth century the transition in parish churches was complete. The way that liturgical changes altered the design of churches is summarised in Theodor Klauser *A short History of the Western Liturgy*, 1969, pages 97-101. The particular design of friary churches also exemplifies the effect of function on church design. Friary churches were in effect two churches separated by the walking place – the one to the east for the community, the one to the west for the laity, designed for public preaching. This is exactly the arrangement at Burnham, as far as is known.

27 A published version of *The Lay Folks Mass Book: or the manner of hearing Mass in four texts*, which included some additional material such as the Offices and notes by Thomas Frederick Simmons, was published by the Early English Text Society in 1879.

28 The concept of purgatory and the theological reasoning behind it are complicated. It basically concerns the perfection of the individual whose sins are forgiven and has in that sense been 'justified', but has not yet reached that stage of perfection needed to be capable of the beatific vision (coming face to face with God). (See Rahner and Vorgrimler 1983: 426-7). The possibility of the salvation of the human soul was believed to be made possible through the passion, death and resurrection of Jesus Christ (the Act of Redemption), which opened up the possibility for humankind to receive (as a free gift – grace) the necessary justification. What was called the Last Judgement indicated the final confirmation of the fate of each individual soul.

29 Likewise, the seven sacraments of the Church, which were seen as essential to salvation for the Christian, were difficult theologically to represent pictorially since the fundamental essence of the sacraments were to be found in the words uttered, whilst the actions had the secondary function of helping to make clear what the words signified.

Consequently, as the meaning of these essential liturgical actions were not easily explained iconographically, they were only infrequently represented in church art or architectural form, although the fonts in some churches did attempt to do so (for example at Great Witchingham and Little Walsingham, both in Norfolk). Such representations as there are record some aspects of the enactment of ritual rather than the full meaning of the sacrament itself. For this reason, reliance on artistic survivals alone is an inadequate source for understanding what ordinary people thought and believed. In practice, therefore, it is necessary to look elsewhere than the iconography for an understanding of the common belief system at the time.

30 The wills recorded in Alban's paper go into considerable detail regarding their contents. It is not the intention, therefore, to repeat that detail here but rather to offer a general summary and how this reflects upon the relationship of lay, religious and secular clergy.

31 Since at least the fifth century the Catholic Church had taught that the κοινωνια, the New Testament concept of the 'community' of God's people, included both those still living and those who had departed. Thus it was believed that the living could pray for the souls of those who had died, and conversely, the 'saints' (those who had died and were justified by God) could intercede for the living. Saying Masses for the souls of the dead became a common practice in the later Middle Ages and often led to the establishment of 'chantries' – special arrangements that ensured that the departed soul would be prayed for. The wealthy might even pay for a special chapel to be constructed within the church, but often the money was simply used to pay the stipend of the priest who undertook the task.

32 *Cal. Papal Letters*, (London, 1902), iv, 433. A translation of the Latin text can be found in the Annex, in Fr Copsey's Chronology for the year 1392. An 'indulgence' was originally the remission of public penance imposed by the Church for a certain period (thus it is often expressed in years and days). Indulgences were associated with the performance of good works and logically applied to the penance imposed for sins for which the recipient had already repented. However, the system was open to abuse and misunderstanding and became the target for criticism in the period leading up to the Reformation. (Rahner & Vorgrimler 1983: 238-9)

33 'The guilds also could have their monthly dinners in the community refectory and there is a record (in Coventry) of the Carmelite novices singing during the meals.' (Fr Copsey, personal comment 28/08/19.

Bibliography

Note: the bibliography to the Annex is provided separately on page 248.

Primary sources *(with abbreviations used in the text)*

UNPUBLISHED

Kew: The National Archives

C143/26/12 Grant by Walter de Calthorpe and William Reynald of land in Burnham to the prior and Carmelite friars there, 1297.

E40/5971 Will of Thomas Gigges of Brunham St Clements, 1467.

E40/11071 Feoffment by Robert Gygges of Wyghton to Thomas Gygges of Brunham Overey, 'gentilman', 1505.

E40/12352 Probate copy of the last will and testament of Olyve Gygges, 1510.

E40/12778 Items relating to the will of Thomas Gegges, 1505-6.

E40/13389 Probate copy of the testament of Nicholas Esthawe, of Bishop's Thornham, 1457.

E42/340 Grant of the manor called 'Veautres' in Burnham by John Drewe, clerk to John Jygg, 1423.

PROB 11/1/32 Will of Sir Robert de Hamenhale of Brunham, 1391.

WARD 2/51/177/39 Letters of attorney of John Drewe, clerk, appointing Thomas Jygges to take seisin of the manor of Veautres, Burnham, 1423.

WARD 2/51/177/50 Quitclaim by Sir Richard Veutre to Thomas Jiggys, gentleman, of land in the manor called Veutres in Burnham, 1446.

WARD 2/52A/178/66 Quitclaim and release by Simon Veautre to Richard Athellbald of South Creake et al. of the manor of Vewters, Burnham, 1419.

WARD 2/52A/178/70 Grant by John Gygges of Wighton to Thomas Gygges of Burnham St Clement of the manor of Vewters, Burnham, 1423.

WARD 2/52A/178/76 Grant by Thomas Gygges of Burnham Overy, gentleman, to Roger Townsend, esquire, et al. of the manor called Veutris in Burnham, 1442.

WARD 2/53/178/242 Letter of complaint to the lord of the manor of Vewters, Burnham St Clement by William Ossant, n.d. [early 16th cent.].

WARD 2/53/179/70 Grant by William Osant of Burnham Norton, yeoman, to Alice Goldale his sister, of 2 acres of land, 1559.

BIBLIOGRAPHY

Norwich: Norfolk Record Office

ANF will register Liber 4 (Grey) Archdeaconry of Norfolk Probate Records, Will Register 1459-87.

C/Sca 2/60 Burnham Enclosure Award (Burnham Deepdale, Burnham Norton, Burnham Overy) 1821, attested 1826.

C/Sca 2/60 Burnham Norton Enclosure Map 1825.

DN/TA 229 Burnham Norton Tithe Map (no date) and Apportionment, 1840.

DN/TA 349 Burnham Overy Tithe Map and Apportionment, 1840.

DN/TA 358 Burnham Sutton Tithe Map, 1840; Apportionment, 1841.

DN/TA 386 Burnham Westgate alias Burnham Market Tithe Map, 1837, and Apportionment, 1841.

HARE 5975, 227X3 Copy will of Nicholas Esthagh of Thornham Episcopi, 1457.

HARE 5976, 227X3 Copy of Probate copy of will of Nicholas Esthagh of Thornham Episcopi, 1457/8.

MC 106/11 Manuscript of W. Rye, 'Maritime History of Norfolk'.

MC 1830/1, 852X7 Plan of Westgate Manorial Lands c. 1796.

NCC will register Cobald Norwich Consistory Court Probate Records, Will Register 12 1465--8.

NCC will register Coppinger Norwich Consistory Court Probate Records, Will Register 30 1511-20.

NCC will register Harsyk Norwich Consistory Court Probate Records, Will Register 2 1384-1415.

NCC will register Heydon Norwich Consistory Court Probate Records, Will Register 1 1370-86.

NCC will register Hirning Norwich Consistory Court Probate Records, Will Register 3 1416-27.

NCC will register Johnson Norwich Consistory Court Probate Records, Will Register 29 1510-13.

NCC will register Mingaye Norwich Consistory Court Probate Records, Will Register 48 1532-44.

NCC will register Norman Norwich Consistory Court Probate Records, Will Register 17 1485-93.

NCC will register Popy Norwich Consistory Court Probate Records, Will Register 25 1501-4.

NCC will register Robinson Norwich Consistory Court Probate Records, Will Register 33 1513-20.

NCC Will Register Sayve Norwich Consistory Court Probate Records, Will Register 22 1498-9.

NCC will register Surflete Norwich Consistory Court Probate Records, Will Register 4 1426-36.

NCC will register Wolman Norwich Consistory Court Probate Records, Will Register 20 1487–96.

NCR, 24B/2 Testament of Walter de Suffield, bishop of Norwich, 1256.

NRO 523 'A Survey of the ports, creeks and landing places of Norfolk 1565' (facsimiles and transcripts of selected folios from TNA, SP12/38).

PUBLISHED

The National Archives, Handbooks, Catalogues and Guides

Bliss, W. H. and Twemlow, J. A. (eds). 1902. *Calendar of Papal Registers Relating to Great Britain and Ireland: Vol. 4, 1362-1404*. London: HMSO.

Calendar of Charter Rolls. London: HMSO. (CChR)

    CChR 1906: Henry III-Edward I Vol. 2, 1257-1300.

Calendar of Close Rolls. London: HMSO. (CCR)

    CCR 1895: Edward II Vol. 3, 1318-1323.

    CCR 1898: Edward II Vol. 4, 1323-1327.

    CCR 1906: Henry III-Edward I Vol. 2, 1257-1300.

    CCR 1938: Henry III, 1268-1272.

Calendar of Inquisitions Miscellaneous (Chancery). London: HMSO. (CIM)

    CIM 1972: Vol. I.

Calendar of Letters and Papers, Foreign and Domestic, Henry VIII. (L&P HVIII)

    L&P HVIII, 1892, Vol 13, part 1.

Calendar of Liberate Rolls. London: HMSO. (CLR)

    CLR 1937: Henry III, Vol 3, 1245-1251.

    CLR 1964: Henry III, Vol 6, 1267-1272: with appendices 1220-1267.

Calendar of Papal Letters. London: HMSO. (CPL)

    CPL 1902: iv, 433.

Calendar of Patent Rolls. London: HMSO. (CPR) 201

    CPR 1895: Edward I Vol. 3, 1292-1301.

    CPR 1901: Edward I 1272-1281. 200

    CPR 1904: Edward II Vol. 4, 1321-1324.

    CPR 1905: Edward III Vol. 8, 1348-1350.

Calendar of State Papers, Domestic:

    CSPD 1856: Edward VI, Mary and Elizabeth Vol. 1, 1547-80.

    CSPD 1871: Edward VI, Mary and Elizabeth Vol. 7, Addenda 1547-80.

Index Chronologicus: In primum partem bullarii Carmelitani. Rome: 1715.

Maxwell Lyte, Henry Churchill (ed.). 1900. 'Deeds A.5901–A.6000', in *A Descriptive Catalogue of Ancient Deeds, Vol. 3.* London: HMSO.

Maxwell Lyte, Henry Churchill (ed.). 1906. 'Deeds: A.13301–A.13400', in *A Descriptive Catalogue of Ancient Deeds, Vol. 5.* London: HMSO.

Parliamentary Archives (formerly House of Lords Record Office) Publications

Parliamentary Archives (PA)

1846. '2nd Report of the Tidal Harbours Commission 1846', in Sessional Papers (1846) [692] [756] 18, parts 1 & 2 and Appendix A, no. 239.

Publications of the Records Commissioners

Caley, John and Hunter, Joseph (eds). 1810-34. *Valor Ecclesiasticus tempus Henrici VIII, Auctoritate Regia Institutus.* 6 vols. London: Record Commission.

Other published primary sources

Brewer, J. S. (ed.). 1862. *Letters and Papers, Foreign and Domestic, of the Reign of Henry VIII, Vol. 1.* London: Longman, Green, Longman, Roberts & Green.

Brewer, J. S. (ed.) 1875. *Letters and Papers, Foreign and Domestic, of the Reign of Henry VIII, Vol. 4.* London: HMSO.

Dodwell, Barbara (ed.). 1958. *Feet of Fines for the County of Norfolk for the Reign of King John, 1201-1215, for the County of Suffolk for the Reign of King John 1199-1214,* new series no. 32. London: Pipe Roll Society.

Fenwick, Carolyn C. (ed.) 2001. *The Poll Taxes of 1377,1379 and 1381, Part 2, Lincolnshire-Westmorland.* London: British Academy.

Glasscock, Robin E. (ed.) 1975. *The Lay Subsidy of 1334.* Oxford: Oxford University Press.

Harper-Bill, Christopher (ed.). 2000. *The Register of John Morton, Archbishop of Canterbury 1486-1500, vol. 3.* Martlesham: Boydell & Brewer, for the Canterbury and York Society.

Harper-Bill, Christopher (ed.). 2007. *English Episcopal Acta, vol. 32: Norwich 1244-1266.* Oxford: Oxford University Press, for the British Academy.

Historic England. 2015. Schedule Entry copy: St Mary's Carmelite Friary and holy well (monument 21389) (unpublished) accessed https://historicengland.org.uk/listing/the-list/list-entry/1013095 (accessed 22 May 2019).

Holinshed's Chronicles of England, Scotland and Ireland. 1807–8, Vol. 4 of 6 vols. London: J. Johnson et al.

Jacob, Ernest Fraser and Johnson, Harold Cottam (eds). 1938. *The Register of Henry Chichele, Archbishop of Canterbury 1414-43, Vol. 2: Wills proved before the Archbishop or his Commissaries.* London: Canterbury and York Society.

Linguistic Geographies. n.d. *The Gough Map of Great Britain.* www.goughmap.org (accessed 6 May 2019).

Marshall, William. 1787 and 1795. *The Rural Economy of Norfolk*, Vols 1 and 2, 1st and 2nd edn.

Oblique Aerial Photograph: CUCAP. 1951. NHER TF 8342ABK (CUCAP FQ20) 15-JUN-1951

Paris, M. 1852. *Matthew Paris's English history: From the Year 1235 to 1273*, trans. J. A. Giles. https://archive.org/details/matthewparissen0lrishgoog/page/n9 (accessed 6 May 2019).

Raine, J. (ed.). 1856. *The Obituary Roll of William Ebchester and John Burnby, Priors of Durham*, Surtees Society Vol. 31. Durham: Surtees Society.

Worcester, William. 1969. *Itineraries*, ed. J. H. Harvey. Oxford: Oxford University Press.

Secondary sources

Albone, J., Massey, S. and Tremlett, T. 2007. *The Archaeology of Norfolk's Coastal Zone: Results of the National Mapping Programme.* London: English Heritage.

Allison, K. J. 1955. 'The lost villages of Norfolk', *Norfolk Archaeology*, vol. 31, pp. 116–62.

Anderson, S. forthcoming. 'The ceramic building material', in R Clarke, *Norwich Whitefriars: Medieval Friary and Baptist Burial Ground. Excavations at Jarrold's Printing Works, Norwich, 2002-03.* Cambridge: East Anglian Archaeology.

Andrews, F. 2006 (rev. edn 2015). *The Other Friars: Carmelite, Augustinian, Sack and Pied Friars in the Middle Ages.* Woodbridge: Boydell Press.

Andrews, J. et al. 1999. 'Sedimentary evolution of the north Norfolk barrier coastline in the context of Holocene sea-level change', in I. Shennan and J. Andrews (eds), *Holocene Land-Ocean Interaction and Environmental Change around the North Sea.* London: Geological Society.

Andrews, Phil. 1992. 'Middle Saxon Norfolk: evidence for settlement, 650–850', *Norfolk Archaeological and Historical Research Group Annual*, vol. 1, pp. 13–28.

Ashdown-Hill, J. 2000, *Whitefriars. The Priory of Our Lady of Mount Carmel, Norwich.* Privately printed.

Ashwin, Trevor and Davison, Alan (eds). 2005. *An Historical Atlas of Norfolk*, 3rd edn. Chichester: Phillimore.

Atkin, M. and Evans, D. H. 2002, *Excavations in Norwich 1971-1978 Part III.* East Anglian Archaeology, vol. 100. Gressenhall: Norfolk Archaeological Unit.

Ayers, Brian. 1985. *Excavations within the North-East Bailey of Norwich Castle.* East Anglian Archaeology, vol. 28. Gressenhall: Norfolk Archaeological Unit.

Ayers, Brian. 1991. ''Post-medieval archaeology in Norwich: a review', *Norfolk Archaeology*, vol. 25, pp. 1–23.

Ayers, Brian. 2016. *The German Ocean: Medieval Europe around the North Sea.* Sheffield: Equinox.

Ayers, Brian and Murphy, P. 1983. 'Waterfront excavation at Whitefriars Street car park, Norwich, 1979', in P. Wade Martins (ed.),*Waterfront Excavation and Thetford Ware Production, Norwich.* East Anglian Archaeology, vol. 17. Gressenhall: Norfolk Archaeological Unit.

Barringer, J. C. 1989. *Faden's Map of Norfolk.* Dereham: Larks Press.

BIBLIOGRAPHY

Barringer, J. C. 2005. 'Norfolk Hundreds', pp. 96–7 in T. Ashwin and A. Davison (eds), *An Historical Atlas of Norfolk,* 3rd edn. Chichester: Phillimore.

Batcock, Neil. 1991. *The Ruined and Disused Churches of Norfolk*, East Anglian Archaeology, vol. 51. Gressenhall: Norfolk Archaeological Unit.

Bayliss, Alex, Hines, John, Høilund Neilsen, Karen, McCormac, Gerry and Scull, Christopher. 2013. *Anglo-Saxon Graves and Grave Goods of the 6th and 7th Centuries AD: A chronological framework.* Society for Medieval Archaeology Monograph 33. London: Maney.

Bescoby, D. 2017. Imagined Land: St Mary's Friary, Burnham Norton geophysical survey. Report for the Norfolk Archaeological Trust.

Blair, John. 2018. *Building Anglo-Saxon England.* Woodstock, N.J.: Princeton University Press.

Blake, W. J. 1951–2. 'Norfolk manorial lords in 1316', *Norfolk Archaeology*, vol. 30, part 3, pp. 234–61, and vol. 30, part 4, pp. 263–86.

Blinkhorn, Paul. 2012. *The Ipswich Ware Project: Ceramics, trade and society in Middle Saxon England.* Medieval Pottery Research Group Monograph.

Blomefield, Francis. 1805–10. *An Essay Towards a Topographical History of the County of Norfolk*, 11 vols, rev. edn. London: W. Bulmer & Co./W. Miller.

Braun, H. 1950. 'The Carmelite friars of Aylesford', *Archaeologia Cantiana*, vol. 63, pp. 50–60.

Brown, Philippa (ed.). 1984. *Domesday Book: Norfolk.* Chichester: Phillimore.

Bryant, H. 1914. *The Churches of Norfolk.* Norwich: Norwich Mercury.

Burwash, D. 1969. *English Merchant Shipping 1460–1540,* repr. Devon: David & Charles.

Butler, Lawrence. 1986. 'Church dedications and the cults of Anglo-Saxon saints in England', pp. 44–50 in L. A. S. Butler and R. K. Morris (eds), *The Anglo-Saxon Church*, Research Report 60. London: Council for British Archaeology.

Caffell, A. and Holst, M. forthcoming. 'Human skeletal remains: the medieval burials' in R. Clarke, *Norwich Whitefriars: Medieval Friary and Baptist Burial Ground. Excavations at Jarrold's Printing Works, Norwich, 2002–03.* Cambridge: East Anglian Archaeology.

Camp, Anthony J. 1974. *Wills and their Whereabouts,* 4th edn. London: the author.

Campbell, J. 1975. *Historic Towns Atlas: Norwich.* London: Scolar Press in conjunction with Historic Towns Trust.

Chester-Kadwell, B. 2017. 'Changing patterns of routeways in the landscape of the Eastern High Weald from the end of the Roman period to the building of the turnpikes', *Archaeologia Cantiana*, vol. 138, pp. 227–55.

Chester-Kadwell, Mary. 2009. *Early Anglo-Saxon Communities in the Landscape of Norfolk*, British Archaeological Reports British Series 481. Oxford: Archaeopress.

Chroston, P., Jones, R. and Makin, B. 1999. 'Geometry of Quaternary sediments along the Norfolk coast, UK: a shallow seismic study', *Geolocical Magazine*, vol. 136, no. 4.

Claiden-Yardley, Kirsten. 2014. 'Tudor noble commemoration and identity: the Howard family in context, 1485–1572', D.Phil. thesis, University of Oxford.

Clarke, R. forthcoming. *Norwich Whitefriars: Medieval Friary and Baptist Burial Ground. Excavations at Jarrold's Printing Works, Norwich, 2002–03.* Cambridge: East Anglian Archaeology.

Clarke, W. G. 1921. *Norfolk and Suffolk*. London: A & C Black.

Cockayne, George Edward (ed.). *The Complete Peerage by G. E.C.* 1910–98. 14 vols, Vol. 3. London: St Catherine Press.

Coppack, G. 1990. *Abbeys and Priories*. London: Batsford for English Heritage.

Copsey, Richard. 2004. *Carmel in Britain: Studies on the early history of the Carmelite Order, Vol. 3: The Hermits from Mount Carmel*. Faversham: St Albert's Press, and Rome: Edizioni Carmelitane.

Copsey, Richard. 2006. 'The Medieval Carmelite Priory at Norwich: a chronology', unpublished.

Copsey, Richard. 2017. 'The medieval Carmelite Priory at Burnham Norton: a chronology'. Unpublished typescript, rev. edn. Faversham.

Cox, J. C. 1906a. 'Religious houses', pp. 315–466 in William Page (ed.), *The Victoria History of the County of Norfolk, Vol. II*. London: Archibald Constable.

Cracknell, B. 2005. *Outrageous Waves: Global warming and coastal change in Britain*. Stroud: History Press.

Crawley, P. E. 2011. *An Archaeological Excavation and Watching Brief at Friary Cottage, Burnham Norton, Norfolk: Assessment report and updated project design*. Report no. 2265a. Gressenhall: Norfolk Archaeological Unit.

Crowson, A. et al. 2017. *St Mary's Friary, Burnham Norton: Archaeological recording and documentation of the friary precinct walls*. Draft 2017 report (forthcoming) NPS Archaeology Report No. 2016/1231: OASIS ID: norfolka1-233465.

Crummy, N. forthcoming. 'Dress and personal possessions', in R. Clarke, *Norwich Whitefriars: Medieval Friary and Baptist Burial Ground. Excavations at Jarrold's Printing Works, Norwich, 2002-03*. Cambridge: East Anglian Archaeology.

Cullen, Paul, Jones, Richard and Parsons, David N. 2011. *Thorps in a Changing Landscape*. Hatfield: University of Hertfordshire.

Curran, Susan. 2016. *The Wife of Cobham*. Norwich: Lasse Press.

Cushion, B. and Davison, A. 2003. 'Earthworks of Norfolk', *East Anglian Archaeology*, vol. 104, p. 133.

Darby, H. C. (ed.). 1971. *The Domesday Geography of Eastern England*, 3rd edn. Cambridge: Cambridge University Press.

Davies, Gareth. 2010. 'Early medieval "rural centres" and West Norfolk: a growing picture of diversity, complexity and changing lifestyles', *Medieval Archaeology*, vol. 54, pp. 89–122.

Davies, Gareth. 2011. *Settlement, Economy and Lifestyle: The changing social identities of the coastal settlements of West Norfolk, 450-1100 AD*. Ph.D. thesis, University of Nottingham. http://eprints.nottingham.ac.uk/12002/ (accessed 6 May 2019).

Davis, G. R. C. 1958. *Medieval Cartularies of Great Britain and Ireland*. London: Longmans.

Deckers, Pieterjan. 2010. 'An illusory emporium? Small trading places around the southern North Sea', pp. 159–67 in Annemarieke Willemsen and Hanneke Kik (eds), *Dorestad in an International Framework: New research on centres of trade and coinage in Carolingian times*. Turnhout, Belgium: Brepols.

BIBLIOGRAPHY

Doubleday, H. A. and Page, W. (eds). 1906. *Victoria History of the County of Norfolk, Vol. 2*. London: Victoria County Histories.

Duffy, E. 1992. *The Stripping of the Altars: Traditional religion in England 1400-1580*. New Haven and London: Yale University Press.

Duffy, E. 1997. *Saints and Sinners: a History of the Popes*. Yale University Press in association with S4C.

Duffy, E. 2017. *Reformation Divided: Catholics, Protestants and the conversion of England*. London: Bloomsbury.

Dugdale, William. 1665–73[1846]. *Monasticon Anglicanum: A history of the abbies and other monasteries, hospitals, frieries, and cathedral and collegiate churches, with their dependencies, in England and Wales*, 3 vols, London, repr. London: Bohn, 1846, 6 vols.

Dymond, David. 1985. *The Norfolk Landscape*. London: Hodder & Stoughton.

Dymond, David. 2005. 'Medieval and later markets', pp. 76–7 in T. Ashwin and A. Davison (eds), *An Historical Atlas of Norfolk*, 3rd edn. Chichester: Phillimore.

Egan, K. J. 1972. 'An essay towards a historiography of the origin of the Carmelite Province in England,' *Carmelus*, vol. 19, pp. 67, 100.

Egan, K. J. 1992a. 'An essay towards a historiography of the origin of the Carmelite Province in England', pp. 86–119 in P. Fitzgerald-Lombard (ed.), *Carmel in Britain, Vol. 1: Essays on the Medieval English Province*. Rome: Casa Editrice Institutum Carmelitanum.

Egan, K. J. 1992b. 'Medieval Carmelite houses: England and Wales', pp. 1–85 in P. Fitzgerald-Lombard (ed.), *Carmel in Britain, Vol. 1: Essays on the Medieval English Province*. Rome: Casa Editrice Institutum Carmelitanum.

Ekwall, Eilert. 1960. *The Concise Oxford Dictionary of English Place-names*, 4th edn. London: Oxford University Press.

Emery, G. 2019a. *A Community Archaeological Test-Pitting Project at Burnham Norton, Norfolk. Part of the Imagined Land Project*. Norvic Archaeology Report 120. OASIS ID: norvicar1-342594

Emery, G. 2019b. *Archaeological Monitoring and Targeted Investigation Work of the Precinct Wall and the Installation of a Culvert at St Mary's Friary, Burnham Norton, Norfolk*. Norvic Archaeology Report 122. OASIS ID: norvicar1-349496.

Emery, P. A. and Ayers, B. S. 1999. 'Excavations at the Jarrold's Printing Works, Whitefriars, Norwich, 1992', *Norfolk Archaeology*, vol. 43, pp. 275–86.

English Heritage. 1995. Schedule entry copy: St Mary's Carmelite Friary and holy well (monument 21389) (unpublished).

Farnhill, Ken. 2001. *Guilds and the Parish Community in Late Medieval East Anglia, c. 1470-1550*. Woodbridge: York Medieval Press/Boydell Press.

Fitzgerald-Lombard, P. (ed.). 1992. *Carmel in Britain, Vol. 1: Essays on The Medieval English Province*. Rome: Casa Editrice Institutum Carmelitanum.

Foss, David Blair. 1986. *The Canterbury Archiepiscopates of John Stafford (1443-52) and John Kemp (1452-4) with Editions of their Registers*, 3 vols in 4. Ph.D. thesis, University of London.

Francis, Sally. 2003, repr. 2018. *Burnham Norton: One of the Seven Burnhams by the Sea*. Burnham Norton: Sally Francis.

Fraser, C. M. (ed.). 1987. *The Accounts of the Chamberlains of Newcastle upon Tyne 1508-1511*. Newcastle: Society of Antiquaries of Newcastle upon Tyne.

Friedman, E. 1979. *The Latin Hermits of Mount Carmel: A study in Carmelite origins, Vol. 1*. Rome: Institutum Historicum Teresianum Studia.

Gilchrist, R. and Sloane, B. 2005. *Requiem. The medieval monastic cemetery in Britain*. London: Museum of London Archaeology Service.

Greene, J. P. 2005. *Medieval Monasteries*. London: Continuum.

Hadley, D. M. and Richards, J. D. 2018. 'In search of the Viking Great Army: beyond the winter camps', *Medieval Settlement Research*, vol. 33, pp. 1–17.

Hadwin, J. F. 1983. 'The medieval lay subsidies and economic history', *Economic History Review*, new series 36, pp. 200–17.

Hamerow, Helena. 2012. *Rural Settlements and Society in Anglo-Saxon England*. Oxford: Oxford University Press.

Harper-Bill, C. 2004. 'Suffield [Calthorpe], Walter of (d. 1257)', *Oxford Dictionary of National Biography*, https://doi.org/10.1093/ref: odnb/26763

Harper-Bill, C. and Rawcliffe, C. 2004, 'The religious houses', pp. 73–120 in C. Rawcliffe and R. Wilson (eds), *Medieval Norwich*. London and New York: Hambledon and London.

Harvey, Barbara. 1977. *Westminster Abbey and its Estates in the Middle Ages*. Oxford: Oxford University Press.

Hassell, William and Beauroy, Jacques (eds). 1993. *Lordship and Landscape in Norfolk, 1250-1350: Early records of Holkham*. Oxford: Oxford University Press.

Hasted, E. 1797–1801. *The History and Topographical Survey of the County of Kent*, 12 vols. Canterbury: R. Bristow.

Hawes, Timothy L. M. 2000-1. *The Inhabitants of Norfolk in the Fourteenth Century: The lay subsidies of 1327 and 1332 preserved in the Public Record Office*. Norwich: Timothy Hawes.

Heywood, Stephen. 1989. 'The Priory of St Mary in the Meadow of the Order of Peterstone, Beeston next the Sea, Norfolk', *Norfolk Archaeology*, vol. 40, pp. 226–59.

Heywood, Stephen. 1996. 'The Bishop's Palace' in chapter on 'The Romanesque building', in I. Atherton, E. Fernie, C. Harper-Bill and A. Hassell Smith (eds), *Norwich Cathedral: Church, city and diocese, 1096-1996*. London: Hambledon Press.

Heywood, Stephen. 2012. Historic building report for Friary Cottage, Burnham Norton (NHER 43988). Historic Environment Service, September.

Heywood, Stephen. 2013. 'Stone building in Romanesque East Anglia', pp. 256–69 in David Bates and Robert Liddiard (eds), *East Anglia and its North Sea World in the Middle Ages*. Woodbridge: Boydell.

Heywood, Stephen. 2014a. 'The Greyfriars, Little Walsingham', NHER 2036, September. Gressenhall: Norfolk County Council Historic Environment Service. http://hbsmrgateway2.esdm.co.uk/norfolk/DataFiles/Docs/AssocDoc62095.pdf (accessed 6 May 2019).

Heywood, Stephen. 2014b. 'Castle Acre Priory precinct wall', NHER 4096, October. Gressenhall: Norfolk County Council Historic Environment Service. www.heritage.norfolk.gov.uk/record-details?mnf4096 (accessed 6 May 2019).

BIBLIOGRAPHY

Heywood, Stephen and Rogerson, Andrew. 1995. Carmelite Friary Gatehouse, Burnham Norton: Scheduled Monument No. 21389: Excavations prior to installation of staircase, 18 December.

Hickling, S. and Crowson, A. 2015. 'Archaeological watching brief at Friary Cottage, Friar's Lane, Burnham Norton, Norfolk. NPS Archaeology report 3011. Monument No. 21389: Excavations prior to installation of staircase, 18 December 1995'.

Hillen, Henry J. 1907. *History of the Borough of King's Lynn, vol. 1.* Norwich: East of England Newspapers.

Hines, John and Caruth, Jo. forthcoming. 'Excavations in the Anglo-Saxon burial grounds at RAF Lakenheath, Eriswell, Suffolk', *East Anglian Archaeology.*

Hoggett, Richard. 2010. *The Archaeology of the East Anglian Conversion.* Woodbridge: Boydell.

Holder, Nick. 2011. *The Medieval Friaries of London. A topographic and archaeological history, before and after the Dissolution.* Ph.D. thesis, University of London.

Holder, Nick. 2017. *The Friaries of Medieval London: From foundation to dissolution.* Woodbridge: Boydell Press.

Hooton, J. J. 1996. *The Glaven Ports.* Blakeney: Blakeney History Group.

Hudson, W. 1910. 'The "Norwich Taxation" of 1254, so far as relates to the Diocese of Norwich', *Norfolk Archaeology,* vol. 17, pp. 46–157.

Hudson, W. 1895. 'The assessment of the townships of the County of Norfolk for the King's tenths and fifteenths, as settled in 1334', *Norfolk Archaeology,* vol. 12, pp. 243–97.

Hussey, A. 1852. *Notes on the Churches in the Counties of Kent, Sussex and Surrey.* London: John Russell Smith.

Hutcheson, A. J. H. 2000. 'Report on an archaeological evaluation at 71–75 Barrack Street, Norwich,' Norfolk Archaeological Unit Report no. 496, unpublished.

Jotischky, Andrew. 2002. *The Carmelites and Antiquity: Mendicants and their pasts in the Middle Ages.* Oxford: Oxford University Press.

Jungmann, J. A. 1992. *The Mass of the Roman Rite: Its origin and development, Vols 1 and 2.* Westminster, Maryland: Christian Classics Inc.

King, D. 2004. 'Medieval glass-painting,' pp. 121-36 in Carole Rawcliffe and Richard Wilson (eds), *Medieval Norwich.* London and New York: Hambledon and London.

King, D. forthcoming. 'Window glass', in R. Clarke, *Norwich Whitefriars: Medieval Friary and Baptist Burial Ground. Excavations at Jarrold's Printing Works, Norwich, 2002-03.* Cambridge: East Anglian Archaeology.

Kirkpatrick, J. 1845. *History of the Religious Orders and Communities and of the Hospitals and Castle of Norwich.* ed. D. Turner. Yarmouth.

Klauser, T. 1969. *A Short History of the Western Liturgy: an Account and Some Reflections.* Oxford: Oxford University Press.

Knowles, David, 1950. *The Religious Orders in England.* Cambridge: Cambridge University Press.

Knowles, David, 1961. *The Religious Orders in England Volume II: the end of the Middle Ages.* Cambridge: Cambridge University Press.

Knowles, David, 1971. *The Religious Orders in England Volume III: the Tudor Age.* Cambridge: Cambridge University Press.

Knowles, David and Hadcock, Neville R. 1953 (rev. edn 1971). *Medieval Religious Houses of England and Wales.* London: Longmans, Green.

Lamb, H. H. 1977. *Climate: Present, past and future.* London and New York: Methuen.

Latham, R. E. 1999. *Revised Medieval Latin Word List from British and Irish Sources.* London: Oxford University Press for the British Academy.

Le Strange, Hamon. 1890. *Norfolk Official Lists from the Earliest Period to the Present Day.* Norwich: Agas H. Goose.

Le Strange, Richard. 1973. *Monasteries of Norfolk.* King's Lynn: Yates.

Lee, R. 2006. 'A report on the archaeological excavation of "Blakeney Chapel"', *Glaven Historian*, no. 9 (Blakeney Area Historical Society).

Letters, Samantha (ed.). 2002. *Gazetteer of Markets and Fairs in England and Wales to 1516, Part 1,* Special Series vol. 32. Kew: List and Index Society.

Lindley, P. G. 1987. 'The "Arminghall Arch" and contemporary sculpture in Norwich', *Norfolk Archaeology*, vol. 40, pp. 19-43.

Linguistic Geographies. n.d. The Gough Map of Great Britain. www.goughmap.org (accessed 6 May 2019).

Linnell, C. L. S. 1962. *Norfolk Church Dedications.* York: St Anthony's.

MacCulloch, D. 2017. *All Things Made New: Writings on the Reformation.* Harmondsworth: Penguin.

Macnair, A. 2005. Faden's Map of Norfolk digitally redrawn. www.fadensmapofnorfolk.co.uk (accessed 6 May 2019).

May, V. J. 2003. 'North Norfolk coast', ch. 11. of V. J. May and J. D. Hansom, *Coastal Morphology of Great Britain. Geological Conservation Review*, vol. 28. Peterborough: Joint Nature Conservation Committee.

McKerracher, M. 2018. *Farming Transformed in Anglo-Saxon England: Agriculture in the long eighth century.* Oxford: Windgather.

Metzger, M. 1997. *History of the Liturgy: The major stages.* Collegeville, Minn.: Liturgical Press.

Moreland, John. 2000. 'The significance of production in eighth-century England', pp. 69-104 in Inge Lyse Hansen and Chris Wickham (eds), *The Long Eighth Century: Production, distribution and demand.* Leiden, Netherlands: Brill.

Morris, Richard. 1989. *Churches in the Landscape.* London: J. M. Dent.

Nenk, B. S., Margeson, S. and Hurley, M. 1995. 'Medieval Britain and Ireland in 1994', *Medieval Archaeology*, vol. 39, pp. 180-293.

Nitowski, E. (Sister Damien of the Cross). 1987a. *The 1987 Preliminary Season in the Wadi es Siah.* Salt Lake City, Utah: Mount Carmel Project.

Nitowski, E. 1987b. *The Preservation and Restoration of the Monastic Ruins in the Wadi es Siah, Based on the 1987 Preliminary Report.* Salt Lake City, Utah: Mount Carmel Project.

BIBLIOGRAPHY

Nitowski, E. 1989. *The Mount Carmel Project: 1988 Spring Season*. Salt Lake City, Utah: Mount Carmel Project.

Nitowski, E. and Qualls, C. 1991. *Spring 1991 Short Field Report, Mount Carmel Project Sixth Season*. Salt Lake City, Utah: Mount Carmel Project.

Norfolk Heritage Explorer. *Post-Medieval Flood Defences, Burnham Norton*, Report NHER 26676. www.heritage.norfolk.gov.uk/record-details?MNF41900-Post-medieval-flood-defences&Index=2&RecordCount=1&SessionID=e279b450-5922-421b-9869-1b8131d65bb7 (accessed 6 May 2019).

NPS Archaeology. 2016. *St Mary's Friary, Friar's Lane, Burnham Norton, Norfolk, PE31 8JA: Archaeological Recording and Documentation of the Friary Precinct Walls*, Draft Report: Issue 1. Prepared for Norfolk Archaeological Trust.

O'Sullivan, Deirdre. 2013. *In the Company of Preachers: The archaeology of medieval friaries in England and Wales*, Monograph 23. Leicester: Leicester Archaeology.

Oxford English Dictionary (OED). Online edn. https://www.oed.com/

Page, William (ed). 1906. *A History of the County of Norfolk, Vol. II*. London: Victoria County History.

Page, William (ed). 1926. 'Friaries: the Carmelite friars of Aylesford', in *A History of the County of Kent, Vol. 2*. London: Victoria County History.

Peake, John. 2005. 'A snapshot of Blakeney Haven in 1565: a survey of the ports, creeks and landing places of Norfolk', *The Glaven Historian*, vol 8, pp. 58–68. www.bahs.uk/GH-Files/GH8/GH8-Article6.pdf

Penn, Kenneth. 2001. 'Jarrold's Printing Works, Whitefriars, Norwich', Norfolk Archaeological Unit report 630, unpublished.

Penn, Kenneth. 2005. 'Medieval unplanned towns', pp. 72–3 in T. Ashwin and A. Davison (eds), *An Historical Atlas of Norfolk*, 3rd edn. Chichester: Phillimore.

Percival, Sarah and Williamson, Tom. 2005. 'Early fields and medieval furlongs: excavations at Creake Road, Burnham Sutton, Norfolk', *Landscapes*, vol. 6, no. 1, pp. 1–17.

Pestell, Tim. 2003. 'The afterlife of 'productive' sites in East Anglia', pp. 122–37 in Tim Pestell and Katharina Ulmschneider (eds), *Markets in Early Medieval Europe: Trading and 'productive' sites, 650-850*. Macclesfield: Windgather.

Pestell, Tim. 2004. *Landscapes of Monastic Foundation: The establishment of religious houses in East Anglia c. 650-1200*. Woodbridge: Boydell.

Pestell, Tim. 2019. *Viking East Anglia*. Norwich: Norfolk Museums Service.

Pestell, Tim and Ulmschneider, Katharina (eds). 2003. *Markets in Early Medieval Europe: Trading and 'productive' sites, 650–850*. Macclesfield: Windgather.

Pethick, J. 2000. 'Coastal change in Norfolk: the wider perspective and future trends', report for the Norfolk Coast Community Conference, 'The Changing Coast' (Norfolk Coast Project).

Pevsner, Nikolaus. 1958. *Shropshire* (Buildings of England). Harmondsworth: Penguin.

Pevsner, Nikolaus. 1963. *N.W. and S. Norfolk* (Buildings of England). Harmondsworth: Penguin.

Pevsner, Nikolaus. 1970. *Northumberland* (Buildings of England), repr. Harmondsworth: Penguin.

Postan, M.M., 1975. *The Medieval Economy and Society.* Harmondsworth: Penguin.

Pringle, D. 1984. 'Thirteenth-century pottery from the monastery of St Mary of Carmel', *Levant*, vol. 16, pp. 91–111.

Pringle, D. 1998. 'St Mary of Carmel', pp. 249–57 in *The Churches of the Crusader Kingdom of Jerusalem, Vol. 2.* Cambridge: Cambridge University Press.

Rahner, K. and Vorgrimler, H. 1983. *Concise Theological Dictionary*, 2nd edn. London: Burns & Oates.

Richards, Julian D. and Haldenby, Dave. 2018. 'The scale and impact of Viking settlement in Northumbria', *Medieval Archaeology*, vol. 62, no. 2, pp. 322–50.

Rigold, S. E. 1965. 'Two Kentish Carmelite friaries: Aylesford and Sandwich', *Archaeologia Cantiana*, vol. 80, pp. 1–28.

Robertson, David and Ames, John. 2010. 'Early medieval intertidal fishwiers at Holme beach, Norfolk', *Medieval Archaeology*, vol. 54, pp. 329–46.

Robertson, W. 1882. 'Inventory made at the Dissolution of St Mary's, Lossenham, Carmelite Friary', *Archaeologia Cantiana*, vol. 14, pp. 311–12.

Rogerson, Andrew. 2003. 'Six middle Anglo-Saxon sites in West Norfolk', pp. 110–21 in Tim Pestell and Katharina Ulmschneider (eds), *Markets in Early Medieval Europe: Trading and 'productive' sites, 650-850.* Macclesfield: Windgather.

Rogerson, Andrew. 2005. 'Middle Saxon Norfolk (c. AD 650-850)', pp. 32–3 in T. Ashwin and A. Davison (eds), *An Historical Atlas of Norfolk*, 3rd edn. Chichester: Phillimore.

Röhrkasten, Jens. 2004. *The Mendicant Houses of Medieval London, 1221-1539.* Münster, Germany: Lit Verlag, p. 467.

Runciman, S. 1955. *A History of the Crusades, vol 3: the Kingdom of Acre and the Later Crusades.* Cambridge: Cambridge University Press.

Rutledge, E. 2005. 'Medieval and later ports, trade and fishing, up to 1600', pp. 78–9 in Tim Pestell and Katharina Ulmschneider (eds), *Markets in Early Medieval Europe: Trading and 'productive' sites, 650-850.* Macclesfield: Windgather.

Rutledge, E. 2007. 'Documentary evidence', pp. 46–58 in P. Emery (ed.), *Norwich Greyfriars: Pre-conquest town and medieval friary*, East Anglian Archaeology Vol. 120. Gressenhall: Norfolk Museums and Archaeology Service.

Rutledge, E. forthcoming. 'The documented friary', in R. Clarke, *Norwich Whitefriars: Medieval Friary and Baptist Burial Ground. Excavations at Jarrold's Printing Works, Norwich, 2002-03.* Cambridge: East Anglian Archaeology.

Rye, Walter. 1913. *Norfolk Families.* Norwich: Goose & Co.

Sabin, V. 1994. 'Bare ruin'd choirs: the Carmelite Friary at Burnham Norton', pp. 1–10 in *Burnham Market Records and Recollections.* Burnham Market: Burnham Market Society.

Sandred, K. I. and Lindström, B. 1989. *The Place-names of Norfolk: Norwich.* Nottingham: English Place Names Society.

BIBLIOGRAPHY

Saul, Nigel. 2001. *Death, Art, and Memory in Medieval England: The Cobham family and their monuments, 1300-1500*. Oxford: Oxford University Press.

Schroeder, H. J. 1937. *Discplinary Degrees of the General Councils*. St Louis: B.Herder

Sheehan, Michael McMahon. 1963. *The Will in Medieval England*. Toronto, Ont.: Pontifical Institute of Mediaeval Studies.

Shelley, Andrew. 2004. *Excavations and Building Recording at Jarrolds Printing Works, Whitefriars, Norwich 2002-3, Post-Excavation Assessment*. Norfolk Archaeological Unit Report no. 908, unpublished.

Shepherd Popescu, Elizabeth. 2009. *Norwich Castle: Excavations and historical survey 1987-98, Part I: Anglo-Saxon to c.1345*. East Anglian Archaeology, Vol. 132. Gressenhall: East Anglian Archaeology.

Simmons, T. F. (ed.) 1897. *The Lay Folks Mass Book*. London: Early English Text Society.

Smith, Hassell A. and Baker, G. M. 1982/83. *The Papers of Nathaniel Bacon of Stiffkey, Vol. 2, 1578-1585*, NRS Vol. 19. Norwich: Norfolk Record Society.

Smith, P. 2012. *Petitionary Negotiation in a Community in Conflict: King's Lynn and West Norfolk c.1575 to 1662*. Ph.D. thesis, University of East Anglia.

Smith, P. 2014. 'Beyond the sea wall: the case of the fishermen of Burnham marshes', *Norfolk Archaeology*, vol. 46, pp. 37–44.

St John Hope, W. H. 1890. 'On the Whitefriars or Carmelites of Hulne, Northumberland', *Archaeological Journal*, vol. 47, pp. 105–29.

Steers, J. A. 1934 (rev. edn 1960). *Scolt Head Island*. Cambridge: Cambridge University Press.

Steers, J. A. 1948. *The Coastline of England and Wales*. Cambridge: Cambridge University Press.

Steers, J. A. 1981. *The Coastal Features of England and Wales: Eight essays*. Cambridge: Cambridge University Press.

Stöber, Karen. 2007. *Late Medieval Monasteries and their Patrons: England and Wales, c.1300-1540*, Studies in the History of Medieval Religion 29. Woodbridge: Boydell Press.

Tanner, N. 1984. *The Church in Late Medieval Norwich 1370-1532*. Toronto, Ont.: Pontifical Institute of Medieval Studies.

Tanner, N. 2004. 'Religious practice,' pp. 137-56 in Carole Rawcliffe and Richard Wilson (eds), *Medieval Norwich*. London and New York: Hambledon and London.

Tanner, N. 2016. *The Councils of the Church: A short history*. New York: Crossroad.

Thompson, Benjamin. 1994. 'Monasteries and their patrons at foundation and dissolution', *Transactions of the Royal Historical Society*, 6th series, vol. 4, pp. 103–25.

Trend, Nicholas Andrew. 2017. 'Wighton: the church, the village and its people, 1400–1500', Ph.D. thesis, University of East Anglia.

Victoria History of the County of Kent. (VCH Kent).

Virgoe, Roger. 1969. 'The divorce of Thomas Tuddenham', *Norfolk Archaeology*, vol. 34, pp. 406–18.

Weever, John. 1767. *Antient Funeral Monuments, of Great-Britain, Ireland, and the Islands Adjacent*. London: William Tooke.

Williams, N. J. 1988. *The Maritime Trade of the East Anglian Ports 1550-1590*. Oxford: Clarendon Press.

Williamson, Tom. 1993. *The Origins of Norfolk*. Manchester: Manchester University Press.

Williamson, Tom. 2005. 'Place-name patterns', pp. 34–5 in T. Ashwin and A. Davison (eds), *An Historical Atlas of Norfolk*, 3rd edn. Chichester: Phillimore.

Williamson, Tom. 2006. *East Anglia: English Heritage.* England's Landscape Vol. 2. London: Collins.

Williamson, Tom and Skipper, Kate. 2005. 'Late Saxon population densities', pp. 38–9 in T. Ashwin and A. Davison (eds), *An Historical Atlas of Norfolk,* 3rd edn. Chichester: Phillimore.

Woodfield, C. 2005. *The Church of Our Lady of Mount Carmel, Whitefriars Coventry,* British Archaeological Reprint no. 389. Oxford: British Archaeological Reports.

Wright, Duncan W. 2015. *'Middle Saxon' Settlement and Society.* Oxford: Archaeopress.

Wright, J. 2000. 'Coals from Newcastle', *Glaven Historian*, no. 3 (Blakeney Area Historical Society).

Yaxley, David. 1977. *Portrait of Norfolk.* London: Robert Hale.

PART III

ANNEX

The Medieval Carmelite priory at Burnham Norton: a chronology

The Medieval Carmelite priory at Burnham Norton: a chronology

Richard Copsey, O.Carm.

Part I: INTRODUCTION

These chronological notes started life as part of a database of historical information on the Carmelite Province of England and Wales up to the suppression of the province under King Henry VIII in 1538-39. The text which follows here contains all the references and information derived from a number of sources about the Carmelite friary of Burnham Norton. The information is arranged in chronological order in Part II. Part II A gives the general information on the house, Part II B gives a list of known priors of the house and Part II C gives some brief notes on the fate of the buildings and the site after the dissolution of the Order.

A list of those friars known to have been members of the community has been added, taken from my A Biographical Register of Carmelites in England and Wales 1240-1540, (St Albert's Press, in press), in Part III. These entries give all the known biographical information on the individual friars and a list of known works. However, the bibliographies which come at the end of the longer entries have been omitted here. Part IV contains a list of abbreviations used, manuscript sources and a bibliography.

My grateful thanks are due to Brendan Chester-Kadwell, John Alban and Sally Francis for some insightful comments and very helpful additions to the following Chronology. If the reader finds any errors in these notes or knows of any omissions or facts which relate to the house, then I would be very grateful to be informed so that they can be added to our province archives. Our archives also include photos of the remaining buildings, etc.

Part II A: CHRONOLOGY

Unless otherwise indicated, all the Carmelites mentioned in this chronology were, at the time, members of the community of the Carmelite Priory, Burnham Norton. A list of abbreviations used is given at the end of the Annex.

Notes:

From early in the fourteenth century, the English province was divided into four distinctions or regions. From its occurrence in the list of provincial chapters, Burnham Norton was included in the Norwich distinction. Most of the texts in Latin or Norman French have been translated into English.

[1241] Translation: 'Ralph Hempnale and William Calethorpe, noblemen and knights, were the first founders of the convent of Burnham, in the year of the Lord 1241.' [Bale, Cotton Titus D.X. fo. 127: cf. Egan, K. "Medieval Carmelite Houses: England and Wales", Carmelus, 16 (1969), 160].

John Bale mistakenly writes "John" Hempnale as first founder of Burnham Norton. [Bale, Harley 3838, fo. 16].

Note: However, this claim to have been founded in 1241 must be treated with caution as Burnham Norton was the fourth house in order of seniority for the medieval foundations and so came after Hulne Priory, Aylesford and Losenham, the first two founded in 1242 and Losenham soon after 1242. Burnham Norton was founded before 1247.

1253 "In the year 1253, the brothers began to live at the place in Burnham where they now dwell, as appears in the register of the convent. Before this, the brothers had a place in the area called Bardmer (or Bradmer) where they stayed for 30 years, namely from 1223 to 1253." [Bale, Bodley 73, fo. 135: Selden supra 41, fo. 151v: Harley 3838, fos. 1617].

However, Keith Egan in his researches, notes that: "The 1223 date for Burnham cannot be correct. The house could have been founded only between 1242 and 1247, sometime after the foundations at Hulne, Aylesford and Lossenham. It was the last house founded before the revision of the rule in 1247. Bale says that Bradmer was a place not far from Burnham Norton but its location cannot now be determined. However, the general area of Bradmer survives in the name Bradmore Marsh (from Tithe Award for Burnham Norton, 1845)". [Egan, K. "Medieval Carmelite Houses: England and Wales", Carmelus, 16 (1969), 159].

1256	Bishop Walter de Suffield was a benefactor of the house. [H. Bryant, The Churches of Norfolk, (Norwich, 1914), 21].
?	At an unknown date, Sir William Calthorpe bequeathed 20s. to the house. [Bryant, The Churches of Norfolk, 21].
After 1277	Roger Crostwyck, prior provincial from 1272-7, was buried at Burnham Norton. [Bale, Catalogus, ii, 59]
1283, 19 Feb.	Bale, copying probably from a register in Burnham Norton, claims that the provincial Henry of Anna made a visitation of the house on 19 Feb 1283. [Bale, Bodley 73, fo. 135v].
After 1283	Hervey Burnham, vicar provincial 1277-8, was buried at Burnham Norton. [Bale, Catalogus, ii, 59].
1297, 14 May	An inquisition was ordered for a grant of land by Walter de Calthorp. [NA, C 143/26/12, calendared in NA Lists & Indexes, xvii, 42: quoted in Egan, Keith, "Medieval Carmelite Houses: England and Wales", Carmelus, 16 (1969), 160].
1298, 16 June	"Licence for the alienation in mortmain by Walter de Calthorp to the prior and Carmelite Friars of Brunham of a rood of meadow there for the enlargement of their place." [CPR, 1292-1301, 354].
Early 14th c.	From the architectural evidence, the gatehouse of the priory was built about this time. [Pevesner, The Buildings of England: North-East Norfolk and Norwich (1970), 105].
1346	A provincial chapter was held in Burnham presided over by the provincial, John Folsham. [Bale, Bodley 73, fo. 80v].
1350, 29 April	"Licence for the alienation in mortmain by William de Denton, chaplain, to the prior and Carmelite Friars of Brunham Norton of a messuage and a croft for the enlargement of their dwelling place." [CPR, 1348-1350, 497].
1353, 10 Nov	"Licence, for 6s. 8d. to be paid to the king by the prior and Carmelite Friars of Burnham Norton, for the alienation in mortmain by Ralph de Femenhale and Richard Fermen of Burnham Sutton to the said prior and friars of 3 acres of land in Burnham Norton, for the enlargement of their manse. And the 6s. 8d. have been paid in the hanaper." [CPR, 1350-54, 506].
c1357	The Carmelites of Burnham Norton, together with the other religious houses, were asked by the monks of Lilleshull Abbey to pray for the soul of their departed abbot Roger Norries.

ANNEX

	[Dufour, J. & Favier, J., Receuil des rouleaux des morts (VIIIe siècle-vers 1536) – Volume 2 (1181-1399), (Paris: Diffusion de Boccard, 2006) 516].
1365	A provincial chapter was held in Burnham presided over by the provincial, Thomas Brome. [Bale, Bodley 73, fo. 80v]
1370, 13 April	John Rudelond, from this house, was ordained priest at St. Paul's cathedral by Simon Sudbury, bishop of London. [Reg. Sudbury, London, ii, 82]
1374, 23 Feb	John de Berneye, in his will left the following bequest: "... and to the Carmelite brothers at Burnham 1 mark." [Norwich Record Office, NCC will register Heydon 1370-1383, fo. 42].
1385	A provincial chapter was held in Burnham presided over by the provincial, Robert Ivory. [Bale, Bodley 73, fo. 80v].
1387, Feb	In the will of Nicholas Palmere, chaplain, of Great Snoring, Norfolk, dated 17 February 1387 (proved after 25 March 1387), he asked to be buried in the friary, and he made the following bequests: [Translation] "Item I leave to the prior of the brothers of the Order of saint Mary at Burnham, that is Robert of Merston, 6s. 8d.; Item I leave to doctor (magister) brother John Wauncy, 6s. 8d.; Item I leave to doctor brother Adam of Desenham, 6s. 8d.; Item to brother Thomas of Bucham, 6s. 8d.; Item to subprior brother Thomas of Harpelee, 6s. 8d.; Item to brother Thomas of Baunstede, 6s. 8d." In addition, Palmere left 3s. 4d. to each of the other friars of the house not named in the will and 2s. to each of the novices there. Also, he left 6s. 8d. to the Gylde beate Marie de Burnham, otherwise known as "the Friers gild", which was located in the chapel above the gate of the friary. [Norwich Record Office, NCC will register Harsyk, fo. 81v].
1391	Robert Hemenhale, knight, in his will included the following provisions: [Translation] "Firstly I commend my soul to almighty God, the blessed Virgin Mary and all the saints, and my body to be buried in the choir of the brothers of Mount Carmel at Burnham. Item I leave to the said brothers my large black gown. Item, to the same brothers 1 mark in money. ..."]. Dated Sunday before the feast of St. Michael (24 Sept), 1391. [BL, Harley Charter 51 E 14].
1392, 31 Oct	There was a grant from pope Boniface IX: "The like relaxation [of two years and two quarantines of enjoined penance], during ten years, to penitents who on the principal feasts of

the year and that of the dedication, the octaves of certain of them, and the six days of Whitsun week; and of a hundred days to those who during the said octaves and six days visit and give alms for the conservation of the chapel situate over the gate of the Carmelite house of Brunham in the diocese of Norwich." [CPL, (London, 1902), iv, 433].

1406	A provincial chapter was held in Burnham presided over by the provincial, Stephen Patrington. [Bale, Bodley 73, fo. 81].
Before 1410	William Harsyk, who was later a noted theologian, joined the Carmelites at Burnham Norton. [Bale, Catalogus, ii, 88].
1416, 26 Sept	In the will of Isabell Ufford, countess of Suffolk, proved 28 Oct 1416, occurs the bequest: [Trans. "Item, to each house of the four orders of friars in Suffolk and Norfolk, 5 marks to celebrate each year for my soul and for the souls of those named below."]. [Reg. Chichele, Canterbury, ii, 95].
1422 Michelmas	The prior Robert Chyne and brother John Toftys appeared as defendants in a court case brought by John Godfrey.

[Trans. "John Godfrey in his own person himself pleaded on 4th day against brother Robert Chyne, prior of the brothers of the Carmelite Order in Burnham in the said county and brother John Toftys, fellow brother of the same prior and Walter Grene of Burnham St Andrew's in the same county, yoeman, and Joanna his wife for restitution, that they should return to him a certain casket with written papers and other deeds contained in the same casket, which they have unjustly withheld, etc. And they were not present ..."] [Henry VI 1422, CP40/647 (AALT: IMG0670d)].

1429, 27 April	In the will of Thomas Haws, vicar of Burnham p.c. (proved 7 May 1429) occurs the bequest: "Item, I leave to the convent of the Carmelite brothers of the Order of the blessed Mary of Burnham, 40d." [NRO, NCC wills register Surflete, fo. 38v]
1429	A provincial chapter was held in Burnham presided over by the provincial, Thomas Netter. [Bale, Bodley 73, fo. 81v]
1446, 16 Jan	In his will dated 16 Jan 1446, proved 16 Feb 1446, William Fowler of Burnham Norton made the following bequests: "Firstly I commend my soul to almighty God, to the blessed Virgin Mary and to all the saints, and my body to be buried in the convent of the Carmelite brothers in Burnham. ... To the execution of this will that all should be done well

ANNEX

and faithfully, all the remainder of my goods which I have not bequeathed above, I leave to the discretion and the disposition of my executors, that is the prior of the said convent, brother Nicholas Merlow, Margaret Fowler my wife and William Grome, whom I appoint my executors by the present [testament], that they should arrange and dispose for the salvation of my soul as they should see would best please God and the benefit of my soul." [D. Foss, "The Canterbury Archiepiscopates of John Stafford (1443-52) and John Kemp (1452-1454) with editions of their registers", Ph.D. thesis, London University (1986), ii(1), 255].

1446, 1 Feb In a second will of William Fowler (see above), in which he made provision for the sale of his houses, dated 1 Feb 1446 and proved on 16 Feb 1446, he included the following: "Firstly I will that that my house where I now live and the lands which belong to the same house and are in the hands of my tenants, namely John Auntell' and William Grome, so that the sum of money which comes from the sale of the said lands and house may be distributed by the hand of my executors, namely brother Nicholas Merlow prior there, Margaret Fowler and William Grome. I will that the convent of Burnham shall have 20s. Item I will that there shall be held an annual celebration in St Margaret's church for my soul, and that a brother of the same Order shall celebrate the said annual [mass]." [D. Foss, "The Canterbury Archiepiscopates...", ii(1), 256].

When the will was proved, a commission of administration was given to the named executors. They were discharged because of insufficiency of goods.

1457 Nicholas Esthawe gave a legacy to the priory of 26s 8d. [Cox, (1906) "The Carmelite Friars of Burnham Norton", 426]

1457 A provincial chapter was held in Burnham Norton presided over by the provincial, John Milverton. [Bale, Bodley 73, fo. 81v]

1460 Denis Holcan (Holkam), a noted Cambridge scholar and doctor of theology died and was buried at Burnham Norton. [Bale, Catalogus, ii, 98].

After 1464. [Translation] "Title of the Brothers of the Order of the Blessed Mary, Mother of God, of Mount Carmel at Burnham by the Sea, Diocese of Norwich, For the soul of ... etc." (i.e. "Quod decimus vestris et vos impendite nostris; Pergratum munus,

	sic fiet spiritis unus."). [Raine, J., The obituary roll of William Ebchester and John Burnby, Priors of Durham, (Durham: Surtees Society vol. XXXI, 1856) 13].
1467 11 March	Thomas Gigges, of Burnham St. Clement, left a small bequest of money to the priory. [NA E 40/5971: A Descriptive Catalogue of Ancient Deeds, (London, 1906) v, A 11569]. Note: See 1505 and 1510 for other examples of bequests by this family.
1486 Aug	A provincial chapter was held in Burnham presided over by the provincial, John Vynde. [Bale, Bodley 73, fo. 82v].
15 Aug 1486	Thomas Waterpitt, prior of Norwich, presented the agreement of the mayor, aldermen and citizens to be the patrons of the Norwich house to the provincial chapter meeting at Burnham Norton. This petition was granted by the provincial, John Vynde (Carm.) and the definitors in a document dated 11 May 1488. [The document survives in the Guildhall, Norwich: see J. Kirkpatrick, History of Religious Orders in Norwich, (Yarmouth, 1845), 164-6].
1493	The Carmelite William Byntre died and was buried at the friary. [Bale, Catalogus, i, 6323].
1499, 10 Jan	In her will dated 10 Jan 1499 (proved 7 June 1499), Elizabeth Norton, widow of Richard Norton, of Burnham Norton, made the bequest: "to the friars of Burnham, 13s. 4d." [Register of John Morton, iii, 63].
1499, 19 Jan	In his will dated 19 Jan 1499 (proved 4 June 1499), John Gybbys of Brancaster made the bequest: "to the friars of Burnham Norton, 20d." [Register of John Morton, iii, 57].
1499, 10 May	In his will dated 10 May 1499 (proved 25 May 1499), Andrew Horscroft of South Raynham made the bequest: "to the Carmelites of Burnham for celebrating half a Gregorian trental for his soul and those of his benefactors, 5s." [Register of John Morton, iii, 69].
1503	Robert Bale, claimed to be one of the most distinguished Carmelites of his age, was prior of the house. [Cox, "The Carmelite Friars of Burnham Norton", 426].
1505	Thomas Gigges left the friars 6s 8d.: "that is to say, to the prior 12d., and to every friar being a priest 4d., and to every novice 2d., and to their pittance 12d., they to keep a solemn dirige and a mass for my soul and all my friends souls at my burying." [Cox, "The Carmelite Friars of Burnham Norton",

425]. Note: See 1467 and 1510 for other examples of bequests by this family.

1509-10 In a list of general pardons granted by king Henry VIII soon after his accession, there occurs the entry: "John Fakenham, prior, and the convent of the Carmelite Friars of Burnham, Norf. 4 Oct." [L. & P. Henry VIII, i, 2nd. ed., (1), 261].

1510 Olive Gigges, widow of Thomas Gigges, left a bequest of 6 combs of barley to "the whight friers of Burnham". [Cox, "The Carmelite Friars of Burnham Norton", 4256].

1524 A provincial chapter was held in Burnham presided over by the provincial, John Bird. [Bale, Bodley 73, fo. 82v].

1533, 22 April "Andrew prior of the Carmelite Priory and Burnham Norton" signed a letter of attorney as a witness on 22 April 1533. [NA, WARD 2/51/177/20].

1534, April Oath of Obedience: all the friars were compelled to take this:

"All friars of every monastery must be assembled in their chapter house, and examined separately concerning their faith and obedience to Henry VIII, and bound by an oath of allegiance to him, Queen Anne and her present and future issue. They must be bound by oath to preach and persuade the people of the above at every opportunity. They must acknowledge the king as the supreme head of the Church, as Convocation and Parliament have decreed. They must confess that the bishop of Rome has no more authority than other bishops. They shall not call the bishop of Rome pope either privately or publicly, or pray for him as such. They shall not presume to wrest the Scriptures, but preach the words and deeds of Christ sincerely and simply, according to the meaning of the Holy Scripture and Catholic doctors. The sermons of each preacher must be carefully examined and burnt if not Catholic, orthodox and worthy of a Christian preacher.

"Preachers must be warned to commend to God and the prayers of the people, first the King as head of the Church of England, then queen Anne with her child, and lastly the archbishop of Canterbury, with the other orders of the clergy. Each house must be obliged to show their gold, silver and other moveable goods, and deliver an inventory of them. Each house must take an oath under their convent seal to observe the above orders." [L. & P. Henry VIII, vii, 590].

| 1535 | The prior was Robert Reder and the value of the house, as given in the Valor Ecclesiasticus, was as follows: | |

Income:

From 40 acres of land in Burnham Norton	26s. 8d.
From 14 acres of land in the fields of Burnham Westgate	9s. 4d.
From 14 acres of land in the fields of Burnham Sutton	9s. 4d.
Total Income	45s. 4d.

Dues:

Philip Calthorp, knt, per annum	7s. 11d.
Richard Southwell, knt, manor of Lexham	2s. 7d.
Pountfrett College	7 1/2d.
Walsingham Priory	12d.
John Fyncham	19d.
Burnham Norton church	8d.
House of St. John of Carbroke	1d.
Hugh Thurlowe	2d.
Total Dues	14s.7 1/2d.
Remaining clear	30s. 8 1/2d.

[Valor Ecclesiasticus temp. Henr. VIII. Auctoritate Regia Institutus, (1810 34), iii, 371].

1536 10 Feb	Robert Ryder, prior, was granted a dispensation to hold a benefice with cure of souls and to wear his habit beneath that of a secular priest, having resigned the above office. Fee paid £8. [Chambers, D., Faculty Office Registers, 1534-1549, (Oxford, 1966), 44].
1537	In April, popular discontent manifested itself in a serious way in Norfolk. Men met in the streets of Walsingham and 'condemned the suppression of so many religious houses in which God was well served and many good deeds of charity done'. 3040 men of the district were arrested. Their object was to take Lynn and seize it and fortify the Thetford and Brandon bridges. A special commission sitting at Norwich castle on 22nd May tried those arrested. Among them were two Carmelites of Burnham Norton who were both found

ANNEX

guilty. John Pecock was sentenced to death and executed at Lynn on Friday, 1st June, 1537. (Eleven others were executed at different towns in Norfolk). William Gibson, the second Carmelite, was sentenced to life imprisonment for failing to reveal the plot. [An account of this episode is found in Gasquet, Henry VIII and the English Monasteries, (London, 1888-9), 3145].

1537, 27 Nov. William Gybson, of Burnham, Norfolk, clerk, Carmelite friar and co-brother of John, prior of Burnham,...(and others)... Pardon of all treasons, rebellions, etc. committed by them before 1st. August last. [L. & P. Henry VIII, xii, (2), 1150].

1538, 17 May Jane Calthorp wrote to Cromwell asking, "him to obtain licence from the King for her to purchase a house of White Friars, near Polested Hall, in Burneham, Norfolk, which manor the King granted to her and her heirs male. There are only four friars, and being too poor to sustain the charge and repairs of the house, they are willing to part with it. [She] has no house to live in but one poor house in Norwich, from which she is often driven by the plague." [L. & P. Henry VIII, xiii, (1), p. 374].

1538 30 May A dispensation to become a secular priest was granted to Richard Makeyn, "recently of Burnham Norton", for the fee of £4. [Chambers, D., Faculty Office Registers, 1534-1549, (Oxford, 1966)., 135].

1538, 31 Aug Sir Roger Townsend wrote to Thomas Cromwell that he was sending by the prior of the White Friars of Burnham, Norfolk, a book of 'cungerations' and a paper of prophecies rehearsed by one Richard Laund, pinner of Norwich. Townsend asks Cromwell to thank the prior, who was the taker of one of the most rank traitors that were privy to the conspiracy at Walsingham. [L. & P. Henry VIII, xii, (2), 602].

1538 A paper drawn up towards the end of the year, enumerating the friaries in the Eastern Counties: "Hereafter ensueth the causes of such houses as we have not as it defasede ne rasede. The late White Friars of Burneham. The houses are not sold, but stand as they were left by the Visitor (Richard Ingworth) on account of a letter written by Mr. Southwell to Will. Buttes, his deputy, ordering him not to meddle as Sir Ric. Gresham had the preferment of the said house at the King's hands." [L. & P. Henry VIII, xiii, (2), 1212 (p. 508)].

Among the spoils of church plate from the religious houses of Norfolk were: '3 oz. gilt, 58 oz. white and a nutt garnished with silver,' from the White Friars of Burnham. [Cox, "The Carmelite Friars of Burnham Norton", 426].

At the dissolution, the friary possessed 68 acres of land and was valued in 1535 at £2 5s. 4d. [J. Speed, The Historie of Great Britaine, (1623) bk 9, chap. 21, 1082]. Sir William Dugdale gives the value as £1 10s 8 1/2d. [Monasticon Anglicanum, (London 1665-73, repr. London 1846), vi (3), 1573].

Within the Church was an altar to the Virgin Mary, to whom the convent was dedicated. [Bryant, The Churches of Norfolk, 22].

Part II B: KNOWN PRIORS OF THE CARMELITE HOUSE, BURNHAM NORTON

John of St. Faith	-1359
Robert de Merston	1387
William Harsick	1410
Robert Cheyny	1422
Robert Burnham	1425
Nicholas Merlow	16 Jan-1 Feb 1446
William Byntrey	-1493
Robert Bale	-1503
John Fakenham	1509-10
Andrew	1533
Robert Ryder	1535-1536 (resigned)
John -	1537

Part II C: POST-DISSOLUTION HISTORY OF THE HOUSE

1542 — The site was granted to William, Lord Cobham, and Edward Warner, to be held of the King in capite, with certain messuages about it. [Bryant, The Churches of Norfolk, 22].

1544, 21 Feb — Licence to alienate was given to Sir George Broke and Edw. Warner, the King's servant, to lady Anne Calthorpe, widow.

ANNEX

	"Priory of Friars Carmelites of Burneham, Norf. with lands (described and tenants named) in Burneham. P. 4 m 16." [L. & P. Henry VIII, xix (1), p. 85].
1545, 8 Nov	Licence to alienate was granted:
	"Joan Calthorp to Wm. Blenerhayset and Anne his wife. House and site, church, etc. of the late Carmelite Friars of Burneham, Norf. and lands (specified and tenants named) there which belonged to the same. P 17 m 4." [L. & P. Henry VIII, xx (2), p. 454].
1577	Two acres of concealed lands in the tenure of Francis Cobbe, belonging to the Carmelite friars, were granted to Edward Grymston. The property was subsequently owned by William Bromfield. [Bryant, The Churches of Norfolk, 22].
	The friary later passed to Thomas Pepys, a relative of the diarist Samuel, who used to refer to the family as 'my Norfolk cousins'. [Moore, St. Margaret's, Burnham Norton, 14].
late 18th cent.	An engraving survives of the gatehouse and the church. The church was still complete and in use as a barn. Now only the west wall survives. [Reproduced in the panel on the site].
1840	The gateway was repaired in 1840 when some excavations were made and skeletons unearthed. Bryant claims that one of them was found to be in conventual dress. [Bryant, The Churches of Norfolk, 22]. The gatehouse was partly rebuilt and reroofed. [see panel on site]
before 1914	Property later passed to the Earls of Orford and was in their possession in 1914. [Bryant, The Churches of Norfolk, 22].
1967	In 1967, the property belonged to Lord Leicester. [Moore, St. Margaret's Church, Burnham Norton, 14].
1970's	The remains passed into the care of Norfolk County Council and essential repairs were undertaken to preserve the remains (with a contribution from the Carmelite Order).

Part III: FRIARS KNOWN TO HAVE BEEN MEMBERS OF THE COMMUNITY

An asterisk * after the name indicates that the individual is described here.

ALAN DERSYNGHAM

In a printed copy of a work by Nicolaus de Horto Coeli, and others, (Padua, undated), there is the attribution: "libellus fr. Alani Dersyngham, O.C., Burham, Cantabrigiis theologie studentis anno christiani salutis 1511" [BL, IC. 29955-56: Ker, Medieval Libraries, 232].

ANDREW ...

On 22 April 1533, Andrew, prior of the Carmelite Priory at Burnham Norton signed a letter of attorney as a witness. [NA, WARD 2/51/177/20].

DENIS HOLCAN (DENYS, HOLKAM, HOLKEHAM, HOLKHAM)

Carmelite who joined the Order in Burnham Norton. He was sent to study at Cambridge university where he incepted as a D.Th. He taught at Cambridge for many years. [Bale, Harley 3838, fo. 103].

Apparently he retired back to Burnham Norton. He was given the title of magister when he died there on 21 Oct 1467 and was buried in the chapel. [Bale, Bodley 73, fo. 135v].

Lost works:

1. Formalitatum suarum, Lib. 1. [Bale, Harley 3838, fo. 103]

2. Determinationum, Lib. 1. [Bale, Harley 3838, fo. 103]

GODFREY FOLSHAM

Bale, in his early unfinished history of the Carmelite Order, Fasciculus Carmelitarum, compiled c1528-1533, notes that: "Godfrey, Reginald and Peter, all surnamed Folsham, shone in the convent in Burnham, fathers who were worthy of veneration". [Bale, Selden supra 41, fo. 154v]. Peter* and Reginald Folsham* are known for being sent to Lyons by the general chapter to seek the approval of the Rule in 1247. Apart from being an illustrious member of the Carmelite community in Burnham Norton c.1247, nothing is further known about Godfrey Folsham although it seems likely that he was related in some way to the other Folshams. [Bale, Selden supra 41, fo. 154v: Harley 3838, fo. 16].

HENRY OF ANNA (ANRA, ARENA, HANNA, HANNE, HANNONIA, HARENA)

Born in Norfolk but possibly, as Bale suggests, to a family which had its origins in the province of Hainaut in Belgium ('Hannonia' in Latin). He joined the Order in Burnham Norton. [Selden supra 41, fo. 159: Harley 3838, fo. 55]. His correct name, as given in his own letters, is Henry de Anna although most later historians have called him "Henry de Hanna".

His early career in the Order is unknown. In his Anglorum Heliades (written 1536), Bale claims Anna was the "first prior and founder of the convent at Oxford", a house which was founded in 1256. [Bale, Harley 3838, fo. 160v]. However, surviving documents name John of Rochester* as the Carmelite who accepted the house and who was its first procurator (prior). [Cart. Oseney, ed. H. Salter, (Oxf. Hist. Soc., 1929), ii, 344-5]. Bale also states that Anna was elected provincial in 1254, but this cannot be true because the two surviving letters relating to the founding of the house in Oxford, dated 21 Aug 1256 and 24 July 1257 show that the provincial at this date bore a Christian name beginning with the letter W.* [Bale, Harley 3838, fos. 55-55v: Cartulary of. Osney Abbey, ed. H. Salter, (Oxf. Hist. Soc., 1929), ii, 345, 347].

In his Anglorum Heliades, Bale claims that in 1260 whilst Anna was provincial, he was sent by the prior general to France to help found houses there.This commission was possibly connected to the fact that the general chapter was due to meet in Aylesford the following year. Hervey Burnham* was appointed vicar in his absence. Bale adds that Anna did the same in Germany, Scotland and Ireland. [Bale, Bodley 73, fo. 79v: Harley 3838, fo. 21v]. There is no supporting evidence for Bale's account that Anna was provincial during this period but it is possible that Anna acted as vicar for the prior general (possibly Simon Stock*) on various missions during the 1260's, such as presiding at provincial chapters, etc. Bale adds that Anna was also appointed vicar general for England during the period that Roger Crostwyck* was in office. [Bale, Harley 3838, fo. 22v].

Bale's earlier notes, based on some lost registers of the province, record that Anna was elected (or re-elected) provincial at the general chapter in London in 1281. [Bale, Bodley 73, fos. 79v, 133]. As provincial, Anna wrote to king Edward I informing him that the recent provincial chapter at Cambridge had ordered that each of the brethren should pray and offer mass for the king, his family and the realm and asking the king's protection for the Order. This letter survives but is undated and Egan suggests it was written c.1283. [NA, SC 1/15/194: *Egan thesis*, 169, n1]. Bale, copying probably from a register in Burnham Norton, claims that Anna made a visitation of the house there on 19 Feb 1283. [Bale, *Bodley 73*, fo. 135v]. Two documents from the general chapter meeting in Montpellier on 22 July 1287 relating to the adoption of the white cloak list him among the provincials present who signed the decree. [A. Staring, *Medieval Carmelite Heritage*, (Rome, 1989), 54, 66: A.C.G., i, 10]. In 1287, he presided over the provincial chapter at Lincoln which enforced the change in the habit in England. He held other chapters at Oxford in 1289, Lynn, 1291, Oxford again, 15 August 1296 and Ipswich, 1300. [Bale, *Bodley 73*, fo. 79v].

On 27 April 1289, John le Romeyn, archbishop of York, requested him to receive Richard Manlovel*, an Augustine canon of Thurgarton into the Carmelite Order. [*Reg. Romeyn, York*, 123]. Eight appeals from Anna to king Edward I seeking the detention and return of errant friars survive. [NA, C 81/1793/3-8, 10: W. Prynne, *Antiquae constitutiones regni Angliae ...*, (1672) 640-1]. From the places where Anna signed these letters, it's clear that, on 1 Dec 1293, he was in Aylesford but by 9 Dec, he had returned to London. [NA, C 81/1793/4 & 5]. He was in London on 9 Aug 1295 and again on 27 May 1297 and on 16 Aug 1297, the last possibly after returning from the general chapter in Bruges in June. [NA, C 81/1793/7-8: A. Staring, *Medieval Carmelite Heritage*, (Rome, 1989), 296]. On 2 Feb 1299, he was in London but the next letter, dated 23 March 1299, was signed by Humphrey Necton* as vicar general, probably due to Anna being absent. [NA, C 81/1793/6, 9]. On 9 Sept 1299, he signed the final surviving letter from Northampton. [NA, C 81/1793/10].

Bale's later compositions claim that Anna died in office on 28 Nov 1299 at Stamford and was buried in the choir there. [Bale, *Harley 3838*, fo. 26v: Bale, *Catalogus*, i, 308]. However, in an earlier list of chapters, Bale gives the date as "28 Nov 1300", which concurs with the record that Anna presided at the chapter held at Ipswich in 1300. Chapters were normally convened on 15 Aug each year so the fact that the next chapter, called to elect his successor William Ludlington*, took place in Stamford on the 27 Feb 1301 would seem to indicate that it was called early due to the death of Anna. [Bale, *Bodley 73*, fos. 79v, 133].

An epitaph composed by the Italian Carmelite, bl. Baptist of Mantua (†1516), is preserved by Norbert of Saintt-Julian:

> "Here lies Henry of Hanna from Burnham, his full name
> A learned man, who lived a holy life
> Noted for his virtues, this brother gained the highest office,
> Second rector of the British province
> He received the new cloister beside the banks of the Isis:
> then, sent to the French,
> he founded many houses there.
> Returning to his own English, he remained as rector
> Until, old in years, he passed peacefully away."

[*De Scriptoribus Belgicis et Viris Illustribus ex Ordine Carmelitarum*, Bibl. Royale de Belgique Ms. 3818 (16492)].

Surviving Writings:

Bale records a collection of letters with *incipit* which was presumably preserved in the provincial archives. The letter-book itself has been lost but the originals of some letters have survived.

1. *Elegantes epistolas, Lib. 1*: "Dilectus in Christo filiis Londinensibus." [Bale, *Harley 3838*, fo. 55v].

Ms.: surviving letters:

i. *NA*, SC 1/15/194: letter to king Edward I, dated c.1283 assuring him of the prayers of the brethren and asking for his protection:

Appeals to king Edward I for the return of errant friars,

ii. *NA*, C 81/1793/3: undated letter to king for the return of John of Lynn*:

iii. *NA*, C 81/1793/4: 1 Dec 1293, letter to king for the return of John Berkynge* & Philip of Beccles*:

iv. *NA*, C 81/1793/5: 9 Dec 1293, letter to king for the return of William of Offynton*:

v. *NA*, C 81/1793/6: 2 Feb 1299, letter to king for the return of John of Symingham*:

vi. *NA*, C 81/1793/7: 29 May 1297, letter to king for the return of Philip of Beccles*:

vii. *NA*, C 81/1793/8: 16 Aug 1297, letter to king for the return of John Malore*:

viii: *NA*, C 81/1793/10: 9 Sept 1299, letter to king for the return of William of Cobham*:

Ed.:

ix. W. Prynne, *Antiquae constitutiones regni Angliae sub regibus Joanne, Henrico III, et Edoardo I circa jurisdictionem et potestatem ecclesiasticam ...*, (1672) 640-641: 9 Aug 1295, letter to king for the return of Ralph of Snytterell*:

Lost works:

2. *Ordinationes locorum, Lib. 1.* [Bale, *Harley 3838*, fo. 55v].

3. *Conciones aliquot., Lib. 1.* [Bale, *Catalogus*, i, 307-8].

These two titles without *incipit* are probably conventional "additions" by Bale.

Misattribution:

4. Copies of three short sermons by "Meister Hane der Karmelit" are found in Oxford, Bodl. Libr., Ms Laud misc. 479:

a. *Sermo de Adventum:* "*Gaudete in domino semper*" (fos. 8v-10)

b. *Sermo in festum Pentecostes:* "*Emitte spiritum tuum et creabuntur*" (fos. 53r-v)

c. *Sermo de sanctis:* "*Omnes querebant eum tangere, quia virtus de illo exibat et sanabat omnes*" (fos. 96v-97).

    These sermons were thought to be by Henry of Anna but are now judged to be by a later German Carmelite, Johannes Vogolon from Cologne. Vogolon was awarded a doctorate in Paris University and later lectured in Cologne where he died sometime after 1343. These sermons have been printed with an Italian translation by E. Boaga, O.Carm., "I tre sermoni spirituali del 'Meister Hane der Karmelit'", *Analecta Ordinis Carmelitarum,* 41 (1990) 22-33.

HERVEY BURNHAM (HENRY, BRUNHAM)

Following the general chapter held in Aylesford in 1260, Bale notes that Burnham was appointed as vicar provincial to act for the provincial, Henry of Anna*, who was away in France, probably acting as vicar-general. [Bale, *Harley 3838*, fo. 21v].

    On 19 Feb 1283, Burnham was living in Burnham Norton when the provincial, Henry de Anna*, visited the house and described him as "an old and learned man". [Bale, *Bodley 73*, fo. 135v].

    Bale records that Burnham furnished the library at Burnham Norton with various books on canon law and theology for the use of the students there. [Bale, *Selden supra 41*, fo. 159].

JOHN ...

Prior of Burnham Norton on 27th Nov 1537 when, together with William Gybson* and others, he received a pardon for his part in the Walsingham conspiracy. "William Gybson, of Burnham, Norfolk, clerk, Carmelite friar and co-brother of John, prior of Burnham,...(and others)... Pardon of all treasons, rebellions, etc. committed by them before 1st. August last." [*L. & P. Hen. VIII*, xii, (2), 1150].

    Presumably the same person who, on 31st Aug 1538, was mentioned in a letter to Thomas Cromwell by Sir Thomas Townsend: "Sends, by the prior of the White Friars of Burnham, Norfolk, a book of 'cungerations' and a paper of prophecies rehearsed by one Ric. Laund, pinner of Norwich.

    The prior can show him the good service done by Austen Styward, alderman of Norwiche. Asks him to thank the prior, who was the taker of one of the most rank traitors that were privy to the conspiracy at Walsingham. Would have written sooner but has been engaged with the matter between the prior and cellarer of Walsingham, which Cromwell wrote to him to examine, and which he hopes soon to finish. Begs favour for this prior in his suits. 31 Aug. *Signed.*" [*L. & P. Hen. VIII*, xii (2), 602].

JOHN CREYK

Carmelite of Burnham Norton who was taxed 6s. 8d. in the clerical subsidy voted by Parliament in 1449, as he was parochial chaplain at Broomsthorpe parish church. [Jurkowski, M., "Were Friars paid salaries? Evidence from clerical taxation records", in *Fifteenth Century XIII*, ed. L. Clark, (2014) 150].

JOHN FAKENHAM

He was prior of Burnham Norton in 1509-10 (4 Oct) when he was listed with the brothers in the convent in a general pardon issued by Henry VIII. [*L. & P. Hen. VIII*, i, 261].

JOHN PECOCK

From Burnham Norton and involved with another member of the community, William Gibson*, in the Walsingham conspiracy. The conspiracy started in the middle of April 1537 by two singing men at Walsingham priory and quickly involved a number of other people. The plot was betrayed and among those arrested were two Carmelites, Pecock and William Gibson*. They were held in Norwich castle by 10 May. Pecock was indicted with twenty-seven other conspirators at Norwich Assizes on 25 May and charged with treason. It is possible that Pecock was betrayed by his own prior, John (xii)*, who was recorded as "the taker of one of the most rank traitors that were privy to the conspiracy at Walsingham." [*L. & P. Hen. VIII*, xii, (2), 602].

Two of the conspirators, James Hendley and Harry Capron, gave evidence on 10 June 1537 that they were imprisoned with the two Carmelites and five others in a house within the Norwich Castle and that they went with the friars on occasion to the chapel. Evidently they sang the "anthem of Our Lady" there and on some nights the friars knelt together at the altar. [*L. & P. Hen. VIII*, xii (2), 23].

Pecock was found guilty and condemned, with eleven others, to suffer a traitor's death. On Friday 1st June, after making a "good end", that is expressing his remorse and exhorting the onlookers to obey the king in all things, he was hung, drawn and quartered at Lynn. [*NA*, State Papers, Henry VIII, 1/120, fo. 226, 1/121, fos. 70-2, 86-9: *L. & P. Hen. VIII*, xii, i, 1300 (2), ii, 56, 68: King's Bench Ancient Indictment, 9/538/4-8].

The cause for beatification of John Pecock was put forward by the Carmelite general chapter of 1908. [*Analecta Ordinis Carmelitarum*, 1 (1909), 10].

JOHN RUDELOND

Listed from Burnham Norton when he was ordained priest on 13 April 1370 in St. Paul's, London. [*Reg. Sudbury, London*, ii, 82].

JOHN OF SAINT FAITH (DE S. FIDE, SANCTOFIDENSIS)

(i) Joined the Order in Burnham Norton. [Bale, *Bodley 73*, fo. 135v]. He continued his studies at Oxford University where he incepted as D.Th. Afterwards, he was prior of Burnham Norton until his death on 18 Sept 1359. [Bale, *Selden supra 41*, fo. 168v]

Described by Bale as: "he was held to be an outstanding preacher (as far as time allowed), a not unworthy philosopher, an excellent lawyer and an incomparable theologian". [Bale, *Harley 3838*, fos. 73].

Lost works:

Bale lists the following of his works;

1. *Postilla super evangelium Johannis, Lib. 1*: "*Karissimi doctores et sacrarum litterarum scriptores quilibet libro suo quem scribit vel edit prologum proponere solet. Ut auditoribus suis innotescat que necessitatis scribendi que utilitas etc.*" [Bale, *Bodley 73*, fo. 197v, 199v]. On the first occasion that Bale saw this work, he begins the *incipit* "*Karissimi auctores*". Later, the title becomes *Preconiorum* or *Encomium eiusdem Joannis*. [*Harley 3838*, fo. 73v: Bale, *Catalogus*, i, 441]. Probably the *In laudem Johannis evangeliste, de vocacione paupertate et virtutibus eiusdem, Lib. 1.* noted elsewhere in Bale's notebook. [Bale, *Bodley 73*, fo. 119].

2. *Sermones lxiij de tempore et de sanctis, Lib. 1*: "*Veritas de terra orta est, vas liquore plenum scilicet vino vel aliquo etc.*" [Bale, *Bodley 73*, fo. 197v]. Later, Bale expands this into two works, omitting an *incipit* for the *Sermones de sanctis*. [Bale, *Summarium*, 146v: Bale, *Catalogus*, i, 442].

3. *Collationes varias, Lib. 1*: "*Sufficit tibi gracia mea. 2ª. Ad Corinthios 13ª. Secundum philosophum natura non habundat in superfluis. Nec deficit in necessarijs sed unicuique rei naturali sufficienter providit de medijs quibus possit attingere finem suum. Sic Christus auctor nature.*" [Bale, *Bodley 73*, fo. 199v]. Later entitled *Collationes in Scripturam*. [Bale, *Harley 3838*, fo. 73v].

4. *Tabulam in postillam, Lib. 1*: "*Abimelech prelatus malus est.*" A work Bale describes as "excellent". [*Bodley 73*, fo. 199v]. Later entitled *Eorundem indices* or *Predictorum Elenchos*. [Bale, *Harley 3838*, fo. 73v: Bale, *Catalogus*, i, 442].

It seems likely that the following three works, added in 1536, were parts of

1. above:

5. *Glossemata in Ioannem*, Lib. 1: "Cum iam de prologo mentionem facere." [Bale, Harley 3838, fo. 73v].

6. *In canonicam Joannis*, Lib. 1: "Sicut dicit apostolus Paulus." [Bale, Harley 3838, fo. 73v].

7. *Directorium in Joannem*, Lib. 1: "Accusare peccatorem solet sua." [Bale, Harley 3838, fo. 73v].

The following two works on Matthew's gospel are possibly one composition:

8. *In Evangelium Matthei*, Lib. 1: "Liber generationis, etc. In hoc." [Bale, Harley 3838, fo. 73v].

9. *Super evangelium Matthei indices*, Lib. 1: "Adorare Christum magi venientes." [Harley 3838, fo. 73v].

10. *Tabula juris*, Lib. 1: "Alma mater ecclesia iure suo." [Bale, Harley 3838, fo. 73v].

11. *Concordantie Thomae*, Lib. 1: "Abstinentia, in secunda secunde." [Bale, Harley 3838, fo. 73v].

12. *Loca contrarietatum*, Lib. 1: "Venerabilis doctor Beda in." [Bale, Harley 3838, fo. 73v].

13. *Commentaria in Aristotelem, 'De coelo et mundo'*, Lib. 2: "De natura autem scientia fere plurima, etc. Philosophus in prohemio ostendit." Bale saw a copy of this work in the house of Richard Grafton, c. 1550. [Bale, *Index*, 201].

The last two works, without *incipit*, are doubtful:

14. *Lecturae Scripturarum*, Lib. 1. [Bale, *Catalogus*, i, 442].

15. *Questiones disputatae*, Lib. 1. [Bale, *Summarium*, 146v].

JOHN OF TOFTYS (TOFTES, COSTEYS)

Carmelite at Burnham Norton in 1406 who was taxed 6s. 8d. in the clerical subsidy voted by Parliament that year, indicating that he had a salary or stipend from some source. [Jurkowski, M., "Were Friars paid salaries? Evidence from clerical taxation records", in *Fifteenth Century XIII*, ed. L. Clark, (2014) 147].

Still in Burnham Norton in Michaelmas Term 1422, when he was accompanied his prior Robert Cheyny* and Walter Grene and his wife Joanna when they appeared as defendants in the Court of Common Pleas, sued by a John Godfrey for the return of a casket containing written documents and other charters. [Henry VI: 1422, CP 40/647 (AALT: IMG0670d)].

NICHOLAS MERLOW

Prior of Burnham Norton on 16 Jan 1446 when he was named as an executor in the will of William Fowler. [*Reg. Stafford, Canterbury*, ii(1), 255].

PETER FOLSHAM

Carmelite cleric who, with his companion, Reginald Folsham*, was sent by the general chapter held in 1247 in Aylesford to the papal curia in Lyons to petition pope Innocent IV for the mitigation and papal approval of the Carmelite Rule. Their first names occur in the bull *Quae honorem conditoris*: "*Accedentes ad Apostolicam Sedem fratres clerici Reynaldus et Petrus Ordinis vestri, ex parte vestra a domino papa humiliter postularunt, ...*" [Cicconetti, *La Regola del Carmelo: origine - natura -significato* (Roma, 1973) 202].

Bale, in his early unfinished 'history' *Fasciculus Carmelitarum* compiled c1528-1533, notes that: "Godfrey, Reginald and Peter, all surnamed Folsham, shone in the convent in Burnham, fathers who were worthy of veneration". [Bale, *Selden supra 41*, fo. 154v]. It is unclear whether the three Folsham's were related in any way.

The convent in Burnham Norton, Norfolk, was founded between 1242-1247, so if Peter and Reginald were called 'clerics' then they would have been either secular priests who joined the Order in the new community in Burnham or, more likely, considering that they were selected to undertake such an important mission, that they were English and had joined the Order on Mount Carmel and returned to England with one of the early groups of hermits leaving the Holy Land.

PETER OF SWANYNGTON (SUAVENDUNUS, SUANINGTON, SWAINGTON, SWANTON, SWANINGTON, -IUS, SWANYTON)

Bale claims that he joined the Order in Burnham Norton, in Norfolk. As a young student, he was befriended by Gilbert of Norwich, bishop of Hamar, Norway, who became his patron and probably financed his studies through Oxford University. [Bale, *Summarium*, 113]. Swanyngton was promoted D.Th. in the late 1290's, the first Carmelite to incept there. [Bale, *Bodley 73*, fo. 118v]. Emden and later scholars suggest that he is probably to be identified with the '*Petrus Carmelita*' who engaged in disputations in the faculty of Oxford c.1300-1301 and whose *Quodlibeta* survive in a single manuscript in Worcester Cathedral Library (see below). [A.G. Little & F. Pelster, *Oxford Theology and Theologians c. 1282-1302*, (O.H.S., 1934), 276-277, 375: Emden, *B.R.U.O.*, 1831].

He was one of the Carmelite doctors who supported the Provincial, mag. William Ludlyngton*, in his opposition to any division of the English province. As a result, the prior general, Gerardo da Bologna*, ordered a provincial chapter to be held in London in 1305 and sent two German Carmelites, Conradus a St. Georgio* and Gotfridus de Nussia*, to preside over the chapter. Ludlyngton was deposed and Swanyngton was punished for his resistance by being sent to lecture on the *Sentences* at the Bordeaux convent. [Bale, *Harley 3838*, fos. 27-8, 56-56v].

On the strength of two fragments supposedly written by him relating to St. Simon Stock* and the scapular vision, he has been credited with being the secretary to Simon Stock in 1251 but these texts are a 17th century fabrication by Jean Chéron, the prior of Bordeaux. [A. Staring, 'Simon Stock', *New Catholic Encyclopedia*, (Washington, 1967), 224-5].

Note: It is likely that Peter of Swanyngton* and Peter of Scaryngton* are the same, as Dr. Emden suggests. [Emden, *B.R.U.O.*, 1831].

Surviving work:

1. *Quodlibeta*, "Quaeritur utrum ratio speciei possit attribui Deo sine ratione generis."

Schabel has published the most recent analysis of this *Quodlibet* and gives a revised numbering of the individual questions. C. Schabel, "Carmelite Quodlibeta" in C. Schabel ed., *Theological Quodlibeta in the Middle Ages: The Fourteenth Century*, (Leiden: Brill, 2007), 497-498].

(1) *Quaeritur utrum ratio speciei possit attribui Deo sine ratione generis.*

(2) *Quaeritur an veritas in Deo sit essentialis vel personalis.*

(3) *Quaeritur, posito quod Deus subtrahat praesentiam suam ab intellectu, an possit videre Deum sicut est.*

(4) *Quaeritur utrum expressio formalis in mente angeli vel aliquid intrinsecum habeat rationem principii effectivi respectu actus intelligendi.*

(5) *Quaeritur an specie existens in mente angelica sit principium distincte repraesentativum singularium.*

(6) *Quaeritur an angelius possit intelligere simul plura ut plura, videlicet per plures rationes et plures actus intelligendi simul.*

(7) *Ad quaestionem, cum quaeritur utrum angelus illuminatus videat in Verbo vel in aliquo creato.*

(8) *Quaeritur de actu voluntatis utrum velle quod est actus secundus voluntatis re absoluta differat a voluntate.*

(9) *De voluntate dicitur quod voluntas causat actum suum, quia includit in se duo, et ratione unius est movens et ratione alterius mota.*

(10) *Quaeritur utrum caritas viatoris posset aequari caritati patriae quantum ad habitum, licet non ad fervorem.*

(11) *Quaeritur an angelus posset transire de coelo in terram absque hoc quod transeat per medium.*

(12) *Quaeritur utrum species existens in mente angeli superioris sit universalior et plurium repraesentiva quam species in mente angeli inferioris.*

(13) *Quaeritur an angeli naturaliter possint cognoscere motus nostros interiores.*

(14) *Quaeritur utrum speciei impressio formalis in anima moveat efficienter.*

(15) *Quaeritur utrum angelus cognoscat certitudinaliter futura contingentia.*

(16) *Quaeritur an angelus ex puris naturalibus suis possit attingere ad intelligendum Deum sicut est.*

(17) *Quaeritur utrum intellectus angeli per aliquod donum supernaturale posset elevari ad videndum Deum sicut est.*

(18) *Quaeritur an essentia divina in patria videatur per aliquam speciem aliam ab actu intelligendi.*

(19) *Quaeritur utrum in angelo ad videndum Deum sicut est esse necesse sit ponere aliquod formale principium aliud a lumine gloriae.*

Ms:

Worcester cathedral library Ms. Q. 99, fos. 49rb-54rb.

Note: This Worcester ms. work would seem to be the one which Bale saw and records in his notebook: "*Magister frater Petrus Swanyngton scripsit: Questiones ordinarias et quodlibeta, incipiunt: 'Utrum aliquis spiritus malus possit pati a igne materiali et quod non in omni eo quid patit ab alio'. Questiones xlvii.*" It was probably seen by Bale in the Carmelite library, Oxford. [Bale, *Bodley 73*, fo. 217v].

Ed.:

[Q. 15] C. Schabel, "Carmelite Quodlibeta", 542-543.

Lost works:

2. *Super Summas.* This contained 38 *questiones.* [Bale, *Bodley 73*, fo. 118]. A copy of this work was formerly in Merton College Library. [F.M. Powicke, *Medieval Books of Merton College*, (Oxford, 1931), 56, 97].

3. *Lecturas scripturarum, Lib. 1.* [Bale, *Harley 3838*, fo. 56v].

REGINALD FOLSHAM (RAYMUNDUS, RAYNALDUS, REYNALD, -US)

Carmelite cleric who, with his companion, Peter Folsham*, was sent by the general chapter held in 1247 in Aylesford to the papal curia in Lyons to petition pope Innocent IV for the mitigation and papal approval of the

Carmelite Rule. Their first names occur in the bull *Quae honorem conditoris*: "Accedentes ad Apostolicam Sedem fratres clerici Reynaldus et Petrus Ordinis vestri, ex parte vestra a domino papa humiliter postularunt, ..." [C. Cicconetti, *La Regola del Carmelo: origine - natura -significato* (Roma, 1973) 202].

Bale, in his early unfinished "history" the *Fasciculus Carmelitarum,* compiled c1528-1533, notes that: "Godfrey, Reginald and Peter, all surnamed Folsham, shone in the convent in Burnham, fathers who were worthy of veneration". [Bale, *Selden supra 41*, fo. 154v]. It is not known whether the three Folsham's were related in any way.

The convent in Burnham Norton, Norfolk, was founded between 1242-1247, so if Peter and Reginald were called 'clerics' then they could have been secular priests who joined the Order in the new community in Burnham or, more likely, considering that they were selected to undertake such an important mission, that they were English and had joined the Order on Mount Carmel and returned to England with one of the early groups of hermits leaving the Holy Land.

RICHARD MAKEYN

Described as "recently of Burnham (Norton)" when, on 30 May 1538, he was granted a dispensation to become a secular priest for a fee of £4. [Chambers, D., *Faculty Office Registers, 1534-1549*, (Oxford, 1966), 135].

ROBERT BALE

Born three miles from Walsingham and entered the Order probably at Burnham Norton (not Norwich as some claim). Where he studied is not recorded but it was probably Norwich where he was awarded the title of *lector*. [*Harley 3838*, fo. 109].

John Bale* (no relation), taking his information probably from friars who knew him personally, recorded that, although not an eloquent speaker, he impressed many with his learning and his ability to solve legal problems. A lover of the liturgy and the history of the Order, he collected many works which John Bale saw in the library at Burnham Norton. John Bale adds that Robert's own writings were "unpolished and dull". He is said to have spent a part of each year studying at Oxford or Cambridge, but the surviving texts do little to support any claim to academic prowess although he may have visited the universities, copying manuscripts. [Bale, *Harley 3838*, fo. 109v].

Prior of Burnham Norton at the time of his death on 11 Nov. 1503 and buried there. [Bale, *Bodley 73*, fo. 135v].

Note: Not to be confused with Robert Bale, public notary of London, the supposed author of a chronicle of London 1437-1461.

Surviving works:

1. *Chronica Parva sive Exordium Sacri Ordinis Carmelitarum, Lib. 1,* "Anno mundi 4186. Helias propheta primis patriarcha Carmelitarum." A short chronicle copied by Bale c.1515-1520.

Ms:

Oxford, Bodl. Libr. Selden supra 72, (S.C. 3460), fos. 5-11v.

2. *Historia sancti Heliae Prophetae, Lib. 1,* "Ecce ego mittam vobis Heliam",

Liturgical office with lessons on the life of Elijah and his role as founder of the Carmelites, copied by Bale c.1520.

Ms:

Camb. Univ. Library, Ms. 6.28, fos. 34-42v.

Lost work:

3. *Historiam Symonis Angli, Li. I:* "Ave Symon pater inclitus..."

ROBERT BURNHAM (BRUNHAM)

(ii) Prior of Burnham Norton in the Hilary Term 1425 when he accompanied the former prior Robert Cheyny* and Nicholas Walter, clerk, all executors of the will of John Halcoles of Burnham, when they sued Alexander Balton yeoman of Burnham Overy over a debt. [3 Henry VI 1425, CP 40/656 (AALT IMG 1862d)].

ROBERT CHEYNY (CHYNE, CHYVE)

In Michelmas Term 1422, he was described as the prior of Burnham Norton when he appeared as a defendant in the Court of Common Pleas, accompanied by his fellow friar John Toftys* and Walter Grene and his wife Joanna, when they were all sued by John Godfrey who claimed the return of a casket containing written documents and other charters. [1 Henry VI 1422, CP 40/647 (AALT IMG 0670d)].

He was out of office by Hilary Term 1425 when he accompanied the new prior Robert Burnham* and Nicholas Walter, clerk, all executors of the will of John Halcoles of Burnham, when they sued Alexander Balton yeoman of Burnham Overy over a debt. [3 Henry VI 1425, CP 40/656 (AALT IMG 1862d)].

ROBERT RYDER (REDER)

Listed from Cambridge when he was ordained deacon on 21 Sept 1521 in Buckden preb. church. [*Reg. Longland, Lincoln*, xxvi, fo. 1v].

He was prior of Burnham Norton in 1535. [*Valor Ecclesiasticus temp. Henr.*

VIII. Auctoritate Regia Institutus, (1810-34), iii, 371].

He was still prior on 10 Feb 1536, when he was granted a dispensation to hold a benefice with cure and wear his habit beneath that of a secular priest having resigned the office of prior. Fee of £8. [Chambers, D., *Faculty Office Registers, 1534-1549*, (Oxford, 1966), 44].

ROBERT WALSINGHAM, (JOHN, GALSINGHIN, MALIGRAVA, VALSINGAMIUS, VALSINGHAM, WALSINGAM, WALSINGHAMIUS, WALSINHAM, WALSNGHAMIUS, WALSYNGHAM, -IUS, -US, WALSYNHAYN)

(i) Robert Walsingham was probably born or traced his ancestry from the village of Walsingham in Norfolk, the site of the famous shrine to the Virgin Mary cared for by a priory of Augustinian canons. Born c1270, Walsingham joined the Carmelites in Burnham Norton, 10 miles away, in the mid 1280's. [Bale, *Harley 3838*, fos. 16, 56v: Xiberta, *De scriptoribus*, 114n1]. In some of his notes and his later published works, John Bale* (who joined the Order himself in Norwich) claimed that Walsingham belonged to the Norwich community. [Bale, *Selden supra 41*, fo. 160v: *Harley 3838*, fo. 16: Bale, *Catalogus*, i, 364]. Bale's confusion may be because it is likely that Walsingham completed his initial studies in the Carmelite *studium* in Norwich, returned later to lecture there and was at the end buried in the chapel.

Walsingham's intellectual capability soon became evident and he was sent to study at Oxford where he became a pupil and *socius* (secretary/assistant) of the Carmelite William Pagany de Hanebergh*. [Bale, *Harley 3838*, fo. 60v: Bale, *Catalogus*, i, 341]. Emden suggests that Walsingham incepted as D.Th. c.1305 and, at his vesperies, c. 1305, William of Hecham, O.S.A., acted as his opponent (not Walter of Heyham as in Bale). However, having been awarded his doctorate, Walsingham did not take his place as regent master in the Carmelite *studium* there until later, due to other events. [Bale, *Bodley 73* fo. 208: Emden, *B.R.U.O.*, 1970].

For some years, there had been unrest in the province over the decision of the general chapter to detach the Scottish and Irish houses and form them into a separate province. Walsingham was one of the senior Carmelites who supported William Ludlyngton*, the provincial, in resisting this division of the province. In 1303, two visitators, William Pagany* and William Newenham*, were sent by the prior general to enforce the separation of the Irish and Scottish houses but their attempt failed. Then, in 1305, two senior German Carmelites, Conradus a St. Georgio* and Gotfridus de Nussia* were sent to preside over the provincial chapter held in London. At this chapter, the provincial William Ludlyngton* was deposed and, together with a number of the senior friars who had supported him, he was banished to the continent. Walsingham, however, was allowed to remain in England but was removed from Oxford and sent to lecture elsewhere (probably in Norwich).

Walsingham was back in Oxford and acting as regent master there by 12 Feb 1312 when he was involved in a disputation with *magister* Henry Harclay. This disputation survives in *quaestio* 2 of the second of his *Quodlibeta* which are preserved in Worcester cathedral library (see below). [*Collectanea*, ed. C. Fletcher, (O.H.S., 1885), ii, 240, 241: A. Little & F. Pelster, *Oxford Theology and Theologians c. 1282-1302*, (O.H.S., 1934), 266 n]. Bale records that Walsingham disputed publicly with most of the famous theologians of his time, Alexander of Hales, Gerardo da Bologna*, Giles of Rome, John Duns Scotus, Simon of Faversham, Henry of Ghent, Thomas Sutton, Robert Cowton, Richard of Conington and others. [Bale, *Catalogus*, i, 365: Bale, *Index*, 391].

In a list of Carmelites buried in Norwich, Bale records Walsingham as dying in 1310. [Bale, *Bodley 73*, fo. 51v]. However, Bale must be mistaken in his date as Walsingham was still alive on 17 Feb 1313 when he was involved in the Dominican friars' argument with Oxford University. [*Collectanea*, ed. C. Fletcher, (O.H.S., 1885) ii, 240, 241]. He was still active in the university in 1313-14 when he debated *questio* 6 of his *Quodlibeta 2* in response to the writings of Richard of Conington (see below).

Note: The biographical details of Robert Walsingham have been confused by the fact that Jean Grossi*, who conducted a visitation of the English province in 1413-1414, included a "John Walsingham"* in his list of famous Carmelite writers compiled soon after his return. [Jean Grossi, *De scriptoribus*, 46]. Grossi added the extra details that his "John Walsingham" studied at Paris and was elected provincial for a period. Sadly there is no evidence that this "John Walsingham" ever existed and the change of first name is clearly a mistake by Grossi. However, later Carmelite writers on the continent copied Grossi's mistake and even John Bale believed that there were two separate individuals, Robert and John Walsingham, and constructed biographies for each them, in spite of the fact that the list of provincials which he copied from the provincial archives contained no trace of a John Walsingham and neither did the list of Carmelite doctors at Paris composed by Jean Trisse. The confusion was resolverd by Fr Xiberta in 1931. [Xiberta, *De Scriptoribus Scholasticis*, 111-136]. For further details, see separate entry for John Walsingham*.

Surviving works:

(1) *Quodlibeta I*, " *In disputatione nostra de quolibet querebantur 22 questiones ...; supposito quod res sit presens intellectui ... et rationem rationibus oppositis concedo. Explicit secund quolibet.*",

The *incipit* given in the latest catalogue for the Worcester Cathedral library, has "23" as the number of *questiones* in this collection. [R. Thomson, *A Descriptive Catalogue of the Medieval Manuscripts in Worcester Cathedral Library* (2001) 3]. However, the *incipit* transcribed by Xiberta has the number 22 and so has Bale is his original notes. [Xiberta, *De scriptoribus*, 119-120: Bale, *Bodley 73*, fos. 200v, 217]. For a list of the surviving *questiones* with their *incipit*, see Xiberta, *De scriptoribus*, 119-120.

Ms:

a. Worcester Cathedral library, Ms. F. 3, fos. 220v-252. (Of the 22 *questiones*, nos. 17, 19 & 20 are missing). **Note:** There has been a change in folio nos. in the new catalogue. [R. Thomson, *A Descriptive Catalogue of the Medieval Manuscripts in Worcester Cathedral Library* (2001) 3-4].

b. Florence, Bibl. Laurentiana, Ms. Plut. XVII sin. 10, fos. 24v-27v (*Questio 6* only: in a collection of *questiones* made in Oxford by Stephen Patryngton (see above) and copied in 1393 by Giacopo Fey OFM, from Florence).

Ed.:

[*Questio 1 & 2*] *Questiones* 1 & 2 are extensively quoted by John Baconthorpe* in his *In Primum Librum Sententiarum*, distinctio 27 (*Ioannes Bachonis... Questiones in Quatuor Libros Sententiarum...*, ed. Ioannes Chrysostomus Marasca (Cremona, 1618), i, 284ff.).

[*Questio 5*] C. Schabel & R. L. Friedman, "Trinitarian Theology and Philosophical Issues III: Oxford 1312-1329: Walsingham, Graystanes, Fitzralph, and Rodington", *C.I.M.A.G.L.*, 74 (2003) 39-88 (text: 45-52):

[*Questio 14*] T. Graf, *De subiecto psychico gratiae et virtutum secundum doctrinam scholasticorum usque ad medium saeculum XIV*, Studia Anselmiana 3-4 (Rome, 1935), *104-*110.

(2) *Quolibeta II*, "In disputacione de quodlibet querebantur quedam de Deo et quedam de creatura; de hiis que querebatur de Deo prima quem fuit."

Contains 6 *questiones* which were disputed at Oxford c.1312-1314: *Questio 2* was disputed with magister Henry Harclay in 1312 and *Questio 6* was debated in 1313-14 in response to the doctrines of Richard of Conington. The *questiones* are listed in Xiberta, *De scriptoribus*, 120.

Ms:

Worcester cathedral library, Ms. F. 3, fos. 252-264. [see note above on new folio nos.].

Ed.:

[*Quaestio 6*] W. Goris, "La Critique de Richard de Conington par Robert de Walsingham", *Archives d'Histoire Doctrinale et Littéraire du Moyen Age*, 67 (2000) 269-293 text: 281-293).

Lost copies:

Copies of both *Quodlibeta* were in:

i. Carmelite library, Oxford,

ii. St. Augustine's abbey, Canterbury,

iii. Syon monastery, Isleworth,

iv. the library of Richard Grafton.

[*John Leland: de uiris illustribus*, ed. James Carley, (Toronto, 2010), no. 390: Bale, *Index*, 390].

Lost works:

Bale records seeing the following works by Robert Walsingham in his notebook:

3. *Super .4$^{or.}$ li$^{os.}$ summarum, Lib. 4*: "*Utrum theologia sit sciencia et videtur quod non quia theologie est solum noticia eorum que tenentur per fidem etc.*" [Bale, *Bodley 73*, fo. 200v]. Leland recorded that copies of this work existed in the Carmelite libraries in Oxford & London. [Leland, *De viris illustribus*, no. 390]. Elsewhere this work is attributed to John Walsingham*. [Bale, *Bodley 73*, fo. 1]

4. *Questiones theologie, Lib. 4*: "*Prologus: Verbum dulce multiplicat amicos. Ecclesiastici .6$^{o.}$ Thesaurus delectabilis in agro latens et occultus multos sibi constituit inquisitores et familiares.*" [Bale, *Bodley 73*, fo. 197].

  Later, entitled *Super Sententias* and then *Elucidationes Sententiarum*. [Bale, *Harley 3838*, fo. 56v: Bale, *Catalogus*, i, 365].

5. *XII. Questiones ordinarias, Lib. 1*: "*Utrum respectus vestigialis forme existentis in potencia distinguatur realiter a respectu vestigiali primi principij materialis.*" [Bale, *Bodley 73*, fo. 197]. Leland noted a copy in the Carmelite library, Oxford, and another copy existed in the library of Richard Grafton. [Leland, *De viris illustribus*, no. 390: Bale, *Index*, 391].

6. *Questiones ordinarias, Lib. 1*: "*Queritur utrum in divinis persona producens sit realiter prior persona producta.*" [Bale, *Bodley 73*, fo. 200v].

7. *Quaestiones theologie in vesperijs habitas quibus opposuit magister Wilhelmus de Heyham, Lib. 1*: "*Utrum Christus per suum intellectum creatum cognoscat simul et eodem actu res in seipso ut Deus est et in proprio genere.*" [Bale, *Bodley 73*, fo. 208].

In his *Catalogus*, Bale gives this work the title, *Questiones vesperiales 12*. [Bale, *Catalogus*, i, 365].

8. *Questiones ordinarias .44., Lib. 1:* "Ego sum via veritas et vita, Johannis .9°· Ut dicit Augustinus de creatura Christiana, etc." [Bale, *Bodley 73*, fo. 217]. Later, this is entitled *Determinaciones scripture*. [Bale, *Summarium*, fo. 122: Bale, *Catalogus*, i, 365].

9. *Quodlibeta, Lib. 1:* "Questio in ecclesia olim fuit proposita, utrum ens verum et cetera nomina dicta de Deo significent illum conceptum quiditativum commune univocum Deo et creaturis." [Bale, *Bodley 73*, fo. 217]. Entitled later *Quolibeta maiora*. [Bale, *Catalogus*, i, 365].

10. *In Ecclesiasticum, Lib. 1:* "Omnis scientia a Domino Deo est. Ecclesiastici. 1°· Sicut dicit Augustinus libello de concordia prescencie et gracie Dei cum libero arbitrio. ca. 7. omnis quippe qualiter." [Bale, *Bodley 73*, fo. 200v: Leland, *De viris illustribus*, no. 390].

In his printed works, Bale adds two further titles, without *incipit*, which must be considered doubtful:

11. *Contra Gerardum de Bononia, Lib 1.* [Bale, *Catalogus*, i, 365].

12. *Conciones ad vulgum, Lib. 1.* [Bale, *Summarium*, fo. 122].

"Et alia multa nobis incognita." [Bale, *Catalogus*, i, 365]

[Deletion]

ROGER CROSTWEYT (CROSTWEYTE, CROSTWYK, GROSTWYK)

According to Bale, he joined the Order in Burnham Norton and completed his studies at Cambridge University where he was promoted *baccalarius*. [Bale, *Selden supra 41* fo. 160].

Crostweyt was elected provincial at the provincial chapter held in London in 1272 where the prior general Ralph Fryston* presided and he held office until 1278. [*Cal. Lib. Rolls*, vi, no. 1990: Bale, *Selden supra 41* fo. 160: *Harley 3838*, fo. 22v].

Later in 1278, on 1 Sept, Crostweyt was described as the prior of Oxford when he was present in Oseney Abbey and swore to observe an agreement with the abbey. [*Cartulary of Oseney*, ed. H. Salter, (Oxford, 1929), ii, 349].

Bale claims that he retired after six years of office as provincial, so that he could go to Ireland and help found new houses there but if Crostweyt was in Ireland then his visit to Ireland must have happened after he came out of office as prior of Oxford. [Bale, *Selden supra 41* fo. 160v].

Bale had a high opinion of Crostweyt and he writes about him: "This Roger was of such learning and ability that many came from other provinces to consult him. He often fasted, and always abstained from meat, being content with small portions. Wherever he went, he never used a horse but his only support was a staff. On his preaching journeys he slept on an ordinary woollen blanket, in the same clothes as he wore during the day. Neither the exhortations of the fathers nor of the doctors when he was sick could persuade him to rest more comfortably. For he used to say that hardened soldiers were weakened by such allurements. He wore always simple clothing, a man unfeigned in all things." [Bale, *Harley 3838*, fo. 23]. When and where Crostweyt died is unknown.

THOMAS INGALDESTHORP

Carmelite probably of Burnham Norton who was taxed 6s. 8d. in the clerical subsidy voted by Parliament in 1449, as he was a stipendiary priest at Burnham Norton parish church. [Jurkowski, M., "Were Friars paid salaries? Evidence from clerical taxation records", in *Fifteenth Century XIII*, ed. L. Clark, (2014) 150].

THOMAS THORP

(iv) Listed from Burham Norton when he was ordained priest on 5 June 1512 in Lyddington preb. church. [*Reg. Smith, Lincoln*, xxiv, fo. 88v].

WILLIAM BACHELOR, (BACHELER, BATCHELOR)

John Bale* claims that he joined the Order at Burnham Norton. [Bale, *Harley 1819*, fo. 200].

However, his name first occurs in contemporary records as the prior of the Carmelite community in London when he was a signatory to an agreement on 20 Jan 1507. [NA, E 328/274].

He was still prior in 1512 when he brought an action against Robert Jakson, a brewer, for a debt of £4 and against Thomas Nowers, a gentleman, and Robert Shore, a husbondman, for debts of 40s. each. [Henry VIII 1512, CP40/998 (AALT: IMG0859d)].

Bachelor travelled to Rome early in 1515 where, according to Bale he was consecrated bishop of "Carvaghonensis" (Carvahagonensis) in Greece and destined to be the suffragan and administrator of the diocese of Chichester. Unfortunately, Bachelor died in Rome on 15 July 1515 before he could return to England. [Bale, *Harley 1819*, fo. 200: *Selden supra 41*, fo. 187v].

However, there is no evidence that Bachelor was actually appointed or consecrated as a bishop and the see of Carvahagonensis at this time was occupied by a member of the Order of St. John of Jerusalem. [C. Eubel,

Hierarchia catholica...., (Monasterii, 1913-), iii, 344: *Handbook of British Chronology*, (London: H.M.S.O., 1996), 286].

WILLIAM BYNTREY (BINTREE, BINTREUS, BINTREY, BYNTRE, -US)

Carmelite who joined the Order in Burnham Norton. He was sent to study at Cambridge University and incepted as a doctor there. [*Harley 3838*, fo. 108v].

In 1465, he was appointed prior in Cambridge but he had vacated the office by 1468. [Bale, *Bodley 73*, fo. 79]. Later, he was prior of Burnham Norton, and held this office probably until his death on 3 Sept 1493. [Bale, *Bodley 73*, fo. 135v].

Leland gives the date of his death as 11 Aug 1440 but this is the day on which John Thorpe* died and is much too early for Byntrey. [*John Leland: de uiris illustribus*, ed. James Carley, (Toronto, 2010), no. 546].

Lost works:

1. *Questiones .xlii. ordinarias*, Lib. 1: "Utrum Spiritus Sanctus procedat a Patre et Filio." [Bale, *Bodley 73*, fo. 2v].

Ms.:

Oxford, Bodleian Library, Ms. Bodley 73, fo. 68: (preserves a short excerpt copied by John Bale*, c.1520-25).

2. *Pro defensione mendicitatis pauperum (seu fratrum)*, Lib. 1."Constituit eum super excelsam terram."[Bale, *Bodley 73*, fo. 2v].

Ms.:

Oxford, Bodleian Library, Ms. Bodley 73, fos. 68-68v: (preserves a short excerpt copied by John Bale*, c.1520-25).

Lost works:

3. *Lectiones in Cantica Canticorum)* Lib. 1: "Reverenciarum vestrarum celeberrimi homines." [Bale, *Bodley 73*, fo. 2v].

4. *Determinationes*, Lib. 1: "Prestantissimi, theorie affluentes delicijs." [Bale, *Bodley 73*, fo. 2v].

5. *De laude virginis gloriose sive de eius conceptione*, Lib. 1: "Semper laus eius in ore meo." [Bale, *Bodley 73*, fo. 2v].

6. *De Latini sermonis ornatu*, Lib. 1: "Colores precipui pertinentes ad ornatum diccionis sunt duo scilicet circuicio." [Bale, *Bodley 73*, fo. 197v].

7. *Sermones quoque varios*, Lib. 1. [Bale, *Catalogus*, i, 633].

WILLIAM GIBSON, (GYBSON)

Carmelite at Burnham Norton who was involved with another member of the same community, John Pecock*, in the Walsingham conspiracy. The conspiracy was started in the middle of April 1537 by two men choristers at Walsingham priory who were against the closure of the priory and quickly recruited a number of other conspiritors. The plot was soon betrayed and Gibson and Pecock were among the 25 or so men arrested and held in Norwich castle by 10 May. Gibson was indicted with the other conspirators at Norwich Assizes on 25 May 1537 and charged with misprision for concealment. He was convicted and sentenced to life imprisonment. [NA, State Papers, Henry VIII, 1/120, fo. 226, 1/121, fos. 70-2, 86-9: *L. & P. Hen. VIII*, xii, i, 1300 (2), ii, 56, 68: Kings Bench Ancient Indictments, 9/538/4-8].

James Hendley and Harry Capron gave evidence that, on 10 June 1537, while they were imprisoned with the two Carmelites (i.e. Pecock and Gibson) and five others in a house within Norwich Castle that they went with the friars on occasion to the chapel. There they sang the "anthem of Our Lady" and, on some nights, the friars knelt together at the altar and the others behind them. [*L. & P. Hen. VIII*, xii, ii, 23].

Subsequently, Gibson was linked with another planned insurrection in the village of Fincham, 25 miles away. This conspiracy was planned in April, before the betrayal of the Walsingham plot, but was not learned by the authorities until 27 June. The conspirators were arrested and then tried for treason and condemned on 26 July. Gibson and one other already sentenced for the Walsingham conspiracy were indicted once again for misprision and once more sentenced to life imprisonment. [NA, State Papers, Henry VIII 1/121 173-6: *L. & P. Hen. VIII*, xii, ii, 150: King's Bench Ancient Indictments 9/538/11; 29/170, rot. 33d].

Gibson and five others sentenced to life imprisonment obtained their pardons on 27 Nov 1537 and pleaded them in the King's Bench in the Hilary term of 1538. At the same time they produced an order to the Bench to bind them in sureties for good behaviour and this being done they were all set free. [NA, King's Bench Coram Rege Rolls 27/1105, Rex, rot. 2: *L. & P. Hen. VIII*, xii, (2), 1150].

Note: It would appear that the Carmelite prior of Burnham Norton, John* surname unknown, was involved in the betrayal of the Walsingham conspiracy as he is recorded as the "very taker of one of the most rank traytours that were privy to the conspiracy att Walsyngham." [*L. & P. Hen. VIII*, xii, (2), 602]. This would appear to refer to the Carmelite John Pecock* who was executed for his part in the conspiracy. It is possible that the lenient sentence for Gibson was due to the influence of the prior who may have been his natural brother. See above under John

WILLIAM HARSICK (HARSICKUS, HARSYK, -E, HARYK)

Carmelite who joined the Order in Burnham Norton. [Bale, *Selden supra 41*, fo. 175v]. On 29 Sept 1377, he was in Lynn, probably studying, when he signed an agreement in the cartulary. [Little, *Corrodies*, 20].

Harsick was appointed as prior of Cambridge in 1400 but he had vacated the office during 1401. [Bale, *Bodley 73*, fo. 79]. He had incepted as a doctor, probably shortly after 1401. [Bale, *Selden supra 41*, fo. 175v].

Harsick returned later to Burnham Norton where he was appointed prior. He died there, year unknown. Bale gives him a *floruit* of 1410 which may be the year of his death. [Bale, *Harley 3838*, fo. 90].

Lost works:

Bale apparently saw one work and adds the usual collection of sermons:

1. *Distinctiones theologie, lib. 1:* "Licite aliquis potest diligere." [Bale, *Selden supra 41*, fo. 175v].

2. *Sermones, lib. 1.* [Bale, *Selden supra 41*, fo. 175v].

WILLIAM OF RYSYNG

Carmelite of Burnham Norton who was taxed 6s. 8d. in the clerical subsidy voted by Parliament in 1406, indicating that he had a salary or stipend from some source. [Jurkowski, M., "Were Friars paid salaries? Evidence from clerical taxation records", in Fifteenth Century XIII, ed. L. Clark, (2014) 147].

Part IV: BIBLIOGRAPHY
Abbreviations:

AALT	Anglo-American Legal Texts (http://aalt.law.uh.edu/)
Bodl. Libr.	Bodleian Library, Oxford University
BL	British Library
Cal. Lib. Rolls	Calendar of Liberate Rolls preserved in the Public Record Office: Henry III, (London, 1916-64) 6 vols.
CP	Common Pleas (Plea Rolls: AALT)
CPL	Calendar of Papal Letters
CPR	Calendar of Patent Rolls
Emden, *B.R.U.C.*	Emden, A.B., *Biographical Register of the University of Cambridge to 1500*, (Cambridge,1963).
Emden, *B.R.U.O.*	Emden, A.B., *Biographical Register of the University of Oxford to AD 1500*, (Oxford,1957-1959), 3 vols.
L. & P. Hen. VIII,	*Letters and papers, foreign and domestic, of the reign of Henry VIII: preserved in the Public Record Office, the British Museum and elsewhere in England*, ed. J. S. Brewer et al.., (London: P.R.O., 1862-1932), 22 vols.
NA	The National Archives
NCC	Norwich Consistory Court
NRO	Norwich Record Office

Manuscript sources:

The major source of the manuscript references is a collection of notebooks left by the historian John Bale (1495-1563) who was a Carmelite for the early part of his life.

Bale, Harley 1819   BL, Ms. Harley 1819

[Notes taken by Bale during a journey around France 1526-1527, plus some English notes]

Bale, *Harley 3838*   BL, Ms. Harley 3838

[Three unpublished works written by Bale in 1536-1539 on the history of the Order]

Bale, Cotton Titus D.X   BL, Ms. Cotton Titus D. X.

[A late notebook (c1560+) by Bale after he had left the Order]

Bale, *Bodley 73*   Oxford, Bodl. Libr., Ms. Bodley 73

[An early notebook with entries on the English province and from his visit to the the Low Countries (c1523-24)]

Bale, *Selden supra 41*   Oxford, Bodl. Libr., Ms. Selden supra 41

[A companion notebook like Bodley 73 but with copies of early historical works from the Low Countries and a draft for a history of the Order]

Bale, *Selden supra 72*   Oxford, Bodl. Libr., Ms. Selden supra 72

[The earliest of Bale's notebooks, containing a collection of liturgical offices for Carmelite saints compiled whilst he was a student in Cambridge University c1514-1517]

Bale, *Ms vi, 28*   Cambridge University Library, Ms. vi.28

[Another early notebook, containing short historical works on the Carmelite Order, compiled whilst Bale was the master of students in Cambridge (c1520-1523)].

Bishops' registers are cited from the printed edition, where available, but from the original register when a folio number is given.

Printed Works:

Bale, John, *Illustrium Maioris Britanniae Scriptorum ... Summarium*, (Ipswich, 1548).

Bale, John, *Scriptorum Illustrium Maioris Britanniae ... Catalogus*, (Basle, 1557-59), 2 vols.

Bryant, T. Hugh, *The Churches of Norfolk: Hundred of Brothercross*, (Norwich, 1914), 21-22 + photo.

Cox, J. C., "The Carmelite Friars of Burnham Norton", *A History of Norfolk*, (Victoria County History, London, 1906), ii, 425-6.

Dugdale, Sir William *Monasticon Anglicanum*, 3 vols. (London 166573. repr. London 1846).

Egan, Keith, O.Carm., "Medieval Carmelite Houses; England and Wales" *Carmelus*, 16, (Rome, 1969), 142226.

Egan, Keith, O.Carm., "An Essay towards a Historiography of the Origin of the Carmelite Province in England", *Carmelus*, 19, (Rome, 1972), 67100.

Gasquet, Cardinal, *Henry VIII and the English Monasteries*, (London, 1888-9), 2 vols.

McCaffrey, Rev. P. R., O.Carm., *The White Friars, an outline Carmelite history with special reference to the Englishspeaking provinces*, (Dublin: M.H. Gill, 1926).

Moore, C. N., *St. Margaret's Church, Burnham Norton: with notes on its rectors, the Carmelite friary and Norton village*, (Wells, Norfolk: privately published. undated but after 1967), pp. 16.

Pevsner, N. *The Buildings of England: N.W. And S.*, (Norfolk, 1963).

Villiers, P. Cosmas de *Bibliotheca Carmelitana*, (Aureliana 1752. repr. Rome, 1927), 2 vols.

Wright, T. *Three chapters of letters on the suppression of the monasteries*, (London: Camden Society, xxvi, 1843).